Uneven Re-production

Industry, Space and Society

Policy, Planning and Critical Theory

Series Editor: **Paul Cloke**
University of Bristol, UK

This major new series focuses on the relevance of critical social theory to important contemporary processes and practices in planning and policy-making. It demonstrates the need to incorporate state and governmental activities within these new theoretical approaches, and focuses on current trends in governmental policy in Western states, with particular reference to the relationship between the centre and the locality, the provision of services, and the formulation of government policy.

Titles published in the series include

Policy and Change in Thatcher's Britain
Paul Cloke

The Global Region: Production, State Policies and Uneven Development
David Sadler

Selling Places: the City as Cultural Capital, Past and Present
C Philo and G Kearns

Globalized Agriculture: Political Choice
Richard le Heron

Gender, Planning and the Policy Process
Jo Little

Forthcoming titles in the series

The Power of Apartheid: Territoriality and Government in South African Cities
Jennifer Robinson

Success and Failure in Housing Provision: European Systems Compared
James Barlow and Simon Duncan

Uneven Re-production
Industry, Space and Society

Andy C Pratt
London School of Economics
and Political Science, UK

PERGAMON

UK	Elsevier Science Ltd, The Boulevard, Langford Lane, Kidlington, Oxford OX5 1GB, UK
USA	Elsevier Science Inc., 660 White Plains Road, Tarrytown, New York 10591-5153, USA
JAPAN	Elsevier Science Japan, Tsunashima Building Annex, 3-20-12 Yushima, Bunkyo-ku, Tokyo 113, Japan

First edition 1994

Library of Congress Cataloging in Publication Data
A catalog record for this book is available from the Library of Congress

British Library Cataloguing in Publication Data
Pratt Andy C.
Uneven reproduction: Industry, Space and Society.—
(Policy, planning & critical theory series)
I. Title II. Series
307.12

ISBN (Hardcover) 0 08 040487 1
ISBN (Flexicover) 0 08 040486 3

Printed in Great Britain by Galliard (Printers) Ltd, Great Yarmouth

Contents

Preface

The main theme addressed in this book is the relationship between industry, space and society. The discussion is applied to the analysis of what has become a rather neglected and dusty corner of economic geography: the location of industry in general and the physical form of industrial developments in particular. The form of industrial development which provides the focus for the analysis presented here is the industrial estate. However, as we shall see, the arguments developed here have far wider purchase on the creation and use of the industrial built environment more generally. In short, the book calls for a radical reconsideration of the problem of industrial location and development. Central to this call is a concern with theory and method; more specifically it is concerned with the possibilities of using critical realism to inform this task. It uses critical realism in a novel and explicit way to explore the actually existing form of industrial location and uneven development. In particular it stresses the importance of an analysis of industrial property and its forms: industrial estates, science parks etc. In addition to offering a ground-breaking analysis of the development of industrial estates, this book will be of considerable interest to those concerned with the development of critical realism as a practical research tool, and to those researching and studying the linked issues of industrial location and uneven spatial development.

The book is underpinned by its elaboration of critical realism as a research methodology. There is considerable interest in the social sciences—in geography and sociology in particular—in critical realism[1]

---

[1] Of course critical realists have come under attack from writers supporting post-modernist positions. In a sense realism as an ontological claim is the very anthesis of 'the constant interplay of surface' that is characteristic of much written in the name of postmodernism. My view, one not explored in this book, but one consistent with it, is that there is a possible accommodation between critical realism and postmodernism (or, more correctly, post-structuralism). It is not antithetical to critical realists to consider the importance of language, discourse and signification. The limiting factor for critical realists, and the position of accommodation for poststructuralists, must be on the issue of the nonreducibility of being to language (see Pratt, 1990, p. 1991).

as a theoretical and/or a methodological perspective. In a sense the philosophical arguments against positivism and for critical realism seem to have been 'won'; perhaps too easily, the general acceptance of critical realism—the 'we're all realists now' position—seems on reflection to have been damaging to critical realism, as many of the theoretical, and particularly the methodological, implications have not been worked through. Without a doubt, it is the *application* to particular research projects that has been a stumbling block; indeed it is remarkable that critical realism has received such support given this failure to demonstrate its capabilities. This latter point is somewhat ironic because one of the key tenets of critical realism is the integration of 'abstract and concrete' explanation. It is difficult, if not impossible, to demonstrate such an integration without sustained empirical and conceptual/theoretical work. This book represents an elaboration of how critical realism may be properly 'put to work'.

The notion of uneven re-production used in this book is perhaps an unusual one. It is used here in the context of theorizing social action; specifically to highlight the dynamism of the process of production, but to avoid economic reductionist overtones, thereby to suggest that there is more to the issue than the unevenness of (spatial) outcomes. In short it suggests an unevenness in the *process* of production itself. What is at issue here is an attempt to hold both outcomes and process up to critical analysis at the same time. Hence, the deployment of the concept uneven re-production signals a more nuanced understanding of the nature of uneven development above and beyond its expression as a spatial process. Nevertheless, this book is about space; albeit a reconceptualization of space that encompasses the dynamism of both the social and the economic realm. This concept of space is opposed to the common dualisms: space/society, or space/industry.

Significantly much of the recent debate about space within the sociology and geography journals has been informed by the critical realism. The conventional debates about space reduce it either to an 'absolute' quantity, or to the realm of 'the economic' or 'the social' whereby space is simply portrayed as an outcome of economic or social processes. The critical realist position cuts across this debate by arguing that both draw upon absolutist conceptions of space and substituting instead a socially produced concept.

Some preliminary attempts have been made to weave together the socially produced conception of space and a theory of social action. Scott and Storper (1986) suggest that researchers need to "...grasp the dynamics of the creation, *reproduction* and transformation of territorial complexes of human labour and social activity" (emphasis added). Notably, researchers working under the aegis of the ESRC Changing Urban and Regional System initiative explored this issue (see Bagguley *et al.*, 1990).

Elsewhere, Dear and Wolch (1989) stressing the importance of developing a conception of the reproduction process that is dynamic, discuss the need for an analysis of the "...way that geography facilitates and constrains the practice of everyday life". All of the arguments cited above would seem to offer a hint of the shape of an emergent critical socio–spatial explanation of uneven development.

A further irony of research in this subject area—one that echoes the narrow critique of existing realist research already noted above—is that whilst the 'moment of reproduction' and 'space' are key issues on the theoretical agenda, there is little evidence of an empirical research component to 'ground' these discussions. Even where it exists it is not followed through from initial conception, through methodology, to theory and practice. One research area that would seem to be a prime contender for such an elaboration is the reproduction of the built environment.

Historically, researchers have taken the environment[2] as pregiven or natural. Thus, the focus of debates has been the degree to which the environment determines human action. The materialist stance has given rise to some interesting work on the production of the urban built environment (see Harvey 1982, 1985; Ambrose, 1986). Generally, the weakness of this work lies in its conception of human agency (see Gottdiener, 1985a). Some account has been taken by sector-specific studies of the occupants of the built environment; these have predominantly dealt with office and housing development (see Bateman, 1985; Ball, 1983). A notable gap is work on the industrial built environment. Whilst such research has emphasized the importance of property to industrial development (see Fothergill *et al.*, 1987), it has been expressed within a problematic managerialist framework.

There is a second strand of criticism that can be made here concerning reproduction. The references above emphasize issues of production, in this case the effects of the built environment on the direct users; there is little work on how the built environment affects the restructuring of social relations *outside* the factory, for example, the relative location with regard to the home. Whilst housing researchers seem to have demonstrated an awareness of such issues, much research has to be done yet to elaborate such ideas in other contexts.

The focus of the material presented in this book is on an explanation of the way that the industrial built environment both enables and constrains the potential actions of its occupants as well as those others—for

---

[2]The term 'environment' here refers to the physical context of human interaction. As such it encompasses both the 'built' and the 'natural'; in fact the preferred usage here is that *all* environments are created as physical places or settings for, and of, social interactions.

example employees—dependent upon them.[3] Relations between the providers and the users of buildings are demonstrated to be asymmetric. In fact, it may be suggested, these unequal power relations are 'concreted' in the built environment.[4] Hence, it is argued here, if we are to understand the processes of development it is incumbent upon us to explain how the built environment is actually created in particular places and at particular times. In order to elaborate such an argument this book takes as its example the industrial built environment and, in particular, the emergence of one particular form: the industrial estate.

This book stems from research initially supported by the Economic and Social Research Council (Award No: D00428327103). I would also like to acknowledge the help of Cornwall County Council Planning Department, and Allan Williams and Gareth Shaw all of whom helped to make the empirical research that this book is based upon possible. The practice of writing this book has been rather drawn out, stretching across time, space and institutions: it has accompanied me through four house moves, three different computers and three changes of job; none of which were co-incident in space or time. This acted as a constant reminder—as if it was needed—of the lived experience of both space–time distanciation and the inseparability of production and reproduction. I would also like to thank Paul Cloke both for having the faith in the book from the beginning and the patience to wait for it in the end. Special thanks are also in order for Ros Gill who has read through too many versions of the chapters of this book to mention; she has always been able to come up with a telling point of criticism or praise when it was needed. Our long running arguments about critical realism and poststructuralism will, no doubt, continue. Alas, any omissions or errors remain my own.

Somewhere on the Midland main line
between Beeston and London,
St. Pancras, May 1993

---

[3]There is still a lack of research concerned with the relationship between the providers and the users of industrial property, and the uses to which it is put—in terms of production layout etc. See the collection by Ball and Pratt (1993) for indicative material.

[4]Concreted—that is fixed by, or constrained by, the (relative) permanence of the built environment. Power relations cannot be simply reduced to the built form, although they may well be reinforced and operate through its manifestations. Thus, the locus of concern with how these environments—these settings, these spaces—are created, sustained and recreated.

1

The Built Environment: A Missing Dimension in the Explanation of Industrial Location and Development

Introduction

The aim of this book is a simple one: to explain the actual location and form of contemporary industrial development. As I shall suggest this aim, as is common with many apparently simple and naive questions in the social sciences, is a far from straightforward one to achieve. Of course, the study of industrial location has been a key focus of research activity for geographers, regional economists, economic sociologists and economic planners for a long time. However, a survey of the literature reveals a skewed focus that emphasizes two perspectives. The first is demonstrated by researchers who have been concerned with how industrial activities *should be* located, how they *could be* located given certain conditions, or how they *will be* located as a result of other factors. There may well be pragmatic reasons why researchers have sought to answer these questions, not the least of which is to be 'useful' to society. This concern with pragmatism should not reduce the need for explanation of the existing conditions; presumably any future modification must work from an understanding of how change might be most effectively and efficiently brought about. One of the objectives of this book is to explain the actual location of industrial development.

A second strand to research has been the concern with either the location of an individual firm or the effect of the grouping or agglomeration of firms. In both cases the focus is restricted to the firm and its immediate interactions with other firms, 'the market' or 'labour'. It is almost as if the firm stood outside of society; interactions with a whole range of public and

1

private bodies or institutions and individuals are lost. It is against such explanations, that imply that location is determined by the 'demand' of the individual firm, that this book is partly written. I do not want to suggest that these traditionally considered issues are irrelevant, but rather that they need to be recast in an explanation that creates space for other activities and actors.

The concern with both the actual location and a sensitivity to the wider context has led me to highlight one particular issue in my analysis of the location of industry; the *form* of that location: as a single building, a multi-storey building, an industrial estate or a science park. Perhaps because there has been little consideration previously of the actual location of industry the subject of what form it takes has either not arisen or been assumed away. I will be arguing that in order to address the issue of the form of location there is a need to explore the relationship between the property development process and industrial location. In effect the core of my analysis is concerned with this relationship.

A question that should arise in the reader's mind at this point is "why has the focus on industrial location been skewed in this way?". I have already offered one possible answer: pragmatism. There is another poss-ible answer concerning the way that questions about industrial location and uneven development are formulated; this, in turn, highlights the methodological assumptions of the researcher. I will be arguing that one perspective on the conceptualization and theorization of industrial location — positivism — has emphasized one particular dimension of expla-nation; but that it has not exhausted all dimensions. The example of the lack of concern with the built environment and property development is a case in point. It is for this reason that I will spend some considerable space in this book exploring alternative conceptions of the problem.

The title of this book, *Uneven Re-production*, may strike the reader as a little odd. It is worth explaining what it means. First, it refers to the concept of production; in this case in a different form to that of everyday usage. Within this concept I will include production, distribution, exchange and consumption.[1] Importantly this distinction marks a break from analyses that focus on exchange (market) relations to the exclusion of all others. A good example of such an analytical approach to the economy is neo-classical economics; characterized by its concern with supply, demand and market equilibrium. The concept of production implied by neoclassical economics, besides being narrowly focused on exchange relations, views the world as atomistic and fragmented. By contrast the concept of production that is worked with here stresses the inter-related nature of the components of production; for example, one cannot have production without consumption. In its broadest sense I take this to emphasize the

---

[1] This conceptualization is discussed most clearly in Marx's (1973, p. 100) *Grundrisse.*

social nature of production. Production has to take place in society. Production does not imply fairness or equality. The relative equality of the distribution of benefits of production will depend upon the way that production (and by extension, society) is organized, managed or regulated. Production can be considered to be uneven in two ways: an uneven outcome or/and an uneven process. The implication of adopting such a concept of production is to view industrial location and development in a broader perspective than is common in traditional analyses.

Second, the term 'uneven re-production' captures a sense of the linking of the socioeconomic[2] realm and the spatial realm. Geographers have long argued, quite rightly, that 'space matters'. In its most simplistic form space has been considered as an extension—something that can simply be added on—to existing social and economic analyses. In conceptual terms space and society and space and economy are considered as separate. Recent work in the field of geography, which is now being taken up by sociologists and to a lesser extent economists, has argued in favour of a reformulation of the space–society relationship that accommodates a fundamental inter-relationship. Space and society are both simultaneously the medium and the outcome of one another. This sort of relationship is termed a duality. A duality can be contrasted with a dualism which has two separate elements. One implication of such a reformulation is that space has to be thought of anew; this analytical task has exercised social scientists considerably in recent years. In some respects this book could be seen as an extended reflection on the implications of a radical reconceptualisation of space for one area of geography: industrial location. Finally, uneven re-production captures an important concept of how the inequalities in spatial, social and economic structures are created. It also reminds us that it is not a one-off affair but a continuous and dynamic one; hence the significance of the term *re*-production rather than production.

So far this introduction has been—necessarily—pitched at a high level of abstraction. Abstraction is an important and crucial stage in any analysis that informs the understanding and explanation of concrete phenomena. I will attach particular importance to the process of abstraction and explanation in this book. Nevertheless, it is essential that analyses are grounded in particular concrete occurrences. A key question that the reader may well have at this point is how will such reconceptualization and abstraction relate to particular situations? Does it change our outlook on them? How does it affect the way that we may analyse and evaluate them?

I will be looking at the process of property development; a process which I would like to characterize as a particularly concrete (!) form of the production of space. I want to argue that the outcomes of this process give

---

[2] For ease of reference when I mention society or the social in this context I include the economic and the political under that label.

rise to the new conditions of social and economic development. One aspect of this is an uneven distribution of property development. However, I will be locating my analysis in the context of how the very process of property production is itself unevenly reproduced. The net effect is to constantly reproduce uneven development.

Any analysis of such a grand concept must be by necessity partial. The current account is no exception. I will be stressing the importance of the process of property production; however, the message is that the production of the built environment matters, but that it is only *one* aspect of the uneven reproduction of society as a whole. A second necessity in any analysis such as this is to concentrate on some carefully bounded subject. The subject that I have chosen is the industrial estate. There are several reasons for this choice. First, and foremost, the industrial estate is the most common form of industrial location in Britain, if not the world, today. Second, the industrial estate is a particular example of a form of industrial property development that has a history of less than 100 years. Third, industrial property has only recently developed, within the last 25 years, as a separate property market in its own right. The analysis here elaborates the broad development of industrial estates in Britain. I will also present a detailed analysis of the development of industrial estates in Cornwall. The reason for choosing Cornwall was that it is a classic case of 'the periphery', and crucially of property market failure. I think that there is great value in the exploration of the 'margins', in a social and spatial sense, as it often lays bare the dynamics of the 'core'.

Bringing the analysis through one further stage to methodology, I will be stressing that many of the existing methodological tools that are employed in the analysis of the built environment are not appropriate to the type of analysis sketched out above. Indeed, it might be argued that the lack of critical attention to methodology has left 'blind spots' in many analyses. A novel departure for this book is to elaborate a relatively new methodological terrain termed critical realism.

The initial idea for this book had rather humbler origins, it arose out of frustration—a frustration with existing explanations of industrial location and development. I had noted the emergence of the industrial estate in many parts of the country and the world. Naturally, I wanted to understand how and why such a common form of industrial development came to be. Why were they developed as industrial estates, and why all of a sudden at this particular time? Unfortunately, existing explanations of industrial location and development were of little help. These explanations commonly drew upon idealized forms of development, or were pitched at a very general or abstract theoretical level. What I wanted was an explanation of why this particular form of industrial development, the industrial estate, had emerged. This book is the record of a quest for such an explanation.

The Industrial Estate

The industrial estate is currently the most ubiquitous physical form of industrial development. In Britain, as in most of the developed and developing world, cities, towns and even villages proudly promote the presence of industrial estates established in their environs. The simple term 'industrial estate' is commonly used to refer to a wide variety of developments ranging in size from those of many hundreds of hectares to those of less than one hectare. Whilst some are imaginatively landscaped and developed at low densities, others are simply a bleak collection of industrial 'sheds' huddled together. As with variations in size, shape and aesthetic quality, names also vary; trading estate, industrial estate, industrial park, business park or science park to list the most common.[3] Industrial estates have not always been a significant feature of the industrial landscape, most have been developed since the mid-1960s. The first industrial estate in the world is generally acknowledged to have been developed at Trafford Park, Manchester in 1896. Although there are no statistics available at either a national or regional scale, local surveys indicate that as many as one third of the total number of nonoffice and nonretail employees in the UK work from a site located on an industrial estate. In some localities the industrial estate work force may account for virtually all employment in these categories. This simple fact highlights the point that the industrial estate is important and worthy of further consideration in any explanation of industrial location and economic development. Surprisingly, little attention has been paid to the development of the industrial estate, as these two quotations demonstrate;

"there is no longer any doubt that trading estates now occupy a prominent and permanent place in the industrial and economic life of this country [Britain] and the time is ripe to analyse the reasons for their popularity and to try to assess their future" (Appleyard, 1938, p. 30).

"industrial parks have become such an important component of the locational milieu of the Western industrialised world . . . that their general absence from the geographical literature is remarkable" (Barr, 1983, p. 423).

Given the ubiquitous nature of industrial estate development and the fact that the analysis of industrial location and regional development is situated within the core of three subdisciplines of regional economics, economic geography and land use planning one might have expected that there would be a large and expansive literature on industrial estates. This is not the case. If the industrial estate is mentioned at all it is usually dismissed as the result of agglomeration economies. The point is that such agglomeration economies are those that accrue to the industrialist. The

---

[3] For reasons that will become apparent later in this book the term 'industrial estate' will be used throughout as a generic that incorporates all of these more specialized terms.

assumption would seem to be that the 'demand' of industrialists is simply matched by the 'supply' of industrial buildings. Hence, an agglomeration economy for the industrialist is translated directly into an explanation of the industrial estate. Such a partial argument ignores the internal dynamics of the property development sector: the process of the production of the built environment. A cursory knowledge of the property production industry, even the residential sector, would suggest that there may be a mismatch between the 'demand' and the 'supply' of buildings. An industrialist may want to locate at a certain place and time but there may not be any property available at that location. This is not simply a matter of price. Furthermore, it is rather naive to suppose that the developers themselves are not also going to want to influence the form and location of the eventual building. For both of these reasons it would seem useful to consider the production of the built environment.

It is not only traditional industrial location theories that dismiss the built environment, the problem can also be noted in contemporary work on economic development. The debate about the contemporary re-agglomeration of industry under conditions of productive reorganization, referred to as 'new industrial districts' or 'new industrial spaces', has usefully developed the theoretical terrain and stimulated research into actually existing agglomerations. However, the same problems that have already been noted with respect to traditional industrial location research also apply here: namely a lack of concern with the role of the built environment. Presumably, a reorganization of industrial production requires at one level or another new industrial premises.

This book is concerned with the very problem of explaining the form of actual existing industrial development. This is why the research reported upon in this book is of such wide relevance. It will be argued that the built form itself may be of significance in the explanation of industrial location and aspects of its future development: both in a temporal and spatial sense. It must be emphasized that it is not being argued that the analytical focus should be simply shifted from industrialists to property developers, rather that the need is for a reconceptualization of the relationships between them.

Critical Realism

As well as discussing an unusual topic a relatively new methodological approach is also developed in this book: critical realism. An important characteristic of this approach is the critical examination of the object of interest. Conventional methodological approaches would take the industrial estate's existence as self-evident. The focus of such analyses would be with topics such as the distribution or composition of employment, new firm formation or organizational restructuring. Such approaches have in effect an analytical blind spot for considering the production of the industrial estate itself. A critical examination of the industrial estate must have regard to the particular context in which it was developed and came to be used. In other words it must also consider issues concerned with the processes of property development and financing, as well as land use planning regulation. It is one thing to develop the insight derived from a new methodology, quite another to apply it. Much of the initial work that has drawn upon critical realism has stressed the importance of challenging conventional methods at a philosophical level. Hence, there has been much debate about the validity of positivist and empiricist methods. Much less attention has been paid to dealing with the problems at the practical level. This is an ironic paradox because critical realists are quick to point out the need to link together theory and method in research practice.

One of the points that I make in this book is that the full implications of what it means to do critical realism have not been fully worked out yet. The consequence is that much attention is still needed in order to resolve aspects of putting critical realism into practice. One of these problems relates to information collection. For example, are traditional techniques such as questionnaires applicable or relevant to critical realist practice? Another concern is with how arguments are presented. After all, the narrative form of hypothesis, results and conclusion is peculiar to the practice of positivist science. The possibility of an alternative form for critical realism has yet to be explored.

It is for the above reasons that I will be developing a full treatment of an example of a critical realist research programme in this book. Integral to this aim is the issue of how research questions and research practices are informed by a consistent philosophical and methodological framework. In the remaining part of this chapter I will be establishing what critical realism is, how it emerged and what relation it holds to other philosophical positions.

Philosophy and Methodology

A fundamental stage of any research programme must be to justify and clarify the philosophical and methodological framework to be used. It is the contention of this book that the source of the theoretical problems with industrial location and development theory in general and the explanation of industrial estates in particular lies in the adopted methodological and philosophical positions of researchers. Thus, the first task is to problematize these positions.

Methodology may seem to be a rather strange topic to address as a theme. It will be argued that it is as important as the different theoretical perspectives considered under the themes already discussed. Methodology is the study of the ways in which one carries out research. As such it tends

TABLE 1.1. *The Structure of Theorizing in Social Science (after Johnson* et al. *1984, p. 19)*

		Epistemology (how social reality is known)	
		Materialist	Idealist
Ontology (the nature of social reality)	Nominalist	Empiricist	Subjectivist
	Realist	Substantialist	Rationalist

to be one of the last things addressed in traditional analyses. When all of the theorizing is out of the way and a hypothesis deemed to be worthy of testing has been identified the work of experimental design and information collection follows. Finally, a decision is made as to whether the hypothesis is proven or not. In fact in many analyses this methodological stage is relegated to an appendix, or not reported at all. It is assumed that a standard technique derived from a 'methods text' has been employed.

It might be assumed that the issue of methodology is consensual. What has just been described is what is termed the scientific method. Rather it should be termed *a* scientific method, as it is just one of many approaches to scientific explanation. The scientific method, or positivism, that most researchers will be familiar with, was developed in the context of the physical sciences. There is considerable debate as to the nature and validity of such an approach within the physical sciences (see Harré, 1984; Hacking, 1983; Chalmers, 1982). There is further debate about the validity or appropriateness of extending such an approach to the social sciences. Attempts have been made to codify the different approaches and assumptions to scientific endeavour; for example, Keat and Urry (1975) suggest three positions: realism, positivism and conventionalism.[4] All three approaches are based upon different assumptions and procedures. What method or approach one employs depends upon the position taken on two major issues: epistemology, the nature of social reality; and, ontology, how social reality is known.

The elaboration of any particular position can be quite confusing, particularly as in most circumstances positions are discussed by reference to one another. For this reason Johnson *et al.'s* (1984) characterization of the different positions in relation to theorizing in social science is a useful one to work with, the following section draws upon their argument. Johnson *et al.* develop a matrix that has two positions in each of its two dimensions of epistemology and ontology: materialism and idealism; and nominalism and realism respectively (see Table 1.1).

---

[4] There is a whole discipline concerned with the debates touched on here. One strand is the history and philosophy of science (see Harré, 1994), the other is the sociology of scientific knowledge (see Woolgar, 1988).

The philosophical positions adopted by researchers lie in the cells of this matrix. The epistemological position is perhaps the one most familiar to social scientists. Epistemological questions are those which are concerned with the nature of social reality; whether it exists as a set of material phenomena, or as a set of ideas that people have about their world. The two positions are mutually exclusive. Such a division between the material and the ideal is common both in overviews of sociology (see for example Parsons, 1968) and Marxist critiques. Materialists argue that human behaviour should be understood as taking place within the constraints of the material world: physical and social. Such a position is often also associated with that of naturalism; the contention that there is little difference between the analysis of the behaviour of humans, animals or inanimate objects. As long as the object of interest is a material entity or process it can be analysed in an objective manner.

By contrast, idealists stress the peculiarity and uniqueness of human activity. They stress that human activity is not simply behaviour but a process of the production of meaning. Idealists argue that it is these meanings, ideas and symbols that are the objects of the social world. As such, idealists reject naturalism. Methods that may be appropriate to the analysis of physical events are inappropriate for the social sciences and furthermore misdirect the analytical focus.

The second dimension, that of ontology, is less familiar to social scientists: nominalism and realism. Nominalists take the view that the concepts that we use to describe the world are merely convenient names that summarize what are essentially unique and discrete events.[5] Such general terms are only formal means of getting 'a handle' on reality, not reality itself.[6] The nominalist viewpoint is one that in recent years has held virtually unquestioned authority in the social and physical sciences. The alternative to nominalism is realism. Realists[7] argue that the significance of concepts are that they are able to reveal a social reality not immediately accessible to the observer. Rather than summarizing or generalising, realist analyses penetrate to the underlying reality in order to explain events. As distinct from nominalist analyses they identify fundamental relations of connection between things.

Empiricism is located at the intersection of the materialist and nominalist dimensions. This position, identified by writers such as Talcott Parsons in sociology and much mainstream economics and geography (see Harvey, 1973; Lipsey, 1963) of the past twenty-five years, characterizes human activity as individuals' behaviour taking place in observable

---

[5] It is for this reason that this position is also known as an atomistic one.
[6] When such concepts are taken as reality the error is known as reification.
[7] Note that realism here is being used in a broad sense; it should not be read as critical realism.

circumstances. Knowledge is accumulated via systematic observation. Analyses take the form of probabilistic generalizations about relations between observations, and are validated by the use of consistent logical structures; for example, the hypothetico-deductive method. Results are always tentative, as there is no underlying order to reality. Analyses cannot go beyond observation except in the form of hypotheses. Laws are a form of empirical generalization. The explanation of industrial estates under such a regime might focus on the identification and measurement of a range of factors such as the spatial patterns of location, the size of estates, the firms and their activities, and the local political and social conditions. Some attempt at correlation between the different factors might be used in order to derive a law of industrial estate location and form.

Subjectivism is located at the intersection of the idealist and nominalist dimensions. This position is usually identified with the approach of Max Weber.[8] From this perspective the social world is seen as the outcome of the interpretative activities of *individuals*. The world is a social construction, or rather social constructions. The social scientist is not in a position to hold a privileged account of the world. Thus, science can only aspire to situate these various constructions. The validation of interpretation within the scientific community can only be achieved by agreement or convention.[9] Contrary to empiricism, social events cannot be objectively sensed they are always subjective. Phenomena are not 'things' independent of our means of interpretation; they are those interpretations. From such a perspective the explanation of industrial estates might involve attempts to understand the different meanings that they had for developers, local authorities, or those that work on them. The diverse accounts of industrialists and their justification for locating on them would also be taken as significant. Particular significance might be given to the use of specific names for the industrial estate (such as business park or science park) and the way that these are used in the context of advertising and promotion.

Substantialism is located at the intersection between the materialist and realist dimensions. This position is usually associated with the analytical approach of Karl Marx.[10] From this perspective the social world is conceived of as an objective material structure of *relations*. These relations are not accessible to direct observation. A process of theorization and abstraction is required to explain events. What is observed must be explained by reference to these underlying relationship. Some versions of

---

[8] Of course Max Weber's brother was Alfred Weber the seminal writer on industial location theory. Alfred's philosophical position was closer to empiricism.
[9] Hence the term conventionalism applied to this position. This position also has a lot in common with a position popularized by Rorty'(1980) called pragmatism.
[10] Marx's methodological position was never clearly stated. The closest one gets is the preface to the *Critique of Political Economy*. The later version of this also appears in *The Grundrisse*.

Marxist analyses have, in taking such a position, written out any possibility of human action; they are determinist accounts. Validation of such
analyses is not usually carried out through correspondence to logical
structures—although the argument is logical, or convention—but through
practice and its effectiveness in informing political action. The explanation
of industrial estates from this perspective might stress the fact that they
were one aspect of the range of activities that comprised the production
process. Under the capitalist mode of production this process is premised
upon the antagonistic relations of owners of the means of production and
the sellers of labour. The location may be seen as an attempt to mediate or
diffuse political struggle on behalf of workers. The form might be considered in terms of the tensions within the property production process and
between finance capital and industrial capital.

The rationalist position is located at the intersection of the idealist and
realist dimensions. This position is similar to that elaborated in the work of
Emile Durkheim.[11] From this perspective society is seen as an objective
and constraining structure of ideas. Human activity is considered to be a
symbolic phenomenon but the social is constructed in relationship with
others. Ideas are not considered as attributes of individuals, as with
subjectivism, but as beyond any one individual; as a *collective*. Ideas then
create the framework or limits upon individual's meaningful activities. For
the rationalist, the empirical world is a reflection of ideal reality and
therefore must explained by reference to it. Direct examination of thought
is the route to knowledge of the real world. However, it is not the views of
individuals, as with the subjectivist position, but the structure of the ideas
that lie behind them that is of interest. For the rationalist, industrial estates
might therefore be taken as a manifestation of a form of economic
rationality. Examination of the understandings of industrialists and developers might reveal reasons for acting as they did: locating in a certain
place, or developing a particular type of building. The objective would be
to obtain some insight into the 'collective mind' regarding, for example,
profit maximization that might be the key insight for the rationalist.

Each of the four positions elaborated above have their weaknesses and
strengths. They are presented with their attendant examples as a guide to
clarify the nature of assumptions, mode of theorizing and suggestive of the
nature of methodology that may be involved. The exercise of laying them
out is to examine their relative positions. Few, if any, analysts pursue such
'purist' positions. Most research involves some form of compromise or
resolution of one or more of the cell positions indicated in Table 1. A move
within the social sciences in the post-1970s has been towards a particular
form of synthesis of these different positions. This has been most clearly

---

[11] I follow Johnson *et al.* (1984), p, 147) who argue against the received view (*pace* Giddens,
1976) that characterizes Durkheim as the founding father of positivistic sociology.

elaborated in attempts to resolve the structure–agency problem.[12] The aim is to retain the notion of human agency and that of social structure, to have an analytical space for voluntarism and determinism, without reduction to either side of the dualism. Such approaches must resolve, if they are to be successful, the tensions between the different positions in the matrix. As such they could be considered, figuratively, to lie near to the intersection of the main axes on the matrix in Table 1.1.

Perhaps the best known attempt to achieve such a resolution is to be found in the work of Giddens (1984) in his theory of structuration. Whilst it bears some similarity with structuration, the approach that I will be drawing upon in this book is that of Bhaskar's (1979) transformational model of social activity (TMSA) developed within the context of his work on critical realism. The basic idea shared by both of these approaches is that knowledgeable human actors operate within some form of conscious or unconscious structure (society) that may at turns be enabling or constraining their action. Whilst this may seem to be a simple and commonsensical aim its elaboration has been fraught with problems. Most of this debate has taken place within the discipline of sociology, but it clearly has implications for all of the social sciences. A review of the literature on industrial location and development (Chapter 2) demonstrates that the majority of research falls well short of the aspiration of resolving structure and agency. One aim of this book is to indicate how this position might be improved.

Whilst critical realism has gained some considerable support within the fields of sociology and geography most of this discussion has been confined to an abstract level, as such it has received some criticism concerning its ability to deliver new insights. Furthermore, some doubts have been raised concerning the possibility of operationalizing critical realism. There are important questions to be considered about what form critical realist research takes as part of a full research programme. One aim of this book is to demonstrate a possible resolution of this question. I will be arguing that critical realism can only be effective if it is developed as part of an ongoing dialogue between abstract and concrete research.

Critical Realism and the Social Sciences: A Brief History

For most social scientists critical realism emerged as an alternative mode of science to positivism in the early 1980s.[13] A very useful overview from a general social scientific perspective can be found in Outhwaite's book (1987). The philosophical groundwork for critical realism was carried out

---

[12]This is sometimes referrred to as the micro–macro problem (see Knorr-Certina and Cicourel, 1981; Fielding, 1988).
[13]The key point of reference for sociology was Keat and Urry (1975) and Johnson *et al.* (1984). Whilst Sayer (1982a, 1984) offered a point of entry for geographers.

TABLE 1.2. *The Stratified Nature of 'Reality' (after Bhaskar, 1978, p. 56)*

Domain of the:	Real	Actual	Empirical
Mechanisms	X		
Events	X	X	
Experinces	X	X	X

by Harré and Bhaskar. Harré's work is situated in debates about the history of science and social psychology, it stretches back over many years (Harré 1970, 1979, 1984; Harré and Madden, 1975). However, it is Bhaskar's extension of this project in a philosophical mode that is of key significance to this book.

Bhaskar's realist theory of (natural) science was formulated in the mid-1970s from a debate within the philosophy of science which was critical of the positivist position (Bhaskar, 1978). Bhaskar aimed to weave together two strands of a (then) developing critique of the status of knowledge; the transitive and the intransitive. The first strand draws upon the critique of positivism and was that put forward in different ways by writers such as Kuhn (1970). Kuhn's work stressed the social nature of science and the nature of change and development of scientific knowledge. Drawing upon debates in the history of science, Kuhn highlighted the fact that progress was not a simple process of accumulation of knowledge, sometimes there were 'revolutions' or 'paradigm shifts' that caused a reassessment of what was valid as scientific knowledge. This point of view acknowledged the social basis of science—that what counts for 'truth' is dependent on the current structure of science. So called 'normal science' is carried on as long as the scientific community has a consensus about what problems are defined by the paradigm as worth investigating and how knowledge is validated. During revolutionary periods, the customary methods may begin to provide anomalous results and provide less convincing solutions to problems. The exemplar of what counts for scientific enquiry changes, a new paradigm is established. The key point for Kuhn was that the transition from one paradigm to another was not governed by the rationalistic rules of philosophy. It was not simply a disproval of one set of theories by another, new paradigms are imposed by the scientific community. In Bhaskar's terms such arguments demonstrated the 'transitive' or changeable nature of knowledge.

The second strand was one that Bhaskar drew from Harré's work. This stressed the stratified nature of scientific knowledge. Bhaskar argued that to simply deal with the experience of the immediately perceived world is to collapse three separate domains into one (see Table 1.2). A move from one domain to another is contingent and does not necessarily follow. For example, events can occur without being experienced. Even more significantly causal mechanisms can 'neutralize' one another and hence produce no event or experience. Furthermore, experiences do not necessarily denote causes. Quite simply, there is more to 'reality' than that which is immediately perceived. The view that there is only that which is immediately perceived is termed nominalism. Such a conception is implicit in positivism. It can be confusing because the contention of critical realism— that there are causal mechanisms that produce events—is often used (erroneously) by advocates of positivism. The idea of molecular structure (if it is conceived that molecules actually exist) causing chemical reactions, empirical events, is an example. This (critical realist) position is often referred to as the 'intransitive', or unchanging, nature of knowledge.

Drawing upon these two strands Bhaskar's intervention can best be considered as falling into three parts. The first concerns the nature of being and reality, and their inter-relation. He argues against the collapsing of being into knowledge. By this he is referring to the position that would imply the determination of being by knowledge; a common form of this view is that our perceptions are wholly determined by our theoretical constructs, *not* by the material world: change the idea and you change the world. In its place he argues for a reality as being "non-coterminate with being". This can be best thought of as reality being somehow separate from social constructs that we know it under; constructs, for example, such as space and time. This position is, in a nutshell, the basis of what he terms "transcendental" realism.

This may seem to be a rather abstract point to be arguing. However, it is very important. Bhaskar's point in arguing for this position is that it then allows him to demonstrate how positivism (as a theory of knowledge) serves as an ideology for science. Put simply, he suggests that positivism is how scientists account for their activities, but this does not correspond to the practices through which they derive their explanations. Bhaskar refers to this as the diurnal model of science; a sort of schizophrenic view of scientific practice. We can imagine it as scientists practicing positivism 'by day' doing their experiments, but when they write up their work 'by night' employing a realist mode of explanation. This is not trivial point scoring by the 'purist philosopher', it represents a transgression of the key tenet of positivism. The validity of positivism rests on the following of very strict rules. Bhaskar argues that the diurnal mode of science operates with two incompatible views of the world, by day a nominalist view and by night a realist view. Positivism denies the existence, or the entering into explanations, of a stratified reality.

It is the second of Bhaskar's arguments—for the possibility of naturalism—that has attracted attention amongst the wider social science community (Bhaskar, 1978). This position, which he terms "critical naturalism", is one that maintains that the same methods of analysis can be applied across the natural and social sciences. 'Critical naturalism' is perhaps an unfortunate terminology as Bhaskar means it to refer to the possibility of a unity of method in both the social and natural sciences, not to some form of reductionism or essentialism that the word naturalism may suggest to the social scientist. Paradoxically, naturalism is the position that is held by positivists. Bhaskar's argument is: naturalism yes, positivism no; naturalism is only possible using critical realism.

The perceived failure of positivism to develop adequate explanations in the social sciences has led some (anti-positivists) to suggest that it may not be applicable to that domain (see Johnson *et al.*, 1984, p. 206). Two criticisms can be considered, open systems and human reflexivity. First, open systems. The successful operation of the scientific method is contingent upon there being control over the experimental conditions. The classic example is the artificial bench experiment in the laboratory where all the variables but one are held constant. Thus, any changes in the overall system under investigation can be inferred as caused by the manipulated variable. In the case of social variables closed systems are neither practical nor feasible.

Second, the problem of human reflexivity. Simply, this refers to the process whereby people reflect upon their actions before taking further action. This is an obvious difference between people and inanimate objects. Two issues can be considered here. First, it is one thing to carry out an experiment involving an inanimate object, subjecting it to a certain experimental condition, but quite another to do this with human beings. It raises unacceptable moral issues. Second, human beings are not inanimate but thinking and knowledgeable actors. In order to take account of the human subject's reflections on an experience it is necessary to understand how the subject has understood the experience. It is just such an issue that analysts of hermeneutics focus on: the production of meaning through interaction. Such a position when taken to its extreme can be quite disabling: one ends up in a continuous chain of self reference like in the situation of facing two mirrors towards one another. The case of the research situation adds an extra twist, what Giddens (1984, p. 284) refers to as the "double hermeneutic", i.e. the researcher is attempting to interpret the subject's interpretation of the world. The point is that social research is a far more complex issue than the 'stimulus–response' mode of traditional scientific experiments. Bhaskar resolves the positivists' arguments for naturalism, and the antipositivists' arguments against it, in a unique way. He suggests that naturalism is possible but not within a positivist framework, only within a critical realist framework. It is this position that sets Bhaskar apart from Giddens. This position has the benefit of placing the researcher within the world that is being researched rather than implying that s/he can stand outside it.

The third argument is perhaps the most interesting area for the social scientist. The elaboration of the 'transformational model of social activity' (TMSA) is a surprisingly neglected aspect of Bhaskar's work. The TMSA offers a resolution of a key problem in social theory, the structure–agency debate, that is grounded in a realist philosophy of science. This structure–agency debate concerns the priority given, at turns, to structure or human agency in social explanation. Formulations that stress agency over structure can be criticized for giving too much weight to human action, these are sometimes referred to as voluntarist accounts. In sociology this position is characterized by methodological individualism. This view is also implicit in neoclassical economics and most geographical industrial location theory. Those formulations that stress social or economic structures as the crucial factor can be accused of down-playing human agency. In its extreme form this is termed determinism, that society is prior to individuals. This position is associated with structuralism in sociology. There is a long running debate in sociology to develop theories that offer a satisfactory balance between structure and agency, that accord importance to both societies and individuals. Surprisingly, such an approach has not penetrated the debate concerning the location of industry.

The TMSA is an attempt to balance concern for both structure and agency. In Bhaskar's words

> "the conception that I am proposing is that people, in their conscious human activity, for the most part unconsciously reproduce (or occasionally, transform) the structures that govern their substantive activities of production. Thus, people do not marry to reproduce the nuclear family, or work to reproduce the capitalist economy. But it is nevertheless the unintended consequence (and inexorable result) of, as it is also the necessary condition for, their activity" (Bhaskar, 1989, p. 80).

The comparison with Giddens's structuration project is relevant. At first sight the formulation looks very similar: the acknowledgement of knowledgeable human actors operating within some form of conscious and unconscious structure. Both writers are keen not to prioritize either structures or agents but want to avoid the simple dualism: the either/or. In Giddens's terms it is the 'duality' of structure that encapsulates this idea. It is represented by the notion that structures can be, under different conditions, constraining or enabling. Despite these similarities there are some differences (for discussion see Bhaskar, 1989; Thrift, 1983; and Johnson *et al.*, 1984). First, Giddens has a weak conception of structure in his formulation. Structures are elaborated as the routinized reproduction of activities. Second, Giddens is vague about the philosophical underpinnings of structuration, in particular its ontology. Third, in contrast to Bhaskar and possibly because he does not develop a position on the nature of reality, Giddens does not accept the possibility of naturalism. It is for these three reasons that Bhaskar's rendering of the structure–agency debate is the most satisfying.

It is worth commenting on terminology here. Realism is a philosophical position that has its roots in the Greek classical philosophy of Aristotle and Plato. This position refers to the existence of 'essences' of things or beings;

Bhaskar's concept of transcendental realism is different from this type of realism. It is different due to the notion of stratified reality that admits a real that is not exhausted by the empirical, nor necessarily observable. The causal mechanisms and events are also real. This position is summed up in what Bhaskar first termed scientific realism, to differentiate it from both the Platonic and Aristotlean versions and other naive empiricist versions. The naive empiricist position is almost the opposite of the 'essentialist' one in that the real is exhausted by the empirical domain. With Bhaskar's elaboration of the critical naturalist position, where he considers the application of scientific realism to the social sciences, a further new term was developed to summarize the whole position, a combination of critical naturalism and scientific realism: critical realism. This is now the accepted term to refer to Bhaskar's version of realism and it is the term that will be used throughout this book.

Summary of the Book

The book is substantively concerned with an explanation of the changing role of the industrial built environment in general, and the development of industrial estates in particular. In order to achieve this end the current state of 'theory' concerning industrial location and the industrial built environment is considered (Chapter 2). It is concluded that explanations are generally inadequate, primarily due to the poor conceptualization of the relationship between the use and provision of the built environment. This conceptualization is a hotch-potch of industrial location theory and development theory. Both of these theories leave much to be desired in terms of their conceptualization. It is suggested that if an adequate understanding of industrial built environment can only be achieved then a retheorization is required. The following chapter (Chapter 3) elaborates the form that this theory takes. The critical realist position is developed as well as a discussion of its application to the explanation of the development of the industrial estate. The industrial estate is conceived as a chaotic conception, merely being a particular temporally and spatially specific form of industrial property development and organization.

The concrete research is divided into two parts: what is termed the compositional and the contextual. The compositional analysis is itself broken down into two sections, the development of industrial estates in the UK (Chapter 4), and the development of industrial estates in Cornwall (Chapter 5). This section shows how the industrial estate arose from forms of organization of production themselves related to struggles between the state, capital and civil society. In effect what is being discussed here is the creation and development of the market in industrial property.

The contextual analysis is concerned with the specific nature of the production of industrial estates in Cornwall (Chapter 6). Here an intensive survey of property developers and an extensive survey of industrial property is drawn upon. Details of the relationship between the organization and forms of production and the resultant location and form of industrial estates are given. Chapter 7 is concerned with the issue of evaluation. After a discussion of the theoretical and methodological issues involved in evaluation, the implications for the form, location and occupants of industrial estates for the reproduction of localities are considered. A conclusion comprising of a discussion of the main issues raised in the book constitutes the final chapter.

2

Industry, the Built Environment and Space: A Survey

Introduction

The aim of this chapter is to highlight the consistent failure of existing theories to either explain the particular forms of the built environment or to account for the locations of those firms that eventually occupy it. The chapter identifies as the root cause the nature of the conceptualizations of both the built environment, and of industrial location and development employed in the existing literature. In passing a possible reason for the apparent 'blind spot' concerning particular forms of the built environment—such as industrial estates—in both sets of literature is suggested.

The chapter begins with a brief overview of the only literature that does actually address the concrete form of the industrial built environment; that concerned with industrial estates. The two substantive sections that follow show how two themes—industrial location and development, and industry and the built environment—are dealt with from the two dominant theoretical perspectives; neoclassical economics and Marxism.

The issues raised in this chapter relate to the wider themes highlighted in Chapter 1. The nature of the conceptualization of space would seem to be central in such a re-conceptualization of the process of property development and an explanation of the particular forms of industrial development that result from it. Through discussing the need for more adequate conceptualizations of the built environment and industrial development issues of social reproduction are also broached.

Part I: The Industrial Estate and Its Supporters

Introduction

A review of the existing bibliographies of research on industrial estates and associated developments reveals a broad' range of academic and professional concern:[1] from real estate to geography, and from promotional material to doctoral theses. Commenting upon this 'Pandora's box' of material Barr (1983, p. 428) notes

> "Although some are annotated none classifies studies of industrial parks according to research method. . . . The need for critical evaluation remains".

These comments indicate a problem common to research on the subject of industrial estates: methodological confusion leading to poor explanation. Barr (1983, p. 424) also suggests that past research demonstrates both a semantic and theoretical confusion. Unfortunately, Barr does not clear up this confusion. Considered in such a light, it is not surprising that industrial estates have received the limited attention that academic researchers bemoan.

Previous research on the subject of industrial estates can be further criticized for its concentration on prescription at the expense of explanation. Holford (1938), in what is the earliest analysis of industrial estates, appeared to be aware of the limitations of neoclassical industrial location theory for such purposes. However, the economic underpinning premised in Holford's explanation amounts to little more than a restatement of neoclassical economics with the addition of 'uneconomic factors' such as infrastructure. This exemplifies a problem common to all researchers who may be aware of the inadequacy of their explanations but lack an appropriate conceptual framework within which to rearticulate them, hence, they fall back on the inadequate ones: in this case idealism and empiricism. In order to adequately review the research material written on the subject of industrial estates a clear conception of the methodological underpinnings of the research is needed. Only then can the adequacy of the subsequent explanations be evaluated.

Defining industrial estates: taxonomic gymnastics

Research into the location, form and development of industrial estates has been firmly grounded in positivist methodology and neoclassical theories of industrial location and regional development. Accordingly, a substantial amount of research effort has been expended on definitions and taxonomies of industrial estates.[2] The definitions arrived at concern a range of empirical phenomena: size, ownership, industrial activity and

[1] Specifically on industrial estates: Vance (1961), Karl (1968), Fulcher (1973), Bale (1976), Towse (1985); on science parks: Wilson (1984) and LEDIS (1982, 1983, 1984); on regional development and industrial location: Starbuck (1976), Miller and Miller (1978), and Fisher *et al.* (1979).
[2] This is illustrated by the fact that each of the seven doctoral theses written on industrial estates in Britain have had at least one chapter concerned with this task. (See Kaunitz, 1950; Davis, 1951; Adeolu, 1961; Castree, 1966; Shrewing, 1970; Bale, 1972; and Kay, 1980.) Also see reports compiled by the United Nations (1962a, 1962b, 1965, 1966 and 1968).

employment of occupants, and the purpose of the establishment of the estate. Commonly they are reduced to statements that attempt to include all previous definitions of industrial estates. Taxonomies have been based upon some or all of the empirical phenomena noted above, a practice which Barr (1983, p. 426) terms 'taxonomic gymnastics'. Some of the better examples will give a flavour—

> "An industrial estate is a tract of land which is sub-divided and developed according to a comprehensive plan for the use of a community of industrial enterprises. The plan must make detailed provision for streets and roads, transport facilities and installation of utilities. The plan may provide for the erection of factory buildings in advance of sale or lease to occupants.
> "The plan must ensure adequate control of the site and buildings through zoning, through private restriction incorporated as legal requirements in deeds of sale or leases, and through the provision of continuing management, all with a view to protecting the investments of both the developers of the estate and the tenants." (Bredo, 1960, p. 1).

Names, like definitions, have been variously attached and interchanged e.g. trading estate, industrial estate, industrial park, business park and science park. Several commentators make the case for the consideration of the industrial estate as a generic concept:

> "... the term industrial estate is used as the generic concept to designate a planned clustering of industrial enterprises, offering developed sites, pre-built factory accommodation and provision of services and facilities to the occupants. Terms such as 'industrial park', 'industrial sub-division' and 'trading estate' are employed in different countries to denote the concept of the industrial estate" (United Nations, 1966, p. 4).

Bale makes a similar argument, reviewing all other definitions to date he boils down an essential core which he tries to sum up in a minimal definition.

> "An industrial estate is a grouping of industrial establishments provided with certain common services and utilities laid down in advance of demand, and established as a result of enterprise and planning by an independent organisation" (Bale, 1974a, p. 33).

Some commentators are keen to separate industrial estates out from other developments.

> "While all terms [for industrial estates] are synonymous, they should be distinguished from two other terms, namely, 'industrial area' and 'industrial zone'. An industrial area is a piece of land offering improved sites as an inducement for the establishment of enterprises. An industrial zone is an area restricted to or reserved for industrial use, on which no improvements are made. An industrial estate and an industrial area should in general form part of an industrial zone" (United Nations, 1966, p. 4).

This hierarchical typology is very similar to one developed by Bredo (1960, p. 2), he terms them 'industrial tract', 'industrial subdivision' and the 'fully packaged estate'.

What is common to all of these definitions is that they are *physical* definitions linked primarily to property development, management and urban design issues. It is useful to consider what strategic benefits were considered to flow from industrial estates. Here the early involvement of bodies such as the United Nations and the European Free Trade Association immediately signal the concern with economic development.

Industrial estates: a tool for development

The full title of Bredo's (1960) book is *Industrial Estates: a tool for development*, in this book he clearly states the role that industrial estates may play in development. His main concern is to derive a checklist of what makes for a successful development from worldwide experience.[3] He notes that industrial estates are used to accelerate industrialization and to stimulate small-scale industry (1960, p. xi). Moreover, they are claimed to tap entrepreneurial talent, provide a place for investment and enhance indigenous industrial traditions (Bredo, 1960, p. 8). There was considerable discussion, especially within the context of an emergent UK regional economic policy, that industrial estates could be used as a tool of government policy that might lead to a relocation of industry and the regeneration of depressed localities.

There are other versions of what industrial estates should be. Two early United Nations reports echo Bredo's broad aims, cautioning against a purely physical interpretation of the industrial estate,

> "the establishment of industrial estates, either in large or small countries, is not a substitute for an economic development policy of broader scope" (United Nations 1962a, p. v),

and

> "industrial estate development [is] much more than a real estate development. It was a frequent misconception that all a municipality or even an area or estate authority had to do was to acquire land, provide the infrastructure and erect factories, and the industrialisation would somehow take place" (United Nations, 1968, p. 24)

Despite this concern, the United Nations report clearly has a rather narrower focus than Bredo, concentrating on the firm;

> "industrial estates are intended to influence, through regulations or through positive development measures, locational and investment decisions of industrial entrepreneurs, for whom the determining motive is profitability and efficiency. Consequently, one of the principal criteria for the employment of these devices and of the tests of their efficiency is whether they will satisfy the demand and need of the customer" (United Nations, 1968, p. 141).

Posed in this way the research question is: what do the customers want, and how can it best be delivered? Much of the research that has been carried out on industrial estates accepts this narrower conception of what an industrial estate is. Of course the question is itself premised on a particular conception of what a customer (the firm) is. A substantial amount of the empirical research on industrial estates has sought, in one way or another, to discover the 'ideal' size, layout and management regime

---

[3] This tradition is replicated with the work on science parks.

(see Appendix 1). Other researchers have sought to generalize from these findings in order to arrive at a prescriptive policy.

One thing is clear from the above, as with all empirical taxonomies, that any number of classifications could be employed depending upon the particular criteria used. What is suggested, yet never clearly addressed, is the issue of causality. The matter of agglomeration economies has been referred to in this connection several times. What is interesting is that the conceptualization of the industrial estate as either a physical collection of buildings, or an economic agglomeration simply reproduces a physical–social dualism. In this case, the issue of where exactly the agglomeration economies lie remains: with the firm or with the industrial estate developer? The following sections explore the other side of the dualism by considering the conceptualization of industrial agglomerations drawn from both neoclassical economics and Marxism. These sections highlight that the problem is not only a physical–social dualism but is also related to a methodological commitment to nominalism.

Part IIa: Neoclassical Economics and the Industrial Location Problem

Introduction

The key distinguishing feature of neoclassical economics that marks it off from its predecessor classical economics is the conception of value. Neoclassical economics conceptualizes value as being determined by utility: that is its market price. In contrast classical economics, as espoused in different ways by a range of writers from Smith, to Ricardo and Marx, value is conceptualized as being determined by the input of human effort or labour that went into it. This difference is not simply one of emphasis but crucial to the very grasp of what an economy is and how it can be evaluated. For neoclassical economists the amount and mix of goods produced, prices, wages, and profits are sufficient. For the classical tradition it is the social relations that sustain these phenomena. In short, there is an ontological difference in the conception. As we shall see this fundamental difference, the focus on the immediately observable and measurable, causes neoclassical economists to have a particular perspective on the explanation of industrial estates. There is not a formal exposition of a neoclassical economic explanation for the existence of industrial estates. However, it will have been clear that neoclassical concepts under-pinned the concept of the industrial estate detailed in the introductory section. The aim of this section is to consider what light neoclassical economics can shed on the explanation of the industrial estate.

There are two strands of argument that can be traced in the literature relevant to the potential conceptualization of the industrial estate from a neoclassical perspective. The first strand draws directly on one of the key figures in modern day neoclassical economics, Alfred Marshall, exploring agglomeration though a discussion of the social division of labour and the formation of 'industrial districts'. Contemporary variants of this approach dealing with growth poles and social institutions are also considered. At base this approach is not sensitive to space. The approach attempts to explain agglomeration, and only by implication spatial concentration. Space is conceived, if at all, as a plane upon which economic forces are played out.

The second strand uses a similar conception of space, but it deals with the problem centrally through its conceptualization of the location and agglomeration of industry. This approach, beginning with the work of Alfred Weber, stresses the maximization of costs and profits for the firm. Issues of agglomeration are conceptualized as resulting from the distortion of perfect market conditions that space creates. If only one firm can locate at the ideal location it will gain unfair advantage over others that have to locate in suboptimal locations. Agglomerations are also deemed to bring advantages in terms of reduced transport costs and savings on infrastructure costs. Finally, a modification of 'non-maximizing' firms is introduced via behavioural approaches to industrial location.

The legacy of Alfred Marshall

An important body of work, neglected until recently, draws upon the work, carried out in the latter half of the nineteenth century, of the 'father' of neoclassical economist Alfred Marshall (1974). Marshall pointed out that efficiency was not the sole preserve of large firms, but could also be found in small firms when they were agglomerated in 'industrial districts' (see Bellandi, 1989). Marshall draws upon the writings of Adam Smith to support an argument emphasizing the relationship between a 'social division of labour', the expansion of markets and economic growth.

The 'social division of labour' refers to the division of the production process between several 'craft skilled workers' who may be within the same firm, or within different firms within the same sector of the economy. A key idea was that specialization led to efficiency. Thus, part-finished goods may be passed through a network of small, specialized, but independent, firms in order to produce a final product. The extent of this process would be, it was argued, only limited by the extent of the market.

A central concept elaborated in Marshall's *Industry and Trade* (1919) is the 'industrial atmosphere', or a "thick local texture of inter-dependency which binds together the firm and the local population" in an industrial district. This is a key factor in the acquisition and transfer of skills in the labour force. He drew these ideas from the study of 'industrial districts' in nineteenth century Britain. A detailed and systematic study of the Birmingham industrial district that was influenced by Marshall's work can be found in Allen's (1929) study. Interestingly, this work on industrial districts has gained recent attention in respect to attempts to explain the agglomerations of industry found in present-day Northern Italy. It is suggested by their supporters that these agglomerations are 'industrial districts' as Marshall described them, owing their existence to a 'cultural milieu' and 'social division of labour' found there (see Goodman *et al.*, 1989).

From this perspective, the contemporary 'industrial district' represents a re-emergence of the ideal conditions for economic growth, cast from the shackles of the state. This restores a myriad of autonomous, self-contained, self-regulating product specific localities in a global (free market) context. These localities, due to their comparative advantages, are able to trade with each other on mutually beneficial terms. Furthermore, the 'industrial district' as an entity forms the basis of a flexible local economy that is able to adapt quickly to changes in both product design and market conditions.

Despite this concern with the potential benefits of the social division of labour and the industrial district little, if any, attention has been turned to the consideration of the built environment. The assumption is that the appropriate physical infrastructure will be produced on demand from the firms. Perhaps surprisingly, this strand of work has not been drawn upon by those analysing industrial estates.

A recent modification of Marshall's ideas, linked to an analysis of labour markets can be found in the work of Piore and Sabel (1984; see also Sable, 1989). Their approach differs from the Marshall's work in two important respects. First, in the importance that is laid upon a dynamic historical perspective, namely the transition, in terms of economic organization, from mass production to small batch production . Second, in the stress that is laid upon the development of 'socio-cultural institutional forms' that made such a transition possible.

The history of the organisation of economic activity is presented as one of key branching points, or 'technological divides', in Piore and Sable's work. At such times the organization may change in a variety of possible directions. For example, craft skills might have formed an alternative to the mass production methods adopted in many key industries in the early part of this century. This was, Piore and Sable argue, the essence of the 'first industrial divide'. The period following this technological and organizational divide is characterized by mass production. It is termed the period of 'Fordism', after the exemplar of mass production established by Henry Ford at the River Rouge plant in the USA built to produce the 'Model T' motor car.

Piore and Sabel argue that 'Fordism' is now in disarray, but they are analytically open as to exactly why. On one hand it may be external shocks (inflation, fragmentation of mass markets etc.), on the other hand it may be internal shocks (limits of production capacity, levels and composition of internal demand). Piore and Sabel offer two scenarios for what might follow Fordism at the (current) 'second industrial divide'. Either an attempt to inflate demand for mass produced goods in the Third World to sustain the markets for First World production, or what they term the "flexible specialization" of production based upon craft skills either in emergent small firms or as a result of large firm restructuring.

The principal locational consequence of the adoption of a flexible specialization strategy is localized agglomeration. It is argued that emergent 'industrial districts' are self-contained industrial communities which could replace the large firm as the fundamental economic unit due to the competitive advantages which they have under conditions of political and economic uncertainty. Examples drawn upon by the institutionalist school include Emilia Romagna in Northern Italy and the region of Baden Württemberg in Southern Germany.

Apart from the introduction of an historical perspective to the whole debate Piore and Sabel's work stresses the importance of the development of 'socio-cultural institutional forms'. This refers to a more active emphasis upon the 'cultural milieu' that links firms, community and the state. It is argued that examples might include technical and commercial information exchanges, marketing agencies and research and training institutes. Sabel (1989) argues, for example, that the state has a crucial role in the creation of institutional incentives to ensure the spread of the benefits of flexible specialization to the whole economy. Without this he doubts whether benefits would be spread throughout economies, thus producing greater tendencies toward uneven development.

The sort of institutional incentives favoured relate to such as training, education and technology transfer. Delivery of these would require the creation of new relationships—a confederation—between central and local authorities to ensure that both a pooling and exchange of knowledge occurs between local economies and/or 'industrial districts'. Secondly, there would need to be consistency between the conception and execution of economic strategy (Sabel, 1989).

A version of agglomeration is to be found with the concept of the growth pole. The theoretical conception emanates from the work of Perroux (1950). Perroux argues that industry tends to start off in a particular area because of some natural advantage or even a fortuitous reason. As it grows the industry develops scale economies which will give it a competitive advantage over other similar firms that are just starting up in that locale. Most significantly, industries will be attracted to the locale to supply components or use products produced by the 'propulsive' or 'leading' industry. Other 'interconnected' industries which would create and sustain growth, then transmit it to surrounding industries. In some ways there are similarities with the industrial district in the conception of the 'whole' agglomeration and the focus on one sector. However, there is no attention to the social division of labour; the foci is simply linkages, albeit within one sector. The growth pole concept is, in contradistinction to the industrial district, based upon one large firm and many smaller suppliers.

Darwent (1969) in a review of the growth pole idea emphasizes that the concept has no geographical implications, it is aspatial. Fundamentally, it refers to one sector or even one industry and its organization. He goes on to distinguish another concept, the growth point or centre which does refer to location and space. Darwent stresses the need for clarity suggesting that the growth pole, point or centre is either an observed condition, and/or an instrument of policy to promote such a condition. Accounting for their popularity in the policy literature he concludes that growth points, poles or centres have a

> "... flimsy theoretical background and lack of empirical verification ... [but] ... a great deal of intuitive appeal" (Darwent, 1969, p. 13).

Reviews by Bredo (1960) and the United Nations (1962a) have pointed out that industrial estates are not growth poles even though they may be used as part of a growth pole policy. Even so, the idea has been influential in the research carried out on industrial estates. This is most probably related to an associated idea—that of linkages. This concept will be discussed in the second strand in this part that begins with a discussion of early spatial formulations of industrial location and agglomeration.

The legacy of Alfred Weber

Another way of approaching the conceptualization of agglomerations draws on an explicit spatial factor. Perhaps the best known work is that of Alfred Weber. Weber's work was the first systematic attempt to deal with industrial location. Weber drew upon Von Thünen's (1966) primitive analysis of agricultural location considering the relation between land rent and land use. Whilst the title of Weber's book, written in 1909 and first translated in 1929, refers to a "theory of the location of industries" it is analytically a theory of the location of the firm. It is a partial analysis of location considering the variation of production costs at different locations for the firm: transport, labour and agglomeration costs. The theory attempts to identify the ideal location where all of these costs can be minimized. The ideal location does not necessarily have to be a single point but can be identified as an area or isodopane (a line bounding points of equal cost minimization, like a contour line). Weber's analysis did not address the analysis of agglomeration very closely. Mainly because he did not distinguish between internal and external economies of scale (McCrone, 1969, p. 52). Moreover, the theory was entirely cost-orientated.

Weber's approach was criticized by Lösch (1954) for perhaps the greatest omission of all for a neoclassical economist: ignoring the market. Lösch drew upon the insights developed in Christaller's (1966) central place theory concerning spatial monopoly and market area analysis. Lösch argued that firm location should be based upon profit maximization and cost minimization rather than cost alone. Isard (1956) has attempted to develop this work further in his general theory of space economy.

This line of work demonstrates a commitment to a nominalist conception of the world, characteristic of neoclassical economics, where spatial patterns correspond to resource and exchange arrangements. The conception of the 'whole' system was functionalist, dealing with inter-relationships of the economic elements, and the spatial character of inter-relations. In short, it demonstrated a fundamental cleavage between the spatial and the economic; both elements being conceived in a nominalist manner, with an inadequate causal linkage between them.

A more formal generalization of one element of the concern with cost minimization is that of transfer costs. Here it is argued that spatial agglomerations form because firms all seek to reduce these costs. This issue has been discussed in regional economics and geography under the topic of linkages. Estall and Buchanan (1966, pp. 95–6) identified four types of linkages:

(i)   vertical, between separate firms in different stages of production;
(ii) horizontal, between separate firms at the same stage of production usually for assembly later;
(iii) diagonal, between firms providing inputs at various stages in the production process;
(iv) 'common roots', between firms utilizing sources of materials of production in common.

Economists have been more concerned with forward and backward linkages relating to the production process itself. As such this represents a much narrower conception than that of the industrial district, one that focuses simply on material exchanges. Wood (1969) offers a slightly more encompassing view of the 'total linkage pattern' which may, he suggests, comprise both material and information linkages. The concern with linkages does have some obvious parallels with the aspatial accounts discussed above. What is notable about linkage analysis is its sole focus on immediate costs and the neglect of social and labour market concerns that can be found in the work deriving from Mårshall.

One might have expected that linkages would be an obvious benefit for firms locating upon industrial estates. All of the in-depth academic studies of industrial estates have focused, dutifully, upon this issue. Not one is able to substantiate the existence of agglomeration economies.[4] Nevertheless some researchers still feel that

". . . among the most powerful attributes [of industrial estates] are those that derive from proximity" Hartshorn (1973, p. 36).

In neoclassical economic theory it is argued that the demand for some goods (public goods), such as roads or other infrastructure, is under-revealed. For example, it might be argued that it is not in the interest of a single individual to build a road when others might get the benefit for free or a small toll. Whilst all individuals may benefit from such a road it is not in the interest of one to build it. In fact it is a classic example of market failure. This is often used as an explanation of state intervention; a state intervention to assist the market, to meet an unrevealed demand. One of the consequences of such provision is another case of market distortion. The provision of infrastructure in one place will confer extra benefits on those potential users of it located in that area. For example, industrialists may benefit from reduced connection charges to utilities, or benefit from roads built by other industrialists, the state or developers. These benefits are referred to as externalities (see Bale, 1978). There may be negative externalities as well as positive ones. For example, when too many firms locate in one place the facilities may be over-used (again it is argued that it is not in any one individual's interest to provide more infrastructure) the result may be congestion.

This theoretical material highlights the benefits to be gained from agglomeration economies i.e. improved linkages and infrastructure. The point made through the public good argument is that an independent body will be required to provide the initial investment for an industrial estate, particularly in periods or localities experiencing economic depression. Of course it did not escape the attention of policy makers that intervention of this sort may be required to help propagate agglomeration economies. This takes the argument into the realm of planned developments whereby planning is required to overcome the distortions of 'absolute' space, without planning monopoly conditions and uneven development occur.

Wolton's (1938) edited review of industrial estate developments high-lights the importance of infrastructure as an attraction to firms as does an

---

[4]Neither Adeolu's (1961, p. 25) research on Kirkby industrial estate, Davis' (1951, p. 144), Castree's (1966, p. 251), Shrewing's (1971, p. 203), and Bale's (1972, p. 299) in South Wales, Allen's (1951) in Slough, or Barr and Matthews' (1982, p. 91) in Calgary, Canada were able to establish the significance of linkages in the formation and operation of industrial estates. Nevertheless, Bale (1972, p. 208) does add an interesting caveat, intuitively linkages should build up over time and thus may be underestimated in surveys in one time period. Whilst he is not able to accept the importance of linkages Davis adds that the grouping of large numbers of activities ". . . makes it easier to get things done" Davis (1951, p. 148). This sentiment is also expressed by Shrewing (1971, p. 203), who also stresses the importance of the environment and infrastructure.

early survey by Political and Economic Planning (1939, p. 10). Before we get carried away with such an explanation for the industrial estate we must remember that neoclassical theory takes the firm as its fundamental unit. Thus, any explanation of industrial estates is viewed from the perspective of the individual unit. Neoclassical economic theory is basically aspatial, the introduction of space leads to imperfect competition and monopolies. Nevertheless, benefits can be had from monopolies through the reduced cost of infrastructure provision and reduced transfer costs. These benefits, it is argued, may account for the development of industrial estates. There is an optimum physical size for an estate, where negative externalities such as congestion cause the costs to outweigh the benefits of location. It is interesting to note that there does not seem to be any parallel discussion in the literature concerning the optimum 'total linkage pattern', or if there are negative externalities concerning linkages too.

This section concludes with a discussion of behavioural theories of industrial location. There are two strands to a behavioural approach to industrial location, though they are not always separable in practice—a purely descriptive behaviouralism and a behavioural theory of the firm. At one extreme is the recognition of variety, and at the other

> "... simply a replacement of one abstract formalism ('economic man') with another ('behavioural theory of the firm')" (Massey, 1977, p. 189).

Behavioural approaches to the analysis of industrial location have concentrated on aspects of decision-making processes and the perceptions of decision makers to account for 'suboptimal' location decisions (within a neoclassical paradigm) (Smith, 1981, p. 116). Massey (1977, p. 195) argues that this approach has the ideological effect of legitimating the decision of the locator by causing the reader to identify with their objectives. When studying industrial movement Townroe (1971) emphasized the importance of choices made by industrialists locating factories. Other research has been concerned with the locational attraction of industrial estates over nonestates locations (see Cameron and Clark, 1966 and Keeble, 1965). This sort of approach has also been extensively utilized in 'market research' type approaches seeking to demonstrate the benefits of industrial estates as favourable locational environments.

Much of the academic research work on industrial estates has fallen back on descriptions and taxonomies of the 'advantages and disadvantages' of industrial estates. Whilst primarily concerned with testing prescriptive policies, the research also fits within the behavioural perspective.[5]

Inevitably researchers working with a behavioural perspective have run into difficulties. Bale (1972) has proposed an interesting solution to these

---

[5] See Barrett *et al.* (1978: 15), McNamara (1984, p. 101), Goodchild and Munton (1985, p. 89), Gore and Nicholson (1991) and Healey (1990).

problems, recognizing that industrial estates were set up by bodies other than those located upon them, he suggests that researchers should rather focus on the locational decision-making of the site-providing agency. If one takes a broader conception of 'the firm' than industrial geographers normally do (for example the property development company becomes 'the firm') then this approach is unproblematic, remaining within a neoclassical paradigm, albeit at a different scale. It is perhaps because of the problem of resolving the two different scales of firm that even researchers following Bale's suggestion to concentrate upon the site-providing agency have failed to follow-up the consequences in terms of production. Instead they have preferred to concentrate upon the benefits or otherwise of the industrial estate as a locational environment for 'the firm' (for example see Barr, 1983). This would seem to be indicative of a conceptual 'blind spot' for the production of industrial buildings. This is quite consistent with neoclassical theory.

Much of the recent research has followed this track, being characterized by concern for the general benefits of industrial estates and the local environment for industrialists (see Shaw and Williams 1982, 1985; and Cloke and Edwards, 1983). Apart from factors such as layout of estate and factory units, industrialists have identified elements such as rates, accessibility and provision of services as important (Pratt *et al.*, 1986, pp. 42–43).

This section has surveyed a range of conceptualizations of industrial location and development derived from neoclassical economics. Analytically we can note that they are predicated upon empiricism. The concept of value, central to economics, is derived from its form as a market price — an empirically-derived value. The economy is bounded by concern for these market values.

The concept of agglomeration, and by extension space, seems to have caused neoclassical economists and geographers considerable problems. Stressing the importance of inter-trading and specialization Marshall develops the concept of the milieu that characterizes industrial districts. The result is a cost saving and a competitive advantage. However, the benefits are derived from the social division of labour which seems to hark back to a classical conception of economics where value is derived from labour input. Despite the concern with agglomeration the work is aspatial.

The strand of work derived from Weber is spatial, but only to the extent that space can be represented as a monetary value. Examples are transport costs, infrastructure costs and linkage costs. Behaviouralist approaches simply relax the profit maximizing assumptions of the model. All of the work surveyed in this section is atomistic. Firms are represented as individual isolated units that are analysed in terms of their market relations. As such these conceptualizations are not of general industrial location but more properly of the individual firm. As McCrone perceptively notes, the theory of the firm

". . . cannot explain . . . the spread of economic activity over space" (McCrone, 1969, p. 58).

The conceptualizations discussed above do not permit access to the consideration of space in general or the built environment in particular except via surrogate values. Whilst rental values or location costs may dictate location, the provision of the actual building is invisible to the conceptualization. It is characteristic of the atomistic conception of this approach that the provision of the built environment is dealt with as a quite separate issue. This is considered in the following section.

Part IIb: Industry and the Built Environment
Introduction

This section addresses both the issues of how the built environment has been considered and what relation its users have to it. As in the last section the perspective is primarily empiricist. Two issues arise, one relates to the conceptualization of the relationship between the user and the built environment, the second to the conceptualization of the production of the built environment.

Urbanization and urban ecology

The most influential strand of work concerning the built environment draws upon the work of Park *et al.* (1925) and Wirth (1938). The output of this group, despite its internal differences, is known collectively as the Chicago School. In the Chicago School's work the city was considered to be analogous to an organism, communities being functional units which adapted themselves to the environment in a Darwinian manner i.e. according to a process of natural selection. The methodology adopted was functionalism: an approach which stresses the interdependence of elements in a society. Rather than society as a whole the object of study in this case was the urban. By implication a separate field of social theory was being developed in relation to the urban—urban studies (see Saunders 1981).

The application of functionalism in the Chicago School's work implied the subdivision of the city according to the observable type of activity: for example, residential, retail, office or industrial. In this sense it conforms to a nominalist conception of the urban. The resulting spatial form was thus considered to be the result of interactions between people influenced by their cultural associations. These cultural associations were, in turn, related to factors such as size or density. In this way the social relations of the city were understood to be determined by its physical characteristics. The overall picture of urban structure and growth derives from four principles: dominance, segregation, invasion and succession. The spatial consequences of this process were modelled as five concentric zones: the central business district, zone in transition, zone of working men's homes, zone of better residences and the zone of commuters. From the perspective of this book this emphasis had an unfortunate consequence, namely that the social and the physical domains were conceived to be, analytically, fundamentally separate.

There are strong resonances in the work of the Chicago School's founders with Von Thünen's agricultural land use model. Two developments are worth noting because they stress the economic dimension more strongly. Hoyt's (1939) modifications, in which the zonal model was substituted for the sectoral, attempted to build in an account of the impact of transportation routes and industrial location. This is more clearly elaborated in Alonso's (1964) work which attempts to take account of the monopolies that *space confers on* economic activities. Alonso took the cost of housing or industrial location to be externally given, the cost declining with distance from the centre. The pattern of uses and location thus became a trade-off between the cost of transportation and accommodation costs. This was formally expressed by the 'bid-rent', that is the rent which an activity would pay for a location whilst maintaining the same profit level.

The systems approach to urban analysis developed in the 1960s continued this work, refining it further. The system, defined as the urban area, was classified on the basis of observable morphology or physical function (see McLoughlin, 1969). Once specified, the analyst is only interested in the interactions, or flows, between nodes (areas). It was argued that these interactions could be grouped and modelled as statistical relationships. By implication the conceptualization of city was as a set of interactions discrete from the built environment. The built environment was being represented as a passive container, a distribution of social and/or economic activities.

One of the few approaches that does stress the prime importance of the physical form ignores its production. Urban morphology simply analyses in an empiricist and descriptive manner the accretion of physical urban form through history (see Conzen, 1983). Modifications to this approach have considered aspects of production (building cycles) but only to the extent that the elaboration of architectural styles developed by particular architectural practices help to elaborate a taxonomy of form (see Whitehand, 1987). In its worst excesses, the social comes to be seen as being totally derived from this built form, either in the case of neighbourhoods (see Coleman, 1990) or townscape (Cullen, 1961).

The property pipeline

At first sight a more promising direction of research has been explored by researchers actually concentrating on the property development process.

Generally these approaches take the form of descriptive generalizations. The conceptualization this time is not so concerned with distribution as with exchange of the built environment. The approach is termed 'the property pipeline'.[6] Put simply, property development is conceptualized on the basis of the sequential transition of land through various discrete 'stages' in its development in a strict chronological order. It is interesting to note that the analytical focus is land not property development itself.

Three similar elaborations can be briefly considered. The first by Cadman and Austin-Crowe (1983) is a four-step process: evaluation, preparation, implementation, and disposal. As such this is little more than a project manager's perspective of the process. The Property Advisory Group (1975), comprising of members of the industry, in its report on commercial property development uses a similar model but with six stages. The second approach includes some extra concerns that incorporate the town and country planning process. Here the linear model becomes a branching one incorporating feedback loops (Punter, 1985). The third variant has been most clearly developed by Barrett *et al.* (1978). Here the model is conceived as a triangle, each side representing one dimension: development processes and prospects, development feasibility, and implementation. An extension to this model, making it into a square by including vacancy dimension, to incorporate the public sector development process of reclamation and re-development, has been suggested by Gore and Nicholson (1985).

These pipeline approaches have four problems. First, their conception of causality is a successionist one. This means that it is simply of the form 'if A then B'. There is no notion of what causes the process aside from a functionalism of a preconceived 'need' for these things to happen for development to take place. Second, they are atomistic and voluntaristic. Like neoclassical economics the actors react to stimuli without any form of constraint imposed upon them. Third, the actors are conceptualized in an idealist manner. The developer, for example, is an ideal-typical actor. Whilst being an ideal type we would not expect the actual actor to conform to this ideal, but the conceptualization of the process as broken into these roles for separate actors is questionable. Ogden (1979, p. 33), for example, identified four types of developer in her research: developer–sellers, builder–developers, developer–investors and investor–developers. Finally these models are ahistorical in their formulation.

Alternatives to the property pipeline model are those that have a behavioural basis. Two types can be identified: individualist and interactionist (Gore and Nicholson, 1991). Drewett's work (1973) is a good example of the individualist approaches. Drewett plots the relationships

[6]See Barrett *et al.* (1978: 15), McNamara (1984, p. 101), Goodchild and Munton (1985, p. 89), Gore and Nicholson (1991) and Healey (1990).

between 'decision agents' in the land development process; builders and contractors are not included in this model. A degree of indeterminacy is included in the model highlighting that the outcome is not always a completed development. One problem with this approach is that, as with the pipeline, decision-making process are not really examined by the simple representation of linkages. An advantage with the approach is this it indicates the possibility of 'blockages' in the 'pipeline' that result in supply not meeting demand.

Drewett's work has been criticized and developed by Goodchild and Munton (1985) who focus on the landowner in the development process. They are also keen to include considerations of the constraints on the development process through legal and planning requirements as well as other actors in the process. However, like the other models it is narrowly defined not taking into account 'external factors' such as government policy and economic change.

In contrast to the individualist approaches that as we noted characterized the conceptualizations of industrial location as well as the development models just discussed, interactionist approaches have been developed primarily by Barrett and Whitting (1983). Whilst beginning with the pipeline model they recognize that none of the roles is necessarily filled by any one agent. Functions can be combined by whichever agents can control them, which is in turn dependent upon the resources that they can command. Development is thus reconceived as a process of resource exchange. The exchange is not a straight-forward one but the outcome of negotiation, each actor seeking to balance risk and reward. Those actors with the greatest resources are thus able to negotiate deals that incur the lowest risk. Whilst this approach does offer a significant step forward in the conceptualisation of the development process, it is still unfortunately concerned with an empiricist notion of the world. Furthermore, even though it does develop the notion of interaction and negotiation, it is still rooted in a behaviouralism that focuses on individuals and plays down constraints to an unacceptable extent.

The Notion of Constraint: 'Supply-side' Approaches

The notion of constraint to individual activities is an important counterbalance to voluntarism that characterizes much of the above. An attempt to take the locational environment more seriously and incorporate it within a more general industrial location theory has been made by Norcliffe in his proposal for a theory of 'manufacturing places'. Norcliffe's aim was to

"... develop a theory of manufacturing location that is explicitly concerned with geographical relationships" (Norcliffe, 1975, p. 19).

Rather than actually integrating space into his approach Norcliffe merely emphasizes it as yet another factor in the locational problem. This is done by concentrating on supply rather than demand characteristics. Three elements of supply at the potential location are considered: infrastructure availability, internal and external economies, and communication and linkage patterns. Although Norcliffe suggests that historical change is taken into account the result is a naturalistic formulation whereby one set of environmental determinants (such as cost which is conflated with distance, and natural resources) are replaced by another (such as infrastructure provision, and the existing firms).

Other writers on industrial location have also considered the issue of infrastructure, for example Hoover's (1968) discussion of physical restrictions on location. More specifically, property and sites have long been considered in studies of industrial locational analyses.[7] However, they have been traditionally considered along with the availability of finance to buy them, or the taxes paid on sites as merely additional factors of production; another marginal cost. Norcliffe's contribution was to place the stress on the 'supply-side' factors of location. Clearly, this opens up a potential space for the integration of property development processes.

In summary it can be noted that Norcliffe's work represents an important corrective to traditional research, introducing the idea that firms are not automatically able to locate anywhere, but will be likely to be confined to existing prepared sites. This sentiment is echoed by Bourn:

> "Industrial parks are becoming an overwhelming feature in the geography of economic and industrial development. They currently may be the chief providers of industrial sites . . ." (Bourn, 1978, p. 111).

Norcliffe's idea was quickly taken up and incorporated into Bale's (1977, p. 87) theory, and more recently by Barr (1983, p. 439) concerning industrial estates stressing the importance of analysing the locational environment in order to explain the contemporary locational decisions of industrialists. Whilst this is a step forward, within such a framework the production or distribution of environments is seen as unproblematic, being 'explained' in terms of the demand of individual industrialists for industrial spaces. In effect the focus is once again turned onto the individual firm rather than the producer of the premises and the social context within which the provision occurs. Thus, power differentials between firms, and developers and other agents in society are naturalized and legitimized.

Research by Slowe (1981) and has approached the problem from the perspective of the developing agencies. This research is the sole example of an analysis of state provision of Advance Factory Units (AFU). Disappointingly for the current work, Slowe is centrally concerned with developing an evaluation of the AFU programme using econometric techniques.

---

[7] See Edge (1972), Blunden (1972, p. 68), Smith (1981, p. 263–266) and Watts (1987, p. 103).

Nevertheless, he does conclude that the AFU (and by implication the state as developer) was influential in the location of industry.

Valente and Leigh's (1982) research on industrial property explicitly uses the concept of 'filtering' and property chains which have been developed in social geography. In its original context this concept refers to the process where by ageing housing stock comes to be occupied by different (usually poorer) social groups. The stock comes to be vacant due to forms of obsolescence in the users terms, usually expressed in terms of the building style or quality, or its location. In industrial property terms social class is usually replaced by size, youth or financial weakness of firms. The implicit assumption here, as in Townroe's (1971) earlier work on industrial movement, is that the choice of possible locations for a firm are ultimately restricted by the premises available. Filtering is, in essence, simply a special case of invasion and succession in the urban ecology model.

Several researchers have carried out work on the re-use of industrial premises particularly by small firms in urban areas (Green and Foley, 1982, 1986; Green *et al.*, 1985; Falk, 1982), some research has also been carried out in the rural context (Newman *et al.*, 1982). Basically, this work explores the way that firms can be re-accommodated within existing spaces that previously had either industrial or nonindustrial uses.

An interesting, though relatively neglected piece of work by Ogden (1979) refered to above also highlights how the restrictions on the development of industrial buildings imposed through the interests of the actors in the development process conflict with the 'needs' of the occupants. This problem was not theorized further, however, researchers in the field of urban and housing geography faced with similar problems have turned their attention to institutional constraints on location through work on urban managerialism.

The concept of urban managerialism, developed by Pahl (1975), represents an attempt to avoid the worst excesses of functionalism as displayed by the Chicago School. The approach focuses upon the allocative rules employed by 'urban managers'. The allocation, or distribution, of scarce resources is explained by an analysis of the policies and practices of those who have the power to allocate them: planners, bank managers and housing officers. Pahl's book, in particular the chapter written with Craven (Pahl and Craven, 1975), represents a notable attempt to admit issues relating to the production of the built environment (in this case housing) into the urbanization process. There are two sets of problems associated with urban managerialism. The first is the mark of urban ecology, the social–spatial dualism albeit with a new stress on social and economic issues. The net result is that space is ignored, it being represented as another distribution. The second problem relates to the limits of managerialism. Quite simply this results from attempts to consider the wider social, political and economic contexts of managers' decisions and the constraints that they might be working within. At this point managerialism can disintegrate into a form of structuralism (see Williams, 1982).

Given the relative isolation of those working in the field of industrial location it is a pleasant surprise to find the concept of managerialism being taken up by Bale (1977, p. 91) in his research on industrial estates. Bale moved beyond a consideration of the 'site-providing agencies' to consider the 'urban manager' in order to suggest that an explanation of the location of industrial estates lay within the context of the wider 'urban–industrial land use system'. Regrettably, Bale developed this work no further.

Chalkley and Perry's work (1982) represents another notable attempt to bridge a gap between developments in consideration of urbanization, and residential location in particular, and industrial location. They have suggested that other ideas utilized within social geography could be transferred to the field of industrial geography. Though they do not mention industrial estates specifically, there would seem to be strong parallels with their explanation of the development of small industrial premises. They have considered how the managers of industrial units have influenced small firms' location and occupation of units (Perry and Chalkley, 1982). Cognisant of the problems of managerialism, although still working within the tradition Perry (1986) later expanded the notion of the manager from a simple local landlord to embrace fund managers of financial institutions.

A wider conception of potential restrictions on locations has been the focus of research on the regional dynamics of industrial movement. The research originated was carried out in the form of a series of research projects[8] for the Department of the Environment by Fothergill *et al.*[8] In contrast to traditional location theories that emphasise costs of land, Fothergill and Gudgin (1982) stress land availability. They develop what has been termed the 'constrained location hypothesis' to explain the decline of employment in urban areas and the growth in rural areas in the 1960s and 1970s in the UK. According to this hypothesis the lack of land available for expansion next to existing industrial properties in urban areas acted as a restriction to access, expansion and the development of new technologies that required more space. Fothergill and Gudgin suggested that firms were left with two choices: first, not to expand but to stay at an existing location and displace labour by investing in more capital intensive machinery (this itself might be limited by factory design limitations), or second, to relocate production to areas of greater land availability—rural areas.

Whilst this work has opened up the question of the influence of premises and infrastructure, it has several drawbacks at a more general level of the

---

[8] (See Fothergill and Gudgin, 1982; Fothergill *et al.*, 1982, 1985, 1985a, 1985b, 1987.)

location of industry. The causal structure implied does attempt to provide a linkage between the industrial activity and its property. Whilst the industrial side of the model is a standard neoclassical concern with the firm, the property side of the model is totally inadequate. The reasons why the properties lack expansion space or are only available in green-field or rural locations are not adequately addressed. It is taken as self-evident that land will be available for development in rural areas, even if it is not in urban areas. No account is taken of the planning system. Furthermore, the work of Fothergill *et al.* puts forward an explanation of conditions situated in a particular time and in a particular place. It certainly would not stand generalization.

Some of these issues have been addressed in a later book, significantly after being joined by Perry (Fothergill *et al.*, 1987). Many of the original arguments of the earlier work are given another airing in this book. However, it is notable that there is a far more credible consideration of the property development process incorporated within it. They adopt a fairly standard 'pipeline' approach to property development. In their analysis they discount 'structural rigidities' in the property development process as less significant than the use of existing space by firms (Fothergill *et al.*, 1987, p. 55). From this point of view the problem of the 'mis-match' between productive needs and property availability is more significant.

"The supply of land and buildings does exert an important influence on location of manufacturing firms' activity, and this influence operates not so much through the price mechanism as through physical constraints and availability . . . the main effects on the location of jobs arise because of constraints in the supply of land" (Fothergill *et al.*, 1987, p. 110).

This important point is taken up and developed as part of a case for public sector intervention in land markets. What is quite interesting here is the conceptual confusion that Fothergill *et al.* seem to get themselves into by discounting the property development industry and then suggesting that land availability is crucial. A more satisfactory resolution would view these as part of the same issue. It is revealing that they are unable to see this problem. To their credit they realise that their findings,

". . . raised doubts about the applicability of neo-classical economic models to the role of land and buildings in industrial location" (Fothergill *et al.*, 1987, p. 110).

However, they persevere in a descriptive manner, not exploring alternative conceptualizations of the property development process. Unlike Fothergill *et al.* we turn to the consideration of property development and industrial development from alterative perspectives: namely within Marxist debates about urbanization.

Despite moving the focus of the debate more specifically to the built environment, empiricism has not served researchers well in terms of the development of adequate conceptualizations of the development process.

Analyses are continually in danger of voluntarism, and thereby fail to address wider society. As has been noted in the previous section the relationship between the users of property and the built environment has been particularly poorly conceived. Attempts to resolve this problem seem to be inherently flawed due to the atomistic conceptions of industrial development and property development. As a result the industrial estate continues to be a blind spot for these conceptualizations.

Part III: Materialist Conceptualizations of Economic Development

Introduction

The shortcomings of functionalist approaches, and limited context of managerialism have been overcome by shifting the focus of analysis from the firm or the environment, to the processes that produce them. This work has been pioneered by urban social theorists working in the Marxian tradition, the seminal work being that of Harvey (1973). The concern of this work has not only been with the spatial consequences, but also the generating forces of them — the capitalist system.

A distinguishing mark of Marxian approaches is their attention to the question of the production of value by distinction from neoclassical economics, Marxian economics (and classical economics) relates the production of value to the amount of labour expended on the production of a commodity. Neoclassical accounts look to the market as an answer to value questions. What this difference implies, from a Marxist position, is that there is more to a market price than meets the eye. The process of production that is lost in the neoclassical conceptualisation is recovered in a Marxian one. It must be concluded that one crucial difference between the two approaches concerns ontology. Neoclassical approaches adopt a nominal view, Marxian approaches a real view.

Just as there were differences in approach and emphasis in the neo-classical approaches, so there are within Marxian approaches. However, one should not expect the divisions to be made in the same places. What is being conceptualized is quite different. Gottdeiner (1985) identifies two strands of Marxian-influenced political economy: class conflict theories and capital accumulation theories. This is a useful distinction in the differential stress it places, respectively, on class struggle or accumulation and the circulation of capital. As will be noted below, in general there is more anlaytical space within ontologically real conceptions of the economy for both industrial development and the built environment. However, it will also be argued that none of the existing approaches adequately comes to terms with the production of the built environment in general, or the production of the industrial built environment in particular; nevertheless, there are pointers to possible directions for research.

Capital accumulation theories

Work on the built environment in the 1970s shifted the focus away from the extreme functionalism of the systems approach. Harvey's (1973, 1982, 1985) work in particular, deploying a political economy perspective, was crucial. Harvey stressed the analysis of the whole urban process which created the physical infrastructure that was essential for the production, circulation, exchange and distribution of commodities. In so doing he rejected the idea of continuous interaction of the spatial and the social inherent in the Chicago School's work. For David Harvey the built environment was capital that was deposited or 'fixed' by the process of capitalist accumulation. The function of the built environment was to facilitate capital circulation. The significance of space derives from the agglomeration of capital, in terms of value, in places such as cities.

A distinction that Harvey makes is between use values (usefulness of the building or land) and exchange values (or market prices) in relation to land ownership, land development, land use and land rental. Harvey criticises the neoclassical conception of rent as derived from the 'best use' as it characterises the landowner as passive. Harvey's reconceptualization stresses that the institution of property ownership confers on landowners a monopoly power to extract a slice of any profit (ground rent) from productive activities carried out on that land.

Harvey develops his conception most clearly and concisely in a 1978 paper entitled *The Urban Process under Capitalism: A Framework for Analysis*.[9] Harvey's analysis of the circulation of value (as represented by capital) rests on a three-fold distinction of 'circuits' of capital: primary, secondary and tertiary. In the primary circuit commodities are produced and consumed, and surplus value (profits) produced. Normally surplus value is reinvested and production expanded. However over time, profits decline or/and there is excess production which limits the scope for fresh invest-ment in the primary circuit, so it is switched to the secondary circuit via both state and public institutions. The secondary circuit is the built environment, comprised of all infrastructure, factories and machines, i.e. the means of production. Harvey makes a further distinction between the built environment strictly for production and that for consumption (house-hold goods, houses etc.). The secondary circuit is the arena for investment activity. The end result is the built environment. The tertiary circuit comprises investments in technology and science and social expenditure

---

[9] Harvey develops and elaborates this analysis most comprehensively in Harvey (1982).

(education, police, health etc.) and is primarily comprised of state invest-ment.

In contrast to the empiricist approaches discussed above Harvey's analysis develops a grand conception of the urban process by stressing the issue of *circulation*. Although it clearly situates the property production process the actual production of the built environment in any specific place or time tends to be glossed over. More micro-scale forms of analysis are developed by Lamarche and Boddy. Lamarche attempted to explore the relationship between an economic formulation of 'the urban question' (see below) and property development. He suggests that in order to resolve this issue it is necessary to modify Marx's theoretical categorization of capital by the addition of 'property capital' (Lamarche, 1975, p. 90). Boddy (1981), in a critique of Lamarche's suggestion, rejects the need for a conceptual category of 'property capital' arguing instead that a focus on the circulation of capital is sufficient. Both Boddy's argument and Lamarche's initial proposal rest on a more literal reading of Marx's *Capital*. Here the three circuits of capital identified here are industrial capital, commercial capital and interest-bearing capital. Boddy analyses the nature of the development process in commodity production.

Industrial capital is directed by the builder, and value produced by the labourer. Commercial capital is directed by the property company which subsequently buys the property. Interest-bearing capital is loaned to the property company by a financial institution to finance the purchase of the property. The property company repays its loan through the sale or rent of the property. Interest-bearing capital is also loaned to the builder to buy raw materials to construct the property in the first place. This loan is repaid on sale to the property company.

Although it is conceptualized at different scales, it is a formulation of circulation of capital through the built environment that is characteristic of the capital accumulation approach. Research in this vein has tended to concentrate upon the office sector[10]. However, isolated pieces of work on industrial production and property development can be found else-where[11]. Gottdeiner (1985, p. 126) suggests that a criticism of this work is its functionalism and over reliance upon capital circulation as an expla-nation of the 'equipment of space'. By focusing upon circulation and exchange, the focus is removed from production which is where value is produced in the first place (Clarke, 1991, p. 13). This explains why there is no concern in these conceptualizations with the actual form of the built environment, or the detail of the agents involved in its production. A further criticism is that the approaches are deterministic, they leave no scope for human action or variation in the form of output.

[10] See Barras (1983), Bateman (1985) and Malone (1981).
[11] See Harvey (1982, p. 388), Boddy (1979, 1981, 1982), MacLaren (1986) and MacLaren and Beamish (1985).

Ambrose (1986) has also attempted to conceptualize the property development system and the role of finance capital (which Boddy terms interest-bearing capital) in terms of the relations between the finance industry, the state and the construction industry. At face value the form of this model is similar to a sophisticated 'property pipeline' model, however it is developed on a materialist basis of commodity production. Unfortunately, the net result is an idealist conception of the agents and structures of development (see Ball, 1984). Furthermore, the labour process (construction) is, by nature of it being treated as a flow, ossified and removed from its material basis.

Another line of explanation that has been drawn upon in terms of capital accumulation is that on Long Waves (see Marshall 1987). Very simply long waves are empirically observed boom and slump phases in capitalist economies. Work by the Soviet economist Kondratiev suggested that each peak was some 50 years apart. An explanation for this boom and slump cycle was put forward by Schumpeter, namely that innovation drove the economy into transformation from the slump to the boom periods.

Recent work attempting to account for science parks has drawn upon long wave theory to relate new forms and economic change. The argument put forward by Simmie and James (1986) is that science parks have been developed to 'capture' innovatory production techniques. That science parks have been developed at this point in time is, they argue, related to the fifth Kondratiev cycle of technological development. This is a rather partial explanation of the development of industrial spaces, with no conception of the production of premises or the social relations of their production, which draws on a general economic determinism not so far away from the neoclassical accounts of location. Interestingly, attempts have also been made to tie in activities in the building industry into long cycles, 'Kuznets cycles' of 15–25 year duration and to link them with economic change in space (see Barras and Ferguson, 1985, 1987).

A recent development of Harvey's (1985) work elaborates yet another conceptualization of the changes in the organization of production. Harvey terms this "flexible accumulation". One aspect of this is the shifting of the balance between Fordist (mass production) and nonFordist systems of labour control coupled with an attempt to play one off against the other. Harvey claims that this has resulted in progressive rounds of unemployment and relocation of production facilities in a 'see–saw' motion of uneven geographical development.

More important for Harvey is the transformation, particularly the globalization, of financial markets that began in the 1970s. The financial system has, he claims, developed an autonomy from 'real production'. This has led to new forms of spatial and temporal 'fixes' to the crisis of profit. By this Harvey means that crises in one part of the economic system can be shifted elsewhere, not only within sectors and places but also between them. So, for example, falling profits in manufacturing in one location can be balanced by reinvestment in the property sector in another country.

Whilst Harvey's argument does grasp an important element of the restructuring of the global, not just the urban, economy, his focus of analysis has remained the same. The focus is upon circulation. The property in any one location is as much 'grist for the mill' of continued flexible accumulation. This issue is discussed again in the conclusion of this chapter. The next section switches attention away from an emphasis upon capital accumulation and focuses on class conflict.

Class conflict theories

A significant contributor to urban theory debates in the 1970s was Manuel Castells. Castells (1977, 1983) stresses consumption in his analyses. He argued that in advanced capitalist societies consumption (for example housing) was increasingly organised on a collective basis. Collective consumption, as he termed it, was controlled by the state in order to ensure continued production (or re-production) of labour power. Castells viewed urban space as a site for the struggle over how collective consumption be organised. Different fractions, urban social movements, would be in conflict over the control of particular aspects of urban space. Having begun from a social basis Castells focuses on consumption relations seemingly at the expense of production relations. Indeed, Clarke (1991, p. 15), argues that Castells effectively divorces relations of consumption, as expressed through urban social movements, from the material basis of the city, space and productive relations.

The approach that Castells took was derived from a reading of the French philosopher Louis Althusser. Althusser's (1969) rereading of Marx had sought to offer an epistemological critique, displacing empiricism with a sound 'scientific' foundation. What was suggested by Castells (1977) was a reconceptualization of the object of urban studies, hence the title of his book— *The Urban Question*. Instead of stressing the individual it is 'collective consumption' that is most important. This approach is often characterized as structuralist because it counters explanations that are reducible to the unconstrained actions of individuals. In so doing structuralist analyses stress the significance of structures (rules or institutions) beyond the individual's choosing. An alternative formulation of the industrial location and development problematic draws upon some of the issues raised by Castells in terms of its mode of conceptualization. However, in this case production relations are stressed instead of those of consumption, and an attempt is made to incorporate space in the analysis.

Notable work by Massey and Catalano (1978) analyses the diversity of interests in the fraction of landed capital. In contradistinction to the suggestion of Lamarche, that there should be a fraction of capital called property capital (see above), Massey and Catalano show the multiplicity of coexisting forms of ownership and control. What is most significant is their effective reconceptualization of space as an historically specific form. This form is appropriated, used, commodified and exchanged under capitalism. The focus is on the class domination of land ownership, little is said about property production.

In industrial geography the seminal work in the class conflict framework is to be found in Massey and Meegan (1979) and Cooke (1983). The title of Massey's (1984) seminal *The Spatial Division of Labour* makes it clear where the research focus is located. This approach, discounting a 'traditional' focus of industrial location such as transport and replacing it with the role of labour power, has also been developed by Storper and Walker (1983, 1984). This idea stems from the analysis of class formation and the labour process: how work is organized. Drawing on the work of Wright (1978), Massey explores in some detail the division of tasks within the production process (managers, administrators, engineers, machine operatives etc.) called the technical division of labour. The technical division of labour gives rise to the social division of labour within society as a whole.

Reorganization of large firms leads to a concentration of particular functions in particular places: office activity in a large city, the production line in a smaller town. As a result the technical division of labour becomes a spatial division as well. Particular types of jobs are located in particular places. This stage of the argument meshes well with an argument concerning the 'new international division of labour' (Frobel *et al.*, 1980).

It is argued that particular spatial divisions of labour are associated with particular styles of accumulation. Viewed in this way the structuralist approach is rendered as 'top-down' in operation. However, this extreme view has to be moderated when such processes are considered both over longer time periods as well as across different sectors of production. In this case it is argued that these patterns of accumulation and spatial divisions of labour of each period interact to build up the distinctiveness of place. Whilst Massey's approach does stress that places or locations are produced through the successive reorganization of production, the actual outcome of this process in terms of the development in each locality of particular forms of industrial development is glossed over. The caveat is that economic and social historical factors do stress the diversity of outcomes from the process. However, the particularities of the development of a built environment to accommodate such development are not addressed.

Gottdeiner (1985, p. 82) argues the approaches discussed above, although counter to neoclassical interpretations of industrial location, fall into the same traps, replacing one set of 'factors' with another. Thus, changes in the social relations of production are either played down or conflated with 'industrial structure' or 'sector'. Another weakness in this approach is the conception of space which is structured by labour relations. This ignores or plays down spatial mobility within the workforce which, particularly in periods of substantial job losses, has a tendency to dilute class conflict. Another criticism is the failure to consider fully the role of the state in the attenuation of class conflict. Two recent contributions draw upon this debate but move it on further. First, by a group working on recent forms of the reorganization of production (as all of the authors are from the West Coast of America they will be referred to as the Californian School) and the French Regulation School.

According to the Regulation School, developed by the French writers Lipietz (1987) and Aglietta (1979), the central theme is the relationship between the regulation of production and the regulation of consumption. The regulation of production refers to the way in which work and the production process are organized and managed. The regulation of consumption refers to the means by which consumption is sustained via such means as welfare and taxation.

The Regulation School argue that a delicate balance between the regulation of production and the regulation of consumption is required to achieve a steady stream of profits. Recognizable periods of 'engineered' equilibrium, expanding production, increased profits, social stability and little labour unrest constitute 'regimes of accumulation'.

It is thus argued that the historical evolution of societies is marked by the periodic transformation of these relationships. The two previous 'regimes of accumulation' are named as 'manufacture' and 'machinofacture'. The current regime of accumulation is known as 'Fordism', describing the balance between mass consumption and mass production, with its associated social and political forms such as collective bargaining and unionization. These social forms create high wages for a significant section of the population, thus sustaining both consumption and production. It is suggested that the spatial forms associated with Fordism are the large integrated, stand-alone plants characterized by closed shop unionization and rigid skill demarcation.

According to the Regulation School the crisis of the 'Fordist regime of accumulation' is being brought about by falling profitability due to the saturation of markets and the breakdown of consent in the workplace as a result of falling wages, inflation and the demise of the welfare state. The resolution of the crisis is leading to a new dynamic equilibrium: the 'neoFordist regime of accumulation'.

The Regulation School does not conceive of a great divide existing between Fordism and its successor, rather it views it as a transmutation to a more intensive, but different regime of accumulation. The spatial forms associated with neoFordism derive from complex and contradictory processes, the key being a vertical disintegration of production linked to local agglomeration. This is brought about by the break-up of large firms into smaller units. For example, local agglomerations may take the form of small firms linked to a 'mother plant' via subcontracting links. Again, it is worth noting the implied hierarchical relationship between firms rather than a non-hierarchical network or organic relationship implied in the Marshallian or the Institutionalist School's theories. The use of stock control techniques such as 'just in time' to achieve minimum stock holding implies a tight supplier linkage between firms as well as a significant degree of temporal, if not spatial, proximity.

Whilst there is a formal vertical disintegration of production in organizational terms, there remains an informal or virtual integration of production via centralized control and the large degree of dependency characteristic of subcontractors. It is argued that a restructuring of the distribution of risk is taking place which although it is giving rise to new organizational forms is the maintenance of flexibility of larger firms through domination of smaller ones. The net effect of the intensification of mass production has been, according to the Regulation School, the splintering of local economies: in effect, a combination of localization and globalization. On one hand there is a centrifugal force and on the other a centripetal one (Amin and Robins, 1990). Whilst the apparent change is the emergence of localized agglomerations, this is matched by a process of global corporate integration that is perhaps more significant (Sayer, 1989).

The Californian approach draws upon the work of the Regulation School. However, it has two distinctive emphases. First, a more liberal interpretation of the ideas of the Regulation School. Second, a greater concern with the spatial implications of changes in regulation (Scott, 1988; Storper and Walker, 1989; Castells, 1989; Storper and Scott, 1989). Like the Regulation school they argue that the Fordist regime of accumulation is in disarray. They argue that the emergence of flexible production was both necessitated by pressures in, and has intensified the crisis of, mass production industries. This group of writers emphasize the significance of key periods of technological innovation and the analysis of transaction costs (the costs of transfer of goods between firms and markets) for spatial change. A point to note about this work is the rather liberal 'pick and mix' approach to key terms that have developed particular significance in other authors' texts. Thus, terms such as 'flexible accumulation', 'industrial district', 'flexible production', 'flexible specialization' and 'regimes of accumulation' are interwoven and sometimes shorn of their original meanings.

The key to the 'new geography of flexible accumulation' is the tendency for internal economies within firms to give way to progressive externalization of the structures of production, for example by contracting-out activities such as accounts, cleaning or security, or elements of the production process. This in turn, it is argued, leads to the agglomeration of firms within industries. In short, vertical disintegration of organizations encourages agglomeration of economic activities and vice versa.

These new 'flexible production complexes' or 'new industrial spaces' are identified as Marshallian 'industrial districts' in character by the Californian School. In many ways the Californian School's position is close to that of the Institutionalists. The key difference is that the Californians do not see 'industrial districts' as self-contained but rather as situated within a global division of labour. For example, they differentiate between the high-technology industrial districts of the USA and Europe, and the low-technology production complexes of the Pacific Rim. In contrast to the Regulationist School they differentiate between the branch-plant decentralization characteristic of Fordism and the new agglomerations of postFordism. Furthermore, they stress the elevated significance of the 'cultural milieu' that particular places acquire in postFordism.

By way of criticism we can note that in a now familiar manner the Californians stress space as a container of new distributions. Whilst they do attempt to engage with new social formations around the analysis of the labour market, they still fail to address issues of production and the built environment.

Another piece of work that fits into the class conflict framework is that by Massey *et al.* (1992) that considers the issues of class, technological and organizational change in a novel way. This work is informed by a reading of critical realism (see Massey and Quintas, 1992). Like Massey's earlier work considerable attention is paid to the analysis of the changes in class structures. In this case the debate is linked to the issue of the labour process, in particular its relation to scientific research and industrial innovation. Massey *et al.* argue that the development of science parks is in part explained by a spatial division of one section of the labour force (scientific workers) and a management and policy conception of scientific research as essentially separate from production.

One aspect of the explanation of science parks for Massey *et al.* is that their separation from production activities and proximity to universities that gives status to the workers there. It is not because it is functional for production. This particular social formation implies a particular physical form: the built environment. Whilst the exact nature of production of science parks is not explored, reference is made to the spatial contingency of the relationship between public and private investment. The significance of this work is the relationship drawn between the restructuring of production and the particular form of the built environment. Whilst the actual nature of property development is not explored in their book, Massey *et al.* do create an analytical space within which it might be considered. This point will be taken up in Chapter 3.

Discussion

The survey presented in this chapter has covered a diverse set of material in the attempt to consider the conceptualization of industry and the built environment. Two major conclusions can be drawn from this survey. The first concerns the notion of space that is implicit in many of the conceptualizations. In most cases the form of a strict social–spatial dualism is upheld. When this is combined with empiricism it has two effects. First, it leads to an atomistic conception of industry and the built environment. Second, it leads to a conceptual 'blind spot' for the production of the built environment. It is for these reasons that the conceptual basis for a consideration of the development of industrial estates developed here is particularly inadequate.

The second conclusion concerns the processes of property development. Even when the role of property development is acknowledged the conceptualization of the process is far from adequate. All of the attempts reviewed here veer towards a form of economism: that is, a reduction of the process to the circulation of capital or individual profit maximization. Effectively this creates another form of dualism, the focus on structures that determine action, or a focus on individuals where structural constraints are not considered relevant.

Chapter 3 begins by introducing the critical realist methodological approach, then proceeds to reconceptualize the relationship between the built environment and industry. This yields a more appropriate focus on the social production of property and a sensitivity to historically specific forms of property provision.

3

Critical Realism and the Explanation of the Industrial Built Environment Form

Introduction

The fact that there are many different ways of conceptualizing the built environment in general, as well as things such as industrial estates in particular, has been made in the previous chapter. The fact that one particular type of conception reoccurred was related to the dominance of a particular mode of reasoning based upon positivism. It is the aim of this chapter to introduce in more detail a different approach to conceptualization based upon critical realism.

It may be asked, 'why is the choice of one conception over another of such significance?' The answer is two-fold. First, it depends upon which approach to science is used. In positivism conceptualization and theorization is a means to an end: an accurate prediction. To the extent that there is a 'good fit' of a model with the data, then any concept or theory would do and reliable predictions may follow. For the critical realist this way of proceeding is an anathema as the critical realist is concerned with identifying, via such abstractions, causal mechanisms which although not always visible are held to actually exist and therefore to account for observed events. In this sense conceptualization is the very essence of explanation. For critical realists explanation and prediction are two quite separate things, for positivists they are part-and-parcel of the same thing.

The second reason is that conceptualization is crucial in determining how and what further investigation takes place: it is a guide to analysis hence the great attention paid to methods as an integral part of research activity. Furthermore, the choice between positivism and critical realism is not neutral or arbitrary. Each position implies taking a particular stand on ontological questions. A criticism of positivism is that by taking 'common sense' concepts one is implicitly accepting a particular ontological perspective. It should be beholden upon all scientists to justify their choice of starting point, positivists use chance, critical realists attempt to base their analyses upon causal and logical grounds. It follows that critical realist informed analyses will invariably take a different starting point from positivist analyses.

This chapter is divided into two main parts, the first is used to elaborate the critical realist position first within the philosophy of science, then in social science. The section is rounded off with a discussion of the implications for research methods and practice of taking up a critical realist position. The second part considers how such a position can be used as a starting point for the reconceptualization of the development of the industrial built environment.

Part I: Critical Realism as Theory and Method

Conceptualization and causality

Perhaps the key step in any analysis is that of dividing things up and classifying them into things that are similar or different. In fact whole branches of science are little more that every more sophisticated taxonomic exercises.

> "Classification is, perhaps, the basic procedure by which we impose some order and coherence upon the vast inflow of information from the real world . . ." (Harvey, 1969, p. 326).

This is such a basic activity that we seldom pay it any attention. In empiricist analyses classification is important but dependent upon the objectives of the research rather than the objects themselves. In this sense, one classification is very much as good as another. Researchers have commonly made recourse to 'natural' classifications such as resemblance, homologous characteristics, or descent. Harré (1970, p. 197) suggests that this approach, termed 'description as classification', can be criticized because it fails to recognize that the group may have other capacities, such as causal powers . Sayer (1984, p. 127) echos this argument by stating that classification should be by causal rather than empirical grouping; the latter he terms chaotic conceptions.

A chaotic conception refers to the grouping and abstraction of non-causally (or contingently) related phenomena. This is a mistake that empiricists will often make as their basis for conception and abstraction is confined to a single ontological plane, that of events. Chaotic conceptions can be contrasted with rational abstractions which are causal structures of internally (or necessarily) related things. This sensitivity to both necessary and contingent relationships is important in critical realism. It distances it from two other positions. First, the position that assumes complete contingency and hence no enduring relations, sometimes referred to as atomism. This position is implicit in positivism. Second, the total relational position. Here it is assumed that everything is related to everything else (see Harvey, 1973, pp. 288–290). This position admits structures and mechanisms, but suffers from determinism. This is a position that has been associated with some interpretations of Marxism.[1]

In order to clarify this point it is perhaps useful to take the industrial estate as an example. 'Natural' classifications could be based upon the size of estate (resemblance), or the type of occupants (homologous characteristics), or design and layout (descent). As noted in Chapter 2, this methodology has been common practice amongst researchers of industrial estates, for example, types of industrial estates have primarily been classified using homologous means: science parks, trading estates. Significantly, they do not refer to causal groupings, in the case of industrial estates: property development processes. As noted above, classification by these empirical characteristics simply results in categories that can be arbitrarily reclassified. As Harré (1970, p. 200) notes

> "The science of taxonomy only makes sense if the classification of individuals by their manifest characteristics is under the control of the theory that their are real differences in the internal constitution of things and substance, from which their manifested characters and their difference spring."

Before progressing further it may be useful to explain what is meant by the term concept. A concept allows general discussion of something without specifying in exactly what terms the concept is being applied. Concepts can be used in reference to one of three sorts of things, those that are real, possibly real, or fictitious. Concepts are key building blocks in the creation of explanations. In positivism concepts are linked together into theories and laws. Usually a systematic testing of hypotheses will be used to evaluate alternatives.[2] The important point to make here concerning concepts in positivist reasoning is that they function as logical devices, they only gain meaning from their place in the theory: they are 'place-holders'. Explanation follows through a process of deductive reasoning from a law and supporting premises.[3]

---

[1] It is ironic that this position has become associated with Marxism because Marx's (1973) 'Introduction' to *The Grundrisse* is the main exemplar of the critical realist method of abstraction. This text has been a focus of attention of many researchers attempting to develop realist methodology (see for example Keat and Urry, 1975; D. Sayer, 1979, 1987; A. Sayer, 1979, 1981, 1984, 1985a; Allen, 1983a). It is here, in particular 'The method of political economy', that we first come across terms such as 'chaotic conception'. D. Sayer (1987) is very good on the comparison of 'traditional' nonrealist readings of Marx compared with critical realist ones.

[2] Another term sometimes used to refer to this process of deduction by hypothesis making is the hypothetico–deductive model.

[3] Positivist analysis are termed deductive–nomothetic (sometimes shortened to d–n). This refers to both the means of logic (deduction) and the process of deriving law-like (nomothetic) statements.

In this sense 'false' theories are as good as 'correct' ones. It follows that some predictions will have no explanatory capacity at all, unless, that is, they refer to causal structures. Hence, any such relation of explanation and prediction is chance. More specifically, this problem is sometimes referred to as that of the asymmetric relationship between prediction and explanation. Just because a prediction works does not mean that it explains. Whilst this is consistent with the nominalist view of the world it does not help with the key issue of intervention in process to regulate them in some way. For such acts we need to know how to influence causes.

The question is how are (real) concepts to be derived? Concepts have to be created by thought processes, critical realists refer to this process as rational abstraction as distinct from chaotic conceptions which are simply derived from nominalist or 'natural' classifications. Concepts are first imagined and their attributes derived by analogy (similarity or difference) from entities already known. Models are used to codify these analogies and processes. There are two main sorts of models; heuristic and explanatory. The first type is designed to simplify or to make a problem 'knowable'. There is no need for such a model to correspond to real processes for it to be useful in such a context. The second type is as an explanation where the model represents a real causal process. It is in this sense that models are realist. Having such a (realist) model implies that a search can be made for the entities involved. Anyone familiar with positivism will be aware that there is often confusion, or slippage, between real and either rationalist or idealist conceptions of models. It must be emphasized that within the positivist deductive–nomothetic structure a search for real entities that moves beyond observables is invalid.

Before advancing further, it is useful to elaborate the notion of causality implied by critical realism. Philosophically, there are two approaches to the problem of causality that we may use that differ in their expression of connection between things. The successionist theory (which underpins empiricism) holds that there is no empirical connection between causes and effects. The structure of argument is 'if A then B'. If A and B reoccur in constant conjunction then a causal link can be inferred. Constant conjunctions are usually measured by statistical techniques (correlation or regression analysis). The important thing is that it is a copresence being noted, not a cause. Rigorous statistical handbooks will point this out, too often correlation elides with cause. Using positivist reasoning this is invalid for two reasons. First, to suggest the existence of cause implies an ontological domain that positivism will not admit. Second, that it requires the use of inductive logic. For example if an event has happened ninety-nine times to imply cause and hence constant repetition for the hundredth occasion requires an inductive step for which there is not, and can never be, evidence. Again, such a step is not strictly admissible in the positivist (hypothetico–deductive) model of reasoning.

The problem of explaining causality is central to scientific analysis. As causality is a concept and not empirically observable, it presents some methodological difficulties for the researcher working within the empiricist tradition. It is important here to consider the concept of closure, this is perhaps best understood within the context of the scientific experiment. The experiment takes place in a laboratory under controlled conditions. All of the components of the processes under investigation are isolated from external interference. This is termed the condition of closure. Next, either one component is manipulated or a new one introduced to the closed system. As this is the only change, the conclusion is that logically any change that occurred in the system under observation must be attributed, or inductively inferred, to this new factor. Using induction invalidates the claims of the hypothetico–deductive model of science.[4] Leaving aside the issue of evidence and discovery of causal processes, a further problem for social scientific researchers attempting to utilize such 'natural scientific' methods is that of inadequate control over closure. It may be organizationally impossible, or morally questionable, to subject humans to 'laboratory-like conditions' regarding, say, unemployment.

The aim of scientists has long been the generation of laws or generalizations from their theories. As noted above, generalizations, particularly if they are of physical characteristics, often involve little or no abstraction, are indifferent to structures and relationships and thus are prone to stress contingency and to neglect social dimensions. It is precisely these elements that are less likely to be invariant over time and space. The inference of outcomes from such generalizations will clearly be spurious and misleading, commonly resulting in ecological fallacies. Ecological fallacies arise where spurious inferential attributions are made from the characteristics groups to those of individuals. The value of generalization must be related to the nature of the objects and their inter-relationships. Together these problems of generalization cast doubt upon the possibility of the derivation of 'proto-laws' in the social sciences (Sayer, 1984, p. 93).

The second approach, termed the generative theory of causality, holds that there is a real connection between causes and effects and that in many cases this can be identified with a causal mechanism. (Harré, 1984, pp. 116–7). The generative conception transcends the (nominalist) division of cause and effect. The conception of a causal mechanism is utilized instead. Things are said to have causal powers and liabilities due to their structure which may, or may not depending upon the particular local circumstances, give rise to an event. This basic difference between conception of causality and ontology and their internal relation to taxonomy in generative theories is expressed by the use of the terms 'event ontology' and 'thing

---

[4]Various attempts have been made to 'side-step' this tricky dilemma. One approach, favoured by Popper, is falsification. He argues that science can not progress by verifying hypotheses but only by falsifying them.

ontology'. Event ontologies refer to groupings of things simply by event, from a nominalist perspective. As noted above there need not be a correspondence between causality and event. Thus, event ontologies are unlikely to be of much use in causal explanation. Urry (1985, p. 25) suggests that thing ontologies refer to nonatomistic and relatively enduring structures which persist because of their causal powers.

Thus, for critical realists unlike positivists, taxonomy and causality are inter-related. This leads to the next stage in critical realists' analyses: exploration of the relationships that constitute causal groupings and specifying the mechanisms that produce events. This process is often referred to as making rational abstractions based upon causal groupings. This can be contrasted with abstraction not based upon causal grouping, a common occurrence in positivist analyses, which critical realists term chaotic conceptions. More generally the form of logic implied by critical realism is called retroduction. Quite simply this means that events are explained by reference to the realization (whether partial or total) or causal powers.

Whilst causal mechanisms may be identified, it does not follow that real world events can be simply 'read off' from these abstractions. Dependent upon the particular contingencies, the same causal mechanism may be realized in different ways. Thus, Urry (1985, p. 25) suggests the need to focus analysis on the precise conditions under which causal powers are realized. This necessarily involves empirical investigation. Thus, the implication is that in a critical realist approach abstraction is not an end, but a beginning in the development of an adequate theory and explanation. The following section explores the applicability of, and implications for, the use of critical realism in the analysis of social processes. This is followed by a discussion of the issue of methodological implications of critical realism in such analyses.

Structure and agency: the case of the transformational model of social activity

The statement of the philosophical positions of critical realism represented a first step in our analysis. The second is to consider the particularity of their applicability to the social domain. As noted in Chapter 1 Bhaskar makes a case for a unity of method between the social and natural sciences, however, this does not mean that they are to be treated exactly the same. A defining characteristic of social science is the subject matter, human beings, and their capacity to think and reflect on their actions. It is important to consider what sort of thing society is and whether it is susceptible to the sort of critical realist analysis outlined above. The critical realist argument can be considered in two stages, first what makes society applicable to realist analysis, and second, how to conceptualize the relationship between society and people.

A well known philosophical position with regard to society is that of methodological individualism. From this perspective the facts about society are explained in terms of individuals. Social institutions are merely abstract models that assist in the interpretation of human behaviour. The social is regarded as a synonym for the group, and as such social behaviour is explicable either as the behaviour of groups of individuals or of individuals in groups. What makes methodological individualism attractive is its insight that society is made up of, and only of, people. However, it is not the only theory that contains such an insight. Bhaskar criticizes this position for its failure to address the relations between individuals and groups. He suggests that such relations are relatively enduring but they do not all involve collective or mass behaviour. This alternative position he terms a relational one. Relational concepts of the subject matter of social science suggest that society does not consist of individuals, or groups, but expresses the sum of the relationships within which individuals and groups stand (Bhaskar, 1979, p. 32).

Bhaskar contrasts the relational conception of society with what he calls the collectivist position, this position emphasizes the group. For the collectivist enduring relations are reconstructed from collective phenomena, whereas from a relational perspective collective phenomena are seen as expressions of enduring relationships. Bhaskar suggests that it is the empiricist and idealist epistemology and the individualist ontology of, respectively, the collectivist and the individualist positions that holds them back from making a real advance. Bhaskar concludes that the relational position is preferable because it is neither essentially concerned with the group or behaviour. However, it is the nature of this relationship between people and society that has presented so many problems for social scientists. It is to this issue that we next turn.

It is perhaps easiest to follow the form of Bhaskar's (1989) elaboration of what he terms the "transformational model of social activity" (TMSA). Four models of the relationships between societies and people are examined. The first two characterize stereotypical positions that have been elaborated in the social sciences. The first is the voluntarist model where social objects are constituted solely by (or arise as a result of) intentional or meaningful human behaviour. The second is the reification model where social objects have a life of their own, external to individuals and capable of coercing them. These positions have been discussed extensively in the sociological literature, the first position being associated with (Max) Weber and the second with Durkheim.

The third and fourth models represent the locus of the key sociological debate throughout the last 20 years. The attempt to synthesize the first two positions, or 'two sociologies' (Dawe, 1970). A dialectical model, as represented in Berger and Luckmann's (1972) characterization of the relationship that society and individual have to one another, is put forward as one attempt to resolve these positions. In this third model it is argued that society forms the individual who then creates society in an on-going process. Social structure is not characterized as a thing able to stand apart from the human activity that created it, but equally society is encountered as alien and coercive. It would seem that the pitfalls of both the first and the second model are avoided in this formulation. However, Bhaskar criticizes this model on two grounds. First, that it encourages a voluntaristic idealism in respect of our understanding of social structure. Second, that it has a mechanistic determination with respect to our understanding of people. Bhaskar asserts that people and society are not two moments of the same process but very different kinds of thing.

The fourth model, Bhaskar's TMSA, holds that the natural world as appropriated by people is always already made. This is not to suggest that society is independent of human activity, but that is it not true to say that humans create it, rather that they transform or reproduce it. Society is thus not the product of individuals' acts, but the totality of human acts sustain or change it. As Bhaskar (1989, p. 76) notes that

> "people do not create society. For it always pre-exists them. Rather it is an ensemble of structures, practices and conventions that individuals reproduce of transform. But which would not exist unless that did so. Society does not exist independently of conscious human activity (the error of reification). But it is not the product of the latter (the error of voluntarism)".

If individuals reproduce society, society provides the necessary conditions for human activity (which may be constraining as well as enabling). In this respect the TMSA can be contrasted with; the voluntarist position where there are actions but no conditions; the collectivist position where there are conditions and no actions; and finally, with dialectical position where there is no distinction between action and condition.

The implication of the TMSA, where society pre-exists the individual, is that humans are deemed to be engaged in the process of sustanation and the constant transformation of that society, which is the production of prior individuals. On one hand this emphasizes the difference in nature of societies or social structures, and people. On the other hand, we can also emphasize the difference between natural structures and social structures. Social structures, unlike natural structures, do not exist independently of the activities that they govern or of the agents' conceptions of what they are doing in their activity. Furthermore, that social structures, unlike natural structures, may be only relatively enduring depending in the last instance on the intentional activity of humans (Bhaskar, 1989, p. 79).

People are distinct from social and natural structures in that their action is characterized by intentionality. This intentionality enables the purposeful activities of monitoring and controlling, and the capacity to monitor the monitorings. Thus people are quite different from social structures whose existence is dependent upon individuals' activities. Engagement in a social act can either be described in terms of the agents own reasons, or in terms of its social function or role. Whilst social structures may impose limits upon activity, they do not determine it. Bhaskar suggests that the role of social sciences under such a conception are to lay out the structural conditions for various forms of conscious action. It is not the task of social science to simply describe the cognitive activity that led to those conditions.[5] To paraphrase with respect to the topic of enquiry in this book, the question is: what social and economic process must take place for industrial estates to be possible?

Structuration and the TMSA

Of course Bhaskar's resolution of the structure–agency formulation is not the only one or even the most well known. Other interpretations are to be found in the work of Bourdieu (1977) and Layder (1981). However, it is Giddens' (1984) interpretation elaborated in the theory of structuration that is perhaps the best known attempt. Giddens, like Bhaskar, approvingly paraphrases Marx to describe his project.

> "Men [let us immediately say human beings] make history, but not in circumstances of their own choosing" (Giddens, 1984, p. xvi, after Marx, 1954, p. 10).

The crux of Giddens's theory is that the production and reproduction of social life is the accomplishment of skilled and knowledgeable actors living in society. Furthermore, that no unitary meaning can be given to constraint in social analysis. Giddens deals with this point in terms of what he calls the duality of structure. The term duality is a reconceptualization of the structure–agency dualism. In a duality, structure is both the medium and the outcome of practices which constitute social systems (Giddens, 1981, p. 2).[6]

More generally, structurationist approaches can be characterized by five points. First, antifunctionalism, and second, the rejection of either structural–determinist or voluntarist explanations, reformulating them as a duality. Third, that they consider time and space central to the construction of all social interaction. Fourth, that social reality is produced by both the conscious and unconscious acts of human agents. Finally, there are a set of intended and unintended external conditions (in space and time) each of which may both constrain, and enable the self-same

---

[5] This is discussed by Harré (1979, p. 112) with regard to the analyses of individuals and crowds using traditional 'cognitivist' approaches.
[6] This work is developed in a series of books (Giddens, 1976, 1979, 1981 and 1984). A summary of structuration can be found in Giddens (1984, pp. 281–284).

process. Giddens's work has aroused considerable debate, mostly sympathetic, amongst other social science practitioners, notably geographers.[7]

It is interesting that Giddens is a little reticent about the application of structuration to research problems, suggesting that in many cases it should only be used to 'sensitize' researchers (Giddens, 1984, p. 326). This seems somewhat of a soft option. Whilst Giddens cites several authors' work as exemplars of the type of research he envisages, few seem to have been actually carried out specifically within its framework (see Craib, 1992).

It is worth considering the fate of those who have tried to apply Giddens's approach. Here a group of inter-related problems with the structurationist perspective can be highlighted in relation to questions raised by critical realism, notably the correspondence of categories in abstract and concrete research. Gregson (1987a, p. 82) points to Moos and Dear's (1986, see also Dear and Moos, 1986) attempt to apply structuration and identifies a key issue: idealist conceptions with respect to their selection of concrete categories as the key problem with their analysis. She goes on to suggest that realism makes claims to resolve this sort of problem. The problem is that realism is, she claims, fundamentally incommensurable with structuration.

Gregson is correct to highlight this problem but it must be emphasized that it is primarily the incommensurability between Giddens's interpretation of structuration and scientific realism that she is referring to. As Thrift (1983) notes in his review of 'the structuration school', it is the formulation of the mediating concept between structure and agency that is crucial. If we compare Giddens's (structuration) and Bhaskar's (TMSA) formulations we can note that Giddens sees the mediating concept in terms of institutions that are reproduced by practices. In effect, Thrift (1983, p. 30) argues, Giddens is redefining structure in terms of practices. In their examination and comparison of both Bhaskar's and Giddens's conceptions of structuration Johnson *et al.* (1984, p. 215) argue that Bhaskar places considerable emphasis on 'hidden' structures, and so has a strong idea of structure (see also Bhaskar 1986, p. 122). In other words it is the development of an ontological dimension that is the strength of Bhaskar's resolution of the structure–agency problem. Thus, it is possible to resolve Gregson's criticisms of structuration and the problem of the incommensurability of realism and structuration and its potential application to practical research if one uses Bhaskar's concept of the TMSA.

Truth, knowledge and critical realism

One of the most immediate practicalities of doing critical realist research is the problem of how to evaluate the explanations produced. Even within

---

[7]See Sayer (1983), Gregory (1984), Thrift (1984, 1985), Storper (1985), and Gregson (1986, 1987a).

the empiricist mode evaluation, or verification, it is problematic because the social world is not susceptible to 'closure' and isolation from interference. Critical realist explanations are not directly susceptible to verification due to the different conception of what and how the 'real' is constituted. Indeed, this has been a point of criticism from antirealists (see Saunders, 1986, p. 359). The point of contention concerns the process of abstraction. Critics such as Saunders, who favour Weberian logic that relies upon the construction of ideal types, claim that the criticalrealist concept formation is simply a result of a priori theorizing; usually of a Marxist hue. It is because critical realist knowledge is assertion that it is not susceptible to testing. Burrows (1989, p. 57) commenting upon this dispute suggests that both critical realism and ideal typical constructs bear many similarities in that they are both one-sided elaborations of the concrete social world. Burrows argues that both approaches are likely to be similar in the early stages of research. However, as research continues there is a move towards critical realist operationalizations of phenomena that give credence to the ontological status of causal groups and distinguish between necessary and contingent relations. Burrows suggests that this point emphasize the necessity of the development of a critical realist methodology to the viability or otherwise of critical realism.

Within critical realism the issue of verification is still a problematic one. The issue turns on the question of the nature of knowledge. For Bhaskar (see 1986; 1989, p. 56) this is a central issue which he seeks to link with emancipation. He argues that if emancipation depends upon the transformation of structures then such a transformation must be a practically necessary condition for a more human set of affairs. There are, he argues, potential links between social theory and practice in society. Social theory is practically conditioned by, and potentially has practical consequences for, society. Bhaskar (1989, p. 6) argues that the relationship between social theory and knowledge, and social practices,

> "will take the form of an emancipatory spiral in which deeper understanding makes possible new forms of practice leading to enhanced understanding".

Crucially, the methods of natural science—positivism—by denying natural necessity and causation, or admitting deeper ontological structures act to obscure or obstruct any progress towards enhanced understanding. As such, they should be considered to be antiemancipatory (Bhaskar, 1989, p. 82).

A further problem is that of truth. A common understanding of scientific activity is that it provides some privileged and final access to the truth about the world. This position is referred to as the correspondence version of truth. Critical realists have sought to distance themselves from this position. The implication of knowledge being an accomplished production of knowledgeable actors in the social world is that all knowledge must not only be fallible but necessarily open to immanent critique. Truth must be conditional, perhaps restyled as 'truth'.

Sayer (1984, p. 229) makes the point that all evaluations are for someone, in other words that they cannot simply be taken out of all contexts and made into some eternal judgement. As such empirical testing of theories can demonstrate quantitative errors, but not evaluate truth. Critical realists have substituted the notion of practical-adequacy for that of truth (see D. Sayer, 1979; Bhaskar, 1979; A. Sayer, 1984).

> "To be practically adequate knowledge must generate expectations about the world and about results of our actions which are actually realized" (Sayer, 1984, p. 66).

Whilst also being wary of the simple correspondence version of truth implicit in positivism, Layder (1990, pp. 55–58) also wants to avoid siding (as positivism does) with the coherence version of 'truth' which he claims constitutes practical adequacy. He suggests that such a position lends itself to relativism and hence denies a separation of the world and the knowledge we have of it. Instead, Layder (1990, p. 58) suggests a middle ground which preserves a critical realist notion of real structures and generative mechanisms independent from cognition, but also sustains two other notions. First, that we can only know the world under linguistic or discursive representations of it. As such, knowledge is always encountered as pregiven, already constructed in the shape of theories, concepts and epistemological premises. Second, that in our pursuit of knowledge we must nevertheless attempt to represent objects independent of discursive practices by which they are known.[8]

Methodological implications of critical realism

A key strength of critical realism is that it not only offers a more satisfactory retheorization of the structure–agency problem but that it also supports claims about how to proceed in science. To some extent these two issues have been dealt with quite separately in the literature on critical realism, a consequence of which has been that debates have continued to be carried on in a rarefied and abstract manner. On one hand critical realism is positioned against positivism, on the other it is positioned against both voluntarist and determinist versions of social science. This does not seem to move the argument on much further. The following two comments sum up the situation, first, with respect to structurationist informed analyses—

> "a concentrated programme of theoretically informed empirical research is needed if this theoretical elaboration is not to occur in a vacuum" (Thrift, 1983, p. 42).

---

[8]Represent, that is, in a symbolic rather than an isomorphic fashion.

Second, with specific respect to critical realism—

> "the practicalities of what it means to do critical realist research are still emerging and ought to be the subject of a wider debate" (Sarre, 1987, p. 10).

There is an irony in this state of affairs. A central tenet of a critical realist science must be a (theoretically informed) empirical programme, yet most debate in this field has been carried out in the absence of such research activity. The argument that I want to stress here is that it is only when the two central issues of critical realism—the critique of science and the critique of social ontology—are bought together in a specific research programme that a substantive contribution to knowledge will be made.[9]

A pragmatic question that may legitimately be asked at this point is, 'what, in practice, is so different about research informed by critical realism?' The remainder of this chapter offers a beginning to the answer of this question. This section is divided into two parts, the first reviews some previous attempts to apply critical realism and draws upon their findings in order to elaborate the prospects and problems of such research. The second part explores the question of which research methods are appropriate to critical realist research.

Previous attempts to apply critical realism

One of the big problems for anyone new to critical realism is the lack of a clear and accepted mode of proceeding. With all its conceptual and philosophical problems, the pragmatist will invariably choose the 'tried and tested' positivism. Particularly, the hard-pressed research student. However, the conclusion to be drawn from the arguments already presented in this chapter would suggest two things. First, that such a faith might be misplaced. Second, the conclusion from the previous chapter, that pragmatically nominalism had not been very successful in explaining the development of industrial estates.

A useful starting point with regard to how to carry out critical realist research is provided by Outhwaite (1987, p. 58) who suggests three steps; the postulation of a possible mechanism, the attempt to collect evidence for or against its existence, and the elimination of possible alternatives. The important message implicit in Outhwaite's proposition is the reliance upon retroduction: explanation by reference to mechanisms. The problem is that it is quite difficult to immediately recognize what form that this might take in any actual research programme. For this reason it is useful to consider some previously documented attempts to apply critical realism.

Allen and McDowell's (1989; Allen, 1983b) research on private landlordism and the explanation of change in the private rental housing sector

---

[9]Bhaskar has argued that the role of his interventions in the realm of philosophy should be considered as an 'underlabourer' or ground clearer (see Bhaskar, 1989, Chapter 1).

in Inner London is a clear exemplar of critical realist informed research. Their comments are worth relating at length.

"By looking in detail at landlords in the context of the housing market or markets in which they operated and investigating the nature of their activities, we were able to discern the structure of relations that lay behind their actions. In turn, we were able to use the results of the case studies to assess the validity of our initial six-fold classification of landlords identified from the findings of our extensive research. The results, in our view, corroborated our initial classification, but as anticipated also revealed differences between practices of landlords which we had placed in the same group. We then had to address the possibility that our guiding preconceptions on the structures of landlordism had foreclosed our analysis of the case studies and yielded corroborative evidence. It would be naive to deny that our initial conceptualisation of landlord types did not influence our interpretation of the case studies, indeed the situation could not have been otherwise; but this statement is rather different from accepting that our preconceptions determined our research findings" (Allen and McDowell, 1989, pp. 75–76, Footnote 1).

Leaving aside their substantive research findings, four points can be made about the application of critical realism to this problem. First, that it placed considerable emphasis upon the abstraction and conceptualization of landlords. Second, it stressed the importance of both extensive and intensive information gathering (see below). Third, there was an iterative approach to analysis, a deeper understanding being developed on each reconceptualization. The fourth point expands on the third, in that attention was drawn to the fact that such an iterative approach does not translate well into a readily comprehensible logic of presentation of results, and as such the order of presentation of research may not correspond to the order in that it was actually done (Allen and McDowell, 1989, p. 59).

The second major application of critical realism to a research project has been that of Morgan and Sayer (1988) on the electrical engineering industry in South Wales. In a commentary on their research Sayer and Morgan (1985) discussed a particularly important aspect of their approach, namely the use of intensive and extensive research designs.[10] Extensive methods consist, ideally, of the examination of all members of a population, although in practice a representative sample may be chosen and properties of the whole population derived from it. The common practice of a simple questionnaire survey or census is the best example. The problem with such a method is that empirical properties are likely to dominate classifications, these are not likely to be causally meaningful. Furthermore, if the properties—causal or otherwise—are widely variable within the group any results are likely to be trivialized as there will be little in common between population members.

Intensive methods involve the examination of a typical member of the population in order to discover all, or as many as practicable, properties that a typical member has. A group will consist of a set of individuals who

---

[10]This distinction was first elaborated by Harré (1979, p. 132). The idea is taken up and elaborated further in Sayer (1984, pp. 219–229) and Sayer and Morgan (1985).

are like the typical member in most respects. The key advantages are that structural relations and interactions can be ascertained. The type of methods usually associated with intensive designs are in-depth interview techniques. The criticism of such an approach is that one could derive as many groups as there are individuals.

The resolution is to use both techniques together. Sayer and Morgan (1985, p. 152) suggest that extensive research prioritises information about patterns and intensive research prioritises information about processes. Depending upon the circumstances intensive could follow extensive research or visa versa. Sayer and Morgan used intensive then extensive, Allen and McDowell extensive then intensive.

Commenting further upon his own attempts to apply realism Sayer (1988, p. 24) notes the problems inherent in its reporting, particularly with respect to both the structuring and ordering of the narrative. Bourdieu (1984, p. 503) touches on a similar problem in his presentation of *Distinction*. Forcing such a structure of explanation into the standard linear form clearly presents problems for the researcher. The danger is that common or accepted forms of presentation effectively impose the hegemony of empiricism. Two points arise. First, that the presentation does not represent the research process. Second, that the form of presentation may not be amenable to critical realist elaborations. There is no immediate solution to this problem, aside from drawing the readers attention to the need to consider separately the presentation of results and how they were derived.

A third exemplar of critical realist informed research is that of Doreen Massey and her coresearchers on industrial restructuring.[11] Here critical realism is used with a 'light touch'. It informs analyses by it is seldom, if at all directly referred to. Most useful for the purpose of this analysis are commentaries (see Massey and Meegan 1985; Massey and Quintas, 1992). Two points arise from this material with respect to research methods. First, the detail of conceptualization and reconceptualization. In Massey and Quintas (1992) in particular, the problem of accepting common-sense categorisations such as science parks as already given is highlighted. It is suggested that a particular task of critical realist research can be to consider the causal efficacy of such explanations and to suggest alternatives. Second, is the use of intensive and extensive research techniques, in particular, in the most recent work, the use of detailed interview transcripts.

Finally, a whole body of work has been informed by critical realism: 'localities research'. Basically, this was a research programme funded by the U.K. Economic and Social Research Council between 1984 and 1987

---

[11]See Massey and Meegan (1982), Massey (1984) and Massey *et al.* (1992).

and co-ordinated by Cooke (1986).[12] Seven teams undertook intensive studies of localities chosen for their variety of experiences in the context of broader national and international changes (Cooke, 1989). The whole programme generated a huge amount of debate about the validity of the 'locality study'.[13]

For the purposes of argument here there are two issues to consider.[14] The first, concerns the use of the 'case study'. The work of social anthropologists, in particular Geertz (1973, 1983) was drawn upon to defend this approach. It stressed the necessity of comparing across cases (see Cooke, 1987). There was a general acceptance of the necessity of considering the unique, particularly the spatially unique, but many critics were concerned about a slide into empiricism and/or idiographic studies. This critique stressed the importance of the development of adequate linking concepts between the micro- and the macro-scale. In the absence of this the method was meaningless. Worse, it could be used as a 'cover' for empiricism under the name of critical realism.

The second is related to the first, there was concern expressed about the problem of defining localities. In practical terms a locality, bounded and defined, seemed to be an a priori of this sort of work. The problem was *which* boundary was relevant? Local labour markets were utilized in most research, but critics pointed out that other causal process may lead to other boundaries being relevant. This highlighted the fact that the bounding of a locality might on one hand be considered arbitrary, and/or reductive to just economic relations. This highlighted a third point—a deeper question concerning the spatiality of social relations.

Duncan and Goodwin derived a hierarchy of the spatiality of social relations based upon the distinction between contingent and necessary relations:

> "(1) 'contingent local variation' (where spatial contingency affects how mechanisms operate in practice)
> (2) 'causal local variation', (where the social mechanisms themselves are locally derived) . . .
> (3) 'locality effects', could occur (where a bundle of complementary and locally derived processes and outcomes produce some sort of local social system)." (Duncan and Goodwin, 1988, p. 61).

Whilst emphasizing that 'space matters', this position effectively closes off possibilities of 'localities' *per se* as research objects, except in (3), which

---

[12]The Changing Urban and Regional System initiative. The work grew out of a research fellowship awarded previously to Doreen Massey on industrial restructuring and its explanation.

[13]The flavour of this debate can be gleaned from Smith (1987) and Harvey (1987), Gregson (1987b), Beauregard (1988), Lovering (1989), Urry (1981b), (1986), Duncan (1986), Savage *et al.* (1987), Cooke (1987, 1989), Cox and Mair (1989), Duncan and Savage (1989), and the special issue of *Environment and Planning* **A 23** (1991).

[14]Arguably, there is a third point which concerns the postmodernist debate, spatiality, uniqueness and critical realism. See my discussion in Pratt (1991).

they suggest is very unlikely. In a later paper Duncan and Savage (1989, p. 204) conclude that researchers should concern themselves primarily with the task of exploring how divisions of labour, state relations and civil society combine to produce spatial effects.

By way of summary, three points can be made about the critical realist search for corroboration of models and causal mechanisms that mark it out from positivist methods. First, that the process may not be a direct or linear one, often it is iterative, the model being refined in an on-going process. Whilst this may seem a trivial point it does severely challenge existing modes of scientific endeavour, both implying a far more exploratory structure and a challenge to the common form of presentation of results.

Second, the process of conceptualization is central to the whole endeavour. Several researchers have highlighted a particular problem, that of the micro–macro distinction. This is manifest in respect to individuals and groups and localities and wider systems. In each case the significance of an adequate conception of the mediating concept is crucial if determinism or voluntarism is to be avoided.

Third, the use of retroduction may necessitate the application of new methods of 'detection' for sensing the 'reality' of new causal mechanisms. The issue of research design has already been discussed above, the question of exactly what methods and styles of analysis might be used has not. This is the subject of the second part of this section.

The methodological implications of critical realism

The great challenge posed by critical realism is how to weave together intensive and extensive methods in research. The terms qualitative and quantitative are often used interchangeably with intensive and extensive research.[15] There have been attempts to 'link' or 'combine' quantitative and qualitative approaches in sociology, this has run in parallel with a concern to resolve the micro- and macro-sociological explanations. However, in the absence of a well worked out theoretical programme these attempts are more hopeful than practical (see Silverman, 1985; Fielding and Fielding, 1986; Dale *et al.*, 1988). Burrows (1989, p. 59) raises this problem in the context of a discussion about critical realism and research methods, he concludes that the most appropriate research tools might be those of ethnography. Ethnographic research usually refers to direct observation of activities of particular members of a group, and the description and evaluation of such activities. Such approaches, favoured by social anthropologists and some sociologists, seek to place action in context.

---

[15]The term intensive and extensive is preferable. It can be argued that quantitative analyses are a poor relation of qualitative data. As all data is qualitative, it is the degree and aim of research that is the defining characteristic.

However, such an approach does not directly address the issue of ontology: the nature of the thing under observation, in this case, the interview. There are two points here. First, is the validity of approaches. The preference for capturing long stretches of interaction, common in ethnography seems to play into the trap of assuming that such data is 'unbiased', whereas it might be argued that interviews or questionnaires are 'false' situations (Hammersley and Atkinson, 1983). Positivists would argue that bias in interviews only arises due to 'bad' interviewers or 'bad' interviewees.

What is significant is that there is a continuum of structured interactions. At one end is the structured questionnaire, at the other is the participant observation. In between are structured and unstructured interviews. To be strictly accurate we might add another axis that would describe the presence or absence of interaction on behalf of the interviewer.[16] Of course, in all situations the analyst has some role in framing the situation. The extent to which context is introduced might be variably dependent upon the causal processes under investigation. Two ideal types could be suggested. The first might mean the researcher noting interpersonal interaction, positioning and movement in one room. The second might require the researcher to analyse global flows of commodities.

Second, researchers have to be sensitive to the type of knowledge that the intensive survey, or interview, is. This is crucial to the interpretation of the method. The crucial distinction is between internalist and externalist positions (Silverman, 1985, p. 170). Used in the context of positivist analyses interview data is simply a presentation of facts or (nominalist) realities about the world. This can be termed the externalist position and it is valid as long as correct procedures (called protocols) are followed. Alternatively, in an ethnomethodological context the focus might be upon conversational practices such as turn-taking, pauses or the frequency of the usage of particular words. These are often based upon a conventionalist epistemology. This is termed the internalist position, in these terms the interview data expresses either interpretative procedures or conversational practices present in what both interviewer and interviewee are doing through their talk and nonverbal actions. Silverman (1985, p. 170) argues that critical realists are concerned with both internalist concerns with form and universality *and* the externalist commitment to content and variability.

As has already been suggested a variety of actual surveys may be required to satisfy the information requirements of any particular piece of research. As intensive and qualitative approaches are covered in most

---

[16]The social science literature is well served by 'how to' texts on the various types of structured questionnaires (see Oppenheim, 1966; Bogden and Taylor, 1975; Moser and Kalton, 1979; Labaw, 1980; and in industrial geography Healey, 1991).

social scientific 'methods' texts they are not dealt with here.[17] However, attention should be paid to the context of their usage. The remainder of this section will focus on the problem of the intensive form of research design and interview analysis.

Sayer (1984, p. 223) in a review of research methods suggests that the critical realist researcher should adopt a less formal, less standardized and more interactive kind of interview. The unstructured interview is the most appropriate tool as it facilitates,

> "a meaningful type of communication which maximises the information flow by making use of communicative and social skills, by being willing to adapt preconceived questions and ideas in the course of the interview" (Sayer, 1984, p. 223).

This position recognizes a crucial aspect of the interview, that it, is an interaction between interviewer and interviewee. The same questions asked in a questionnaire may have vastly different significance for different respondents: whilst the rigidity of structured techniques makes it difficult to follow up and respond to such variations. If one accepts that the subject of interest is the very heterogeneity and polyvalency of agents, then it is appropriate to use research techniques that emphasize rather than suppress the differences between subjects. The rationale for sampling follows on from this and is well expressed by Sayer:

> "in intensive studies the individuals need not be typical and they may be selected one by one as the research proceeds and as an understanding of the membership of a *causal* group is built up" (Sayer, 1984, pp. 221–223, emphasis in original).

The use of a loosely structured questionnaire or interview facilitates the collection of a large amount of detailed information, but it can be difficult to analyse. Sayer offers no help here. The whole field of qualitative analysis is a new and relatively unexplored one. The objective is to develop an analytic technique that is both qualitative and exploratory that is also attentive to both agency and structure. One of the key problems of this type of research is categorization, the central problem is how to link such categorizations to conceptualization. A predetermined textual category technique such as content analysis where the occurrence of key words is noted and quantified is clearly not appropriate. Other textual analysis techniques such as conversational analysis and discourse analysis are not appropriate as they deny classification by causal mechanisms that lie outside of the text.

A potential solution lies in the work of Glasser and Strauss (1967) in their explanation of *The Discovery of Grounded Theory*. The aim in their book was to bridge a gap between empirically uninformed theory and theoretically uninformed empirical research by grounding theory in data.

---

[17]See Footnote 16 for examples of such texts.

Grounded Theory is regarded as a key step in the development of qualitative approaches, it is sometimes referred to as a 'middle-range' theory. Much emphasis is put upon the development of new theories in the approach. The practicalities of what Glasser and Strauss advocate as "emergent categories" are identified from interviews and these are treated as categories for analysis. This involves two problems. First, the naive nominalist classification can be represented as individualist as it reduces any structural factors to those of individuals. Second, both the categories and the initial questions are derived from 'the analyst's head' and are not explicitly derived from causal mechanisms.

However, an approach that avoids the use of phenomenologically derived categories, whereby categories are informed by the abstract theoretical analysis of causal mechanisms would seem to offer a useful guide to procedure. Clearly, the exact suite of techniques applied are likely to vary with the particular research topic under investigation. In the approach that I am proposing the researcher is explicit about the derivation of categories and the research questions. By making the research technique open-ended then 'discoveries' from the information gleaned from both intensive and extensive survey modes can be fed back into the theoretical understanding, facilitating a more adequate choice of categories, and thus, a more adequate conceptualization of the object of interest.

The analysis that follows in Chapter 6 draws upon such an approach. First, the interview schedule was derived from a broader analysis of the causal mechanisms drawn both from extensive survey and abstraction. In detail, the following practice was adopted with regard to the analysis of interview material. The interviews were transcribed and then read through several times. Emergent key concepts were then selected and the interviews coded-up paying particular attention to quotes and their context. As may be expected there is an element of self-fulfilling prophecy about the process of the emergent key concepts already implicated in the interview schedule. As this schedule was itself derived from the extensive survey and subsequent abstract theorization this may be considered to be a key bulwark against the use of the naive empiricist approach that may easily result from following Glasser and Strauss's methodology too closely. The emergent key concept areas were similar to those implicated by the abstract theory, but additional topics such as property management, rent and leases, interaction with other agents and spatially specific information were revealed as significant. Furthermore, the emergent key concepts considerably refined the theoretically defined ones.

For each interview a record card was completed for every key concept. Later, all the information on each key concept was collated across all of the interviews and the subsequent analysis was based upon it. Thus, the information collected would dictate the form of the analysis rather than visa versa. In order to retain confidentiality interviewees' names were suppressed and replaced by code numbers.

The abundance of information produced in this type of analysis gives rise to the need to be selective. In this case, it was decided to bracket out all but the immediate development process. In practice this resulted in the interviews with a range of actors—planners, estate agents and advice agents—not being included directly in the final analysis. However, knowledge of these responses gave the researcher confidence that the bracketing out had not excluded important points.

A final problem arising from this type of research methodology is the presentation of the results. Clearly, as this is not a statistical sample or quantitative research, it makes no sense to provide a statistical breakdown of the responses. Some qualitative analysis texts recommend the reproduction of tables, as in quantitative research (see Miles and Hubermann, 1984). However, it was considered important to include actual quotes in this case. These are presented with the knowledge that the causal context has been established, the quotations actually reproduced are included in order to capture the flavour of the responses rather than being 'representative' or 'exhaustive' of the interview texts.

Part II: Reconceptualizing the Industrial Built Environment

Introduction

In the second part of this chapter a move is made to reconceptualize the industrial built environment. This is followed through in two stages, the first considers the nature of the abstraction of production in general terms. The conclusions drawn here highlight the different conceptions of what might be included in the analysis of production. In particular three issues are emphasized; the autonomy of supply and demand, the autonomy of production from society, and the spatiality of social and economic relations. The second stage considers how, within such a context, the reproduction of property in general and the industrial estate in particular might be considered.

Situating re-production

A crucial stage in critical realist informed research is making rational abstractions. In practice, this involves identifying the necessary relationships between things and distinguishing them from merely contingent relationships. The most daunting question to the analyst is 'where to begin?' Already one is thrust into questions about ontology and epistemology. As noted in the previous chapter a common starting point is with the market, this is the starting point for neoclassical economics. It was pointed out that classical economics offered a potential alternative by beginning with the production of value which derive from labour, not exchange. Marx's approach, in particular that set out in his notebooks, namely *Grundrisse*, has often been offered as an exemplar of this approach. It has been pointed out by many critical realists that the method that Marx employs in this book follows that of critical realism very closely.[18] Less attention has been paid to the substantive content in a critical realist context (see Keat and Urry, 1975; Urry, 1981a). It is this latter vein that will be pursued next.

Production in general. In the 'introduction' Marx (1973, p. 85) is particularly concerned with the conception and abstraction of what he terms "production in general". He devotes his attention to an analysis of the nature of the internal relationships between what he terms the "moments of production"; production, consumption, distribution and exchange. What is suggested is that the concept 'production in general' comprises four elements. Whilst, one part may be experienced as separate from another, its existence is dependent upon the other three. In an abstract sense production is to be considered as a whole, and the divisions are but 'distinctions within a unity' (Marx, 1973, p. 99). For example, production necessitates and implies consumption, distribution and exchange. Likewise, exchange necessitates and implies production, consumption and distribution. This last point demonstrates a departure from neoclassical analyses that simply focus on the market. The market cannot exist in isolation from the rest of production, or society. This apparently simple abstraction has a significant consequence for an analysis of production.

Thus, whilst each individual firm in an economy may seem to be separate, to take it as such in an abstraction would be a chaotic conception. It should properly be considered as but one part of production as a whole; the outputs from one industry forming the input to another. Ironically, the analysis of these linkages has formed a substantive focus for industrial geographers and economists. Despite the focus on the linkages, abstractions of firms are still considered as the key to analysis. The next step for Marx was to explore how production was sustained. The transfer of value was integral in his analysis. In its concrete, or phenomenal, form this was money, property, labour and time. The use of the abstraction *capital*, which he termed "value in motion", was another crucial step to grasping the nature of production. Relating such insights back to the problem of understanding the location and spatial form of industrial development raises two issues: first, what might be considered to constitute 'production' in an empirical sense?, second, the issue of the market.

---

[18]See Footnote 1.

Perhaps surprisingly, Marxist industrial geographers have largely confined their attentions to traditional conceptions of production (manufacturing and sometimes the distribution of functions between 'head office or branch plants'). Recent concern with the analysis of the service sector has highlighted this problematic conception. There is considerable acceptance of the fact that many components of 'service sector' activity were formerly carried out as part of manufacturing activities. Good examples might include distribution and marketing services. It is only since they have been 'hived-off' that the service sector has been paid attention. Looked at in this way it does seem obvious that exchange, distribution, production and consumption can only be adequately understood in relation to one another rather than separately. What seems to be lacking are interlinking studies of production, distribution and exchange within this scheme. There has, however, been a growth of interest in the inter-relationship between investment and production.[19] Whilst this research has much to commend it in its breadth of concern, and its coherence of abstraction, it often falls foul of the economic reductionism and functionalism inherent in some versions of the Marxian thesis.

Likewise analyses of finance and property trading are clearly integral to such analyses. Useful pointers to such research have come from those who have concentrated upon analysis of the property and investment sector itself (Thrift, 1986, 1987a). However, conceptualization of the causal processes are, as yet, underdeveloped. Thrift's (1986, p. 145) analysis of property services, for example, draws upon Faegin's (1982) conception of property actors. However, as Faegin (1982, p. 41) notes, such a taxonomy is misleading in that property actors often subsume other activities which might otherwise be separately categorized. Alternatively, research that considers industrial premises from the perspective of the market treat supply and demand as separate entities, and unrelated to their production, can be dismissed as contentless abstractions. 'Supply-side' approaches are merely a special case of this general approach. The 'supply-side' approaches, whilst emphasizing the production of the industrial built environment, are prone to the deterministic and naturalistic conception of the relationship between the occupant and the premises. Furthermore, they do not offer any explanation of the process by which property comes to be developed.

Although the general nature of the abstraction of production has been established and the significance of the inter-relationships has been highlighted, it is still necessary to specify precisely how production and the use of the built environment are structured together. This will necessarily involve situating the processes in space and time, and thus mean that the

---

[19]See Boddy (1981), Walker and Storper (1981), Sayer (1982a), Taylor and Thrift (1983), and Faegin (1987).

specific nature of institutions will have to be considered. This will necessitate, to paraphrase Thrift (1983, p. 24), a theory of, rather than one about, social action. The following section details the abstraction of production with particular respect to the industrial built environment and the firm.

If an individual firm is considered it is clear that its activities have to be accommodated and located in space. At this place; labour, the means of production, commodities, and finance can be structured together in order to create surplus value. This location is both social, socially produced and socially producing (Urry, 1981b, p. 458). A particular location may, for example, make some firms more 'central' to other areas of production, or workers more 'peripheral'. There is a necessary relationship between production and accommodation. However, this does not mean that it is sufficient to explain industrial property provision. The particular resolution of this relationship will depend upon the distribution of power and resources between, on one hand, the firm and, on the other, those institutions responsible for the provision of such accommodation. Whilst we can make statements at an abstract level about production and the need to consider its four moments it must be remembered that production cannot take place in a vacuum: people must be involved—individually and collectively. The very possibility of production presupposes certain necessities. The first of these is that society is commodity producing. This presupposes a particular social division of labour. Second, that labour is free. This applies in two senses, free from slavery or serfdom, and free from the ownership of the means to produce commodities. Third, the means of production are constituted as private property (D. Sayer, 1987, p. 132). Considered in this way it becomes clear that capital is not so much a 'thing' as a social relation. Production is reliant upon the conditions of production pre-existing it.

Urry (1981a, p. 37) notes that private landownership is crucial as it is necessary for the maintenance and reproduction of capitalist society, yet, the capitalist means of production does not create the necessary conditions for its existence. This is a basic problem in the evolution of, and change in, society i.e. how capitalism is reproduced. Furthermore, the relationship between production and the rest of society has to be specified. One solution to this problem is achieved through an analysis of the specific institutions and their spatial manifestations.

Social institutions. The state has received much attention from sociologists and political economists since the resurgence of interest in Marxist state theory in the late 1960s (Jessop, 1987, p. 1). Whilst industrial geographers have long considered the state in studies of industrial location, it has predominantly been as a further factor in location or policy analysis 'bolted on' to existing theories. Such an approach is called the study of the 'capitalist state'. It is only recently that industrial geographers have turned their attention to the 'state in capitalism'.

Dear and Scott's (1981) edited volume *Urbanisation and Urban Planning in Capitalist Society* seems to have been important in popularizing this perspective. The seeds were set in Pickvance's (1976, p. 12) call for an historical materialist approach to urban sociology in which the state is conceptualized in a structuralist manner as the provider of the complex legal, political, and cultural apparatus necessitated by the economic level of the capitalist mode of production. However, as Clarke and Dear (1981, p. 45) point out, this does not adequately explain the purpose, method and degree of intervention of the state. Little guidance to the solution of this problem can be found in Marx, as Jessop (1977, p. 357) in a comprehensive overview of Marxist interpretations of the state notes that

> "nowhere in the Marxist classics do we find a well formulated, coherent sustained theoretical analysis of the state."

The perceived need to fill this theoretical gap has generated a mini-industry of formulations, critiques and reviews of theories of the state.[20] Criticisms of theories of the state focus on two sets of problems with most formulations: first, the lack of explanation of how and why the mode of production and consequentially accumulation changes. Second, a tendency towards functionalism, reductionism or the neglect of social action. In a later review of theories of the state Jessop (1987, p. 3), himself a critical realist, agues that these problems reflect

> "the methodological impossibility of developing a single, all encompassing theory of so complex a phenomena as the nation-state in all its historical specificity."

The conclusion to be drawn here is perhaps surprising, namely that the state is, in terms of abstract theory, a contentless abstraction a phenomenal form or structure that is contingent upon other factors. The state itself cannot be explained without reference to society. As such the state must be constituted and reproduced by the members who constitute a society. This issue, which Giddens (1981, p. 150) terms 'the production of everyday life' will be considered next.

Giddens (1981, p. 4) attempts to plot out the development and organization of societies in his *Contemporary Critique of Historical Materialism*. In it he deploys a structurationist approach in order reconceptualize both existing economic reductionist and power reductionist formulations in terms of the explanation of reproduction. Giddens asserts that power should be regarded as generated in, and through, the reproduction of what he terms 'structures of domination'. Two major types of resources can be drawn into

---

[20]Comprehensive and critical reviews can be found in the work of Jessop (1977, 1982, 1987), with reference to planning in Dear and Clarke (1978), and to geography in Dear and Scott (1981), and Johnston (1982).

these structures of domination: allocative resources, where humans dominate the material world, and authoritative resources, in the domination of the social world. Giddens (1981, pp. 5–6) argues that in capitalist societies the state plays a crucial role in holding and maintaining power throughout time and space. Giddens is attempting to explore and emphasize the importance and role of human actors in engaging in social action to reproduce society. This point is also taken up by Urry (1981a) in his formulation of the state. Urry argues that the state owes its form to this act of reproduction but that, importantly, this reproductive activity takes place 'outside' of the state in civil society. Urry's conception of civil society and its relation to the state takes an important step away from the cruder Marxist conceptualizations and embraces a modified view through the work of Gramsci.

Although there are many conflicting concepts of the state provided by Gramsci,[21] Urry (1981a, p. 10) adopts the position that civil society has relative autonomy from both the state and capital. Thus, the particular nature of struggle in civil society will involve the development of forms of domination and legitimation by the state, particular forms of production by capital, and degrees of fragmentation and organization in civil society. All of which will be spatially and temporally specific. The relationships between the state and civil society take the phenomenal form of laws enacted by the state, whilst the mediation between capital and civil society; is achieved by the use of money (Urry, 1981a, p. 116).

Analysts of the British government system have pointed to the considerable local variations that exist in local government. This observation has given rise to a wide ranging debate about the explanation of such local variation. Much research effort has drawn upon the structural differences between powers and responsibilities. However, there is also a strand that seeks to explore local variation in political action. Clearly, this is of relevance to the debate about civil society and its local variation.

There has been a considerable amount written about the local state in recent years.[22] Perhaps most important in popularizing this was Cockburn (1977), Duncan and Goodwin (1982, p. 160) emphasize the functional and structural relationships instead of the social relationships of Cockburn (1977). Cockburn also features in the debate about the autonomy of the local state. Cockburn's view is characterized as an example of non-autonomous theory: the local agent is more or less an agent of the central state. A departure from this unified state concept is the dual state proposal of Saunders (1981, pp. 264–266), which suggests that a functional hierarchy exists within the state that is manifest in local and central government actions and interests.

---

[21]See Hoare and Nowell-Smith (1971, p. 208).
[22]See Mohun (1989), Cochrane (1989) and Goodwin (1989) for an overview.

Both these approaches are cut across by Duncan and Goodwin (1982, p. 165) who emphasize the importance of social relations. They suggest that both the workplace and the home need to be considered as a realm of local politics if the links between the uneven development of class relationships and consciousness, that they see as vital to the understanding of the local state, are to be made.

Cooke (1983, pp. 189–190), whilst in broad agreement with this idea, suggests a further expansion as he feels that it neglects civil society, popular democratic struggles, circulation and the precise relationship between the state, civil society and production. Adopting a Gramscian position he sees the local state as both beside and outside civil society, which is itself between the state and production relationships (Cooke, 1983, p. 192). Within local civil society there are many bases for struggle, though the detail of these will vary across space and time (see Cooke, 1986).

An example might clarify this point. The local state could be considered as the result of particular struggles between factions of labour and capital over the nature of reproduction. Rather than a transhistorical form, it is a fleeting and changeable institutional form of power of the state. For example the collectivization of housing stock or the provision of 'key-worker housing' (enabling reproduction) to facilitate industrial development (production). Or again, the administration of land use zoning (production), and provision of infrastructure and transportation (production and reproduction).

Power and control of the local state apparatus may be gained through struggle within civil society (see Duncan and Goodwin, 1988). However, historical evidence shows that the central state has control and power enough to quash such rebellion (e.g. rate-capping in Liverpool and the abolition of the metropolitan counties in 1986). Various commentators have noted the reduction in power and activity by the local state that has occurred since the 1930s in Britain (see Saunders, 1983), furthermore, that greater powers have been amassed by central government and the state more generally (Duncan and Goodwin, 1988; Cochrane, 1989).

As noted in the previous chapter there have been recent attempts to reconceptualize the reproduction of society along the lines suggested by the Regulation School. Warde (1988) offers a reinterpretation of the industrial restructuring thesis offered by Massey (1984) from this perspective. Close attention is paid to changes in the labour processes: particularly as they relate to the reproduction of labour outside the factory, and the nature of state intervention (Warde, 1988, p. 78). One dimension yet to be fully addressed is the relationship between changes in the organization of the labour process and its reproduction: the form of development and the use of space.

The constitution of social relations in space. It is not just social structures that result from this struggle for the reproduction of everyday life but the 'created spaces' and 'environmental artifacts' of the built environment (Giddens, 1981, p. 153). These forms can both structure and be structured by social struggle (Urry, 1981b, p. 458). The exact form is contingent upon the specific relations of production, the historically deposited resources, both 'natural' and those which exist as a result of previous transformations of space and society. In short, the specificity of all the previous time and space inter-relationships that 'make up' a locality. This debate is dependent upon a reconceptualization of both space and how social relations are constituted in space. First, we consider space.

There are two and a half positions on the matter: absolute space, relational space and relative space. The latter two are very similar, what divides them is methodology. The traditional perspective is what is termed absolute space. Here space is taken as real, pre-existent—a sort of container into which things are introduced. This conception has intuitive appeal, it can perhaps best be thought of as having a blank piece of paper on to which distributions are mapped. It follows that either physical relations or morphologies are the focus of most geographical analyses. It has already been noted above how the concern with pattern was expressed in the development of theories of industrial location and also urbanization. Space is naturalized, taken for granted, a priori. There are two consequences that commonly flow from such conception. First, when combined with spatial science where the distributions are modelled as geometric structures space is being deployed as the explanation of particular distributions, a circular argument. Secondly, it encourages a separation of spatial structures and processes.

A half-way house is adopted by Harvey (1973) who suggests that space is relational. By which he means that space is contained within objects as far as it contains and represents within itself relationships to other objects. Thus, in a neat turn Smith (1984) is able to argue that spatial analysis must become social analysis. This analytical turn has opened up the possibility of linking space and social theory. Early attempts included Soja's (1980) socio-spatial dialectic. Soja (1985) later reconceptualized this dualism of space and society as a duality: space is society. Sociologists have recently also become interested in these debates, perhaps foremost is the work of Giddens (1984). However, the legacy goes back further; namely to the work of Lefebvre.

Lefebvre's (1991, written in 1974) view of space as both medium and outcome of human agency is relevant to this debate, but it does not sit happily with either the relativist or the relational view. What is particularly noteworthy about Lefebvre's contribution is that whilst feeling able to generalize about space he does stress the need to consider the *production* of space. This he tends to consider, in turns, at a very abstract level or in terms of political action. He views the production of space as a three phase process, a trilectic: space, everyday life and the reproduction of capitalist relations. Space is created by, and infused with, capitalist relations; it is used as an instrument of control in the way that cities are designed and built. Lefebvre's view is essentially a politicization of the notion of space as something that is formed through social struggle, hence the importance of social struggle (everyday life) to gain control of the production of space to enable noncapitalist social relations to exist.

The relativist space approach does not assume that space is pre-existent but that it is constituted through social relations. That social structures have spatial structures is not debated, what is crucial is that one cannot be had without the other (see Urry, 1985). The key idea here draws upon what Giddens (1984) terms distanciation. Very simply this is the stretching of social relations across space and time. The physical manifestation of any one set of social relations is termed the *locale*. The particular and unique combination of a whole set of social relations that intersect at any one place is termed the *locality*. This conception of the locality captures the idea of uniqueness but also the interlinked nature of social and economic life. However, whereas the relational space position accommodates an abstract or generalizable space the relativist position does not. For critical realists, proponents of this position, space 'in the abstract' has little meaning as they argue space can only be constituted in *particular* places and at *particular* times (Sayer, 1985b). These particularities of the 'concrete' may change the outcome of social and economic processes that cannot be anticipated beforehand. It is in such a context that the need for work on the concrete production of space in particular places and times would seem to be necessary.

The crucial link between social practices and the making of 'place' has been an important theme in the elaboration of what has termed 'the new regional geography' (Jonas, 1988; Pudup, 1988; Gilbert, 1988). The concept of locality, closely linked with this focus found early support from those researchers concerned with the 'rural' economy and society (see Bradley and Lowe, 1984). As noted earlier in the discussion about methods, there is considerable debate about the concept of locality. The term has gained some support from those writing in structurationist and critical realist debates in order to stress the significance of time and space in the constitution of human activity (see Giddens, 1984; Bhaskar, 1983). Thus, it is important to be clear concerning the definition of locality, Thrift and Williams (1987, p. 16) define the *locale*, as the physical settings of institutions within which certain social practices are contained. They go on to suggest that in some places there is such a distinctive institutional mix that a local economy or culture can be identified and constituted in a *locality* (Thrift and Williams, 1987, p. 17). Significantly, they also draw upon Giddens's (1984, p. 132) concept of distanciation[23], by stressing that practices that are carried out locally are not necessarily locally generated (Thrift and Williams, 1987, p. 17).

Recent critical realist accounts have reconsidered space, emphasizing its socially created nature.[24] Attempts to integrate social theory and space from a realist perspective can be found in Urry (1981b, 1983). Such accounts warn against the simple reductionism, essentialism, and naturalism in both the traditional and lay conceptions of space. Space is not absolute, or relative, but of created value and significance. In fact space, as a theoretical construct, can be considered a contentless abstraction (Sayer, 1985b, p. 53). Its value can, and does, change by virtue of causal powers and liabilities constituting space *in situ* (Sayer, 1985b, p. 52). It is not enough to simply be satisfied that space is a social creation; instead it is necessary to inquire into *how* it is created.

The ability to control space, or more particularly land, is contingent upon the 'rights' related to it. These 'rights' are not transhistorical but firmly rooted in institutional structure and practices situated in time and space. Furthermore, they are the result of social struggle. In feudal times 'rights' to land were held by the crown, under capitalism they are owned by individuals (Massey and Catalano, 1978). Thus, the nature of space is inter-related to the existing social structure. 'Rights' of ownership are maintained through both the legal sanctions and their reproduction by individuals. In particular societies the nature of these structures leads to a complex articulation of power. The 'rights' in land may be subdivided between numerous individuals and applied to various material forms such as buildings (or parts of them) and land.

Clearly, the relationship between the firm and the producer of the built environment is a complex, inter-related and interdependent one. The eventual form is neither solely dependent on, or necessarily dominated by, the organization of production in the firm or the developer, but in the articulation of power and its legitimation 'on site' in a specific space and time. As the location of the firm is ultimately contingent upon the satisfactory resolution of the production of accommodation (whether it is in the control of the firm or a 'separate' developer) in time and space, it is logical to isolate this for analysis. The re-production of the built environment is clearly situated in the core of this process, in part mediating social reproduction and spatial reproduction. As Gottdeiner (1985a, p. 268) recognizes:

---

[23]Giddens (1984, p. 377) defines time–space distanciation as "the stretching of social systems across time–space, on the basis of mechanisms of social and system integration".
[24]Sack (1973, 1980), though for a differing view in the same vein, see Sayer (1985b) and Soja's (1980) Marxist interpretation.

"the real-estate sector, including the fraction of finance capital organized around investments in land, is the leading edge of the materialisation of this Late Capitalist development process in space".

Understanding the articulation of power and control within and between the institutions involved in the property development process at any one time, and their relationship to the rest of society, will obviously be a key to explaining the form and nature of uneven development. The next part of this chapter deals with the problem of conceptualizing the process of the re-production of the built environment.

The re-production of the industrial built environment

The aim of this section is to conceptualize the production of the industrial-built environment. This analysis focuses upon the property production process and how it may be conceptualized. It will be argued that the industrial estate is a particular outcome of a subgroup of this process, industrial property development. The aim is to build upon the issues identified in the review of conceptualizations presented in the previous chapter by stressing the importance of agency as well as structure, context, space and historical change. Two different approaches are considered. The first is a development of the interactionist approaches considered in the previous chapter. An institutionalist position that incorporates a structurationist conceptualization is developed. The second position develops the Marxian capital–logic approach. The crucial shift away from determinism incorporates a conceptual focus on production rather than circulation.

As noted in the previous chapter one approach to the property development process drew upon the property pipeline approach and stressed the importance of agency in the interactionist conceptualization. Recent work by writers who initially developed this position has suggested a potential modification of the interactionist approach to what they term an institutionalist approach. Basically this is an attempt to incorporate a stronger sense of structure into their analyses (see Healey and Barrett, 1990; Healey, 1991). Healey and Barrett (1990 p. 93) attempt to draw in Harvey's conception of the urban process, but recognize that Harvey's work does not adequately explore the role of agents. The resolution that they offer is to re-cast the process as a problem of structuration. As such the analysis of the development process

"requires the development of an explicit approach to the relation between structure, in terms of what drives the development process and produces distinctive patterns in particular periods, and agency, in terms of the way individual agents develop and pursue their strategies" (Healey and Barrett, 1990, p. 90).

A later paper clarifies what this might mean in practice. Here Healey (1990, p. 20) suggests that an institutionalist approach might proceed through three levels:

"(1) A *mapping* exercise, focusing on *events* in the *production* process of a development project, identifying the *agencies* involved and the outcomes produced.
(2) The identification of the *roles*, in the production and consumption/use of the development, and the *power relations* which evolve between them.
(3) The assessment of the *strategies* and the *interests* of actors, particularly with respect to the most significant sets of relationships within the process, in order to identify what governs the way different roles are played and relationships developed. This assessment may then be related to the *resources*, *rules* and *ideas* governing the development process in the instance examined."

Whilst in agreement with the intentions of this approach three problems can be identified. First, that the use of institution as a mediating concept in the structurationist conception does not capture a 'duality of structure', rather it preserves a dualism of autonomous structures and agents. In fact structures disappear in this formulation and are replaced by institutions, simply relocating the problem of the mediating concept. This is related to a second point, that of ontology. As has been noted Giddens's structuration is weak on ontology, and correspondingly weak on causality. This is compounded in Barrett and Healey's work by the empiricist form that the research is cast within (especially points 1 and 2). Third, the model works with a mixture of voluntarism and collectivism in its conception of society. It will be recalled that this is the criticism that Bhaskar levelled at the 'dialectical' model of structuration (see above). What would be required, from a critical realist perspective, is a relational model.

The second approach that can be considered draws upon the work of Ball who has attempted to incorporate a relational model of society into his analyses. Ball's approach develops out of a critique of Marxian versions of the development process—such as the work of Harvey—that focuses on the circulation of capital.

Attempts to apply the circulation perspective, such as Boddy (1981) and Henneberry (1988), hinge upon the identification of internal conflicts between different fractions of capital: namely between the users and the providers of property. However, it may be argued that by focusing on circulation the political and social dimensions of change are reduced to the economic. Ball's response (1983) has been to carry out a detailed exploration of the nature of property provision in its historical and sectoral (but not spatial) specificity. This work details the delicate compromises and conflicts between the production sector and the development of particular forms of housing provision. This position is perhaps best established in Ball's response to the work of Cardoso and Short (1983) which offered an explanation of evolution and change in the production and form of housing as based upon different forms of housing production. This key concept— housing production—is defined as

"combinations of the conditions of production, elements of the labour process, and relations of production as they are articulated by particular constellations of agents . . ." (Cardoso and Short, 1983, p. 917).

Whilst this approach does seem to disaggregate the property development process, dealing with the specificity of the residential sector, and focusing on production rather than circulation it still has problems. Ball (1984, pp. 265–266) criticizes Cardoso and Short's approach for its reductionism, lack of historical dynamic, and its inapplicability to empirical situations. Ball makes an important point in contrasting this conceptualization of 'forms of housing *production*' with his alternative, 'forms of housing *provision*'.

> "The use of provision rather than production in my work is not simply semantic but is meant to signify that production cannot be seen in isolation from the use of the product and the means by which the user obtains it. In other words, the spheres of production, exchange (or non-market allocation in the absence of exchange), and consumption must be considered as a unity" (Ball, 1984, p. 264).

Ball's argument here ties in neatly with the abstraction of production that we detailed earlier in this chapter, in short a relational approach. Ball (1983, p. 17) outlines his position thus

> "housing provision via specific tenure form is the product of particular, historically determined social relations associated with the product of particular, historically determined social relations associated with the physical processes of land development, building production, the transfer of the completed dwelling to its final user and its subsequent use. They can be defined as 'structures of housing provision'".

In a later paper Ball (1986, p. 456) elaborates the nature of social struggle over building provision; he identifies three forms: conflicts between social agents involved in a structure of building provision, conflicts involving one or more of those agents and wider social and economic processes, and competition between agents in different structures of provision. However, he is reticent to foreclose theoretical debate, suggesting that the analysis of structures of building provision are a means of ordering and evaluating sets of empirical material rather than explanation itself (Ball, 1986, p. 457). By stressing the contingency of the process Ball is distancing himself from a general theory of building provision or the capitalist city (such as that developed by Harvey). Such a position would inevitably fall into a functionalist trap and thereby ignore the ongoing struggles between the social agents involved. Such struggles will be relatively unique to different sectors of the development process. Thus, a theoretically informed starting point is vital, as is empirical analysis (Ball, 1986, p. 462).

Conclusion

An attempt has been made in this chapter to create a firm philosophical foundation for a reconceptualization of the property development process. Implications for the nature of methodology and theory have been derived. More specifically, it has been argued that the production of the built environment should be viewed as being situated within struggles in wider society. As such it was suggested that the property sector cannot be isolated from production, consumption, exchange or distribution. Further, any rational abstraction of the production of that built environment must have reference to those struggles. Development, and its spatially and temporally uneven nature under capitalism, is actively engaged in day after day, each practice re-producing its form.

It follows that particular forms of the built environment — such as industrial estates — should be explained by reference to the struggles noted above and those both between and within the users and the structure of provision of the premises. The specific nature of property provision will be constantly changing dependently upon those struggles. The particular nature of provision must also be related to the potential users, and the distribution of power and resources between them. In turn, the power and resource of the users must also be related to struggles within civil society, as articulated through both the labour process and the actions of the state.

Clearly, the particular nature of the resolution of these struggles will result in a specific form of the industrial built environment. The exact form will depend upon the historical distribution of the resources, as well as the particular social formulation of the locality. The details of these factors, as with all such contingent phenomena must, and can only, be established by empirical research and not simply 'read off' from theory.

Moreover, it is important to bear in mind that we are not simply concerned with a one-off process: production. The notion of re-production should alert us to the fact that we are dealing with the re-creation of the industrial built environment. Each previous built structure and the associated social relations it has enabled are constantly in the process of becoming a new site for further reproductive struggles.

A key point is that theories of industrial estate development *per se* should best be considered as being based upon chaotic conceptions because they do not acknowledge the inter-relationships with the rest of society, between the developer and the occupant. A wider conception of production as a whole is needed. This itself requires the consideration of the spatial and temporal specificity of institutions and social practices. The implication is that any particular development will be linked to particular contexts. Only within such contexts can the particularity of the agents, institutions and their practices be specified.

With particular respect to industrial estates, this line of logic would imply that they are a spatially and temporally specific form of development: they cannot be defined in the abstract. That they emerged at a particular time, and in a particular place, is significant and must be related to the social, economic and cultural context. Likewise, their contemporary form, location and mode of development can only be considered by recourse to particular painstaking empirical analysis. Nevertheless that analysis must necessarily be informed by abstract theory.

Taking the theoretical and methodological framework that has been outlined in this chapter and 'putting it to work' is a difficult task. The contextual and compositional aspects of the account are interwoven. However, it is useful from the point of clarity to untangle them. In Chapter 4 the broader institutional context of the production of the industrial built environment is discussed; as Ball would term it "the structures of provision". England is the relevant locality for most of this chapter. Chapter 5 takes a tighter focus with the consideration of the particular social and economic relationships within the locality of interest: Cornwall. In the remaining chapters the detailed nature of the development process is considered and how it impacts on the occupation and use of the buildings, and the re-production of the locality. Thus, the industrial estate is situated in particular historical and spatial contexts, at some times resolving and at others antagonizing, struggles in civil society.

4

The Political Economy of the Development of the Industrial Estate

Introduction

This chapter explains the emergence of one particular form of the industrial built environment in England over the last 100 years: the industrial estate.[1] It will be argued that, within the wider re-production of the industrial built environment, changes in the structures of provision — the organization of production (in the widest sense) and the character of the agents carrying it out — are sufficient to explain the emergence of a form of development known as the industrial estate. The argument follows a chronological pattern comprising of four periods commencing just prior to the development of the first industrial estate — Trafford Park — in 1896. In order to clarify the structure of the argument presented in this chapter, five interwoven themes can be highlighted: first, the changing relationship of the occupant and the building i.e. tenure; second, the changing organization of production (including distribution), and the materials and technology utilized therein (that is of buildings and within them). These two can be related to a third theme: institutional changes in the composition of the development sector and the emergence of intermediaries (such as

---

[1]The term industrial estate is used as a generic for developments called variously trading estates, industrial estates, business parks and science parks. It is a group of industrial buildings with more than one establishment or firm using them. They are distinguished from other 'haphazard' groupings of industrial buildings in that there is some conscious effort on the part of an actor with a legal interest in the land such as the landowner, developer, or planner who may develop the site as an integrated unit either of land users or industrial activities. As is noted in the chapter the exact definition of an estate may change from time and place, as such it is an indicator of the changing form of production.

This research is specifically concerned with the development of industrial estates in England, as it is this legislative framework that is relevant to Cornwall. Details of Scotland and Wales are only bought in when they are included under the same legislation.

estate agents, financial institutions, and property developers) between the occupant and owner of the land and building. The fourth theme is the state's changing relation to society. Finally, there are issues related to re-production; the people who work in the industries and live in the localities and their relationship to the changing role of the state, economy and the built environment, and how these relationships both mediate and are mediated by their actions.

Weaving together these themes and documenting the empirical changes is a formidable task. It is not the aim of this chapter to go into intimate detail as to the location of each and every industrial estate, but rather to note the extent and tempo of development. This context will provide a starting point for the remaining chapters of this book which are concerned with the emergence of industrial estates in one locality: Cornwall.

1896–1928: The First Industrial Estate

The first industrial estate was developed at Trafford Park (Manchester) in 1896. The national context for its development of was one of economic restructuring that foregrounded a tension between the development of urban and rural localities. The manufacturing sector was restructuring on an expanded scale to facilitate economic exploitation of the new markets opened up with the expansion of the British Empire. The agricultural sector was just recovering from the nineteenth century recession. The decline of agriculturally based incomes from the landed gentry had led to many sales, particularly of urban estates (Canadine, 1980, p. 424).

Significant struggles were taking place with respect to the relationship between state and society at this time. The extension of the franchise created tensions within the class structure. Hall (1984, p. 26) argues that the social unrest of this period obliged the state to take on a more interventionist role. The Liberal budget of 1909 in which land sales and mineral rights were taxed, and elements of a proto-welfare state such as pension and insurance schemes, school meals and 'workingmen's compensation' were introduced. Such intervention can be viewed as a form of concession. Although little of this legislation remained on the statute books, it marked an important precedent in terms of the emergent role of the state.

Two significant pieces of legislation which did remain were, first, the 1909 Development and Road Improvement Act that established the Development Commission (DC). This Act sought to reverse and relieve rural decline and poverty. The DC was given an advisory role with respect to the direction of Treasury expenditure on the development of agricultural and rural industries, and economic development.[2] Whilst the DC has latterly become known for its role as the promoter of economic development in rural localities, particularly as a provider of factory units, little formal aid was provided for these activities in this early period[3] (Minay 1986).

The second piece of legislation, the 1909 Town Planning Act, was a forerunner of the establishment of comprehensive planning legislation. This legislation must be considered in its wider context. According to Cherry (1982, p. 13), the flow of investment away from housing to the Empire had left urban areas in a poor condition. Such conditions had fanned the flames of civil unrest and rent strikes (see Cullingworth, 1983, p. 1). Rose (1985, p. 40) argues that the spur behind the introduction of planning legislation was the concern that the quality of health of (working class) army recruits was falling. It was thought that improved housing might be a means of ensuring an improvement in general health. In a pincer movement further legislation was introduced to restrict collective action in civil society through controls on trade union activities.

There were also tensions between different levels of government. The local government reforms of the 1880s had resulted from anomalies of representation created by the national extension of franchise. Prior to these reforms agricultural workers were able to vote for national government, but not local government. Through this new resolution a secure basis was established for local government. Local government took on the responsibility in this 'Golden Age' of administering health, utilities, the poor law and the early planning legislation (Byrne, 1983).

Trafford Park, the first industrial estate, was characteristic of much property development in this period. Formerly the home of Sir Humphrey de Trafford it was the result of a land sale by gentry vacating the urban area. The original intention was to use the site as a municipal deer park; only later was the idea modified, first to a housing development, then to a trading estate (Farnie, 1980, p. 118). That the site was developed for industrial uses and not housing can be related to wider factors. The site was rejected by the City Council for use as a deer park due to lack of finance as it was heavily indebted in the construction of the Ship Canal. It was the Ship Canal that proved to be Trafford Park's lifeline, guaranteeing a flow of trade through the port (Stevens, 1947, p. 5). The mode of development followed, more or less, the erratic techniques of suburban housing development of the time.

---

[2] The definition of rural industry here is very limited, simply referring to rural 'craft' industries. Later initiatives concentrated on the provision of infrastructure such as electricity to outlying and rural areas.

[3] Development Commission expenditure on manufacturing related activities was just 1% of total funds in 1932/3, this rose to 13% in 1952/3, 75% in 1972/3 and 81% in 1982/3.

Development of such a site for industry in Manchester, the centre of the colonial cotton trade, was perhaps not surprising. The choice of the actual site, the location of the inland port of the Ship Canal which was then under construction, was of strategic importance with respect to the rivalry between Liverpool and Manchester. It was not long before another estate was established at the other end of the canal at Aintree (Liverpool). Little information is available concerning Aintree other than it was, unlike Trafford Park, an example of a planned development to service Hartley's jam manufacture (Rose, 1985, p. 44).

Much of the house building activity after the turn of the century was private in nature and in the form of infill and urban extension. The poor nature of much of the existing housing stock at this time, the growing population and the pressure on agricultural land uses had two consequences. First, state intervention in the provision of housing, and second collective provision in civil society. A key example of the latter was the Garden City movement, inspired by Ebenezer Howard's 1898 polemic *Tomorrow: A Peaceful Path to Real Reform* (Howard, 1965). The 'back-to-nature' element of the movement held great appeal for the middle classes recoiling from urbanization and industrialization. Other experiments were also being carried out at this time by philanthropically minded industrialists such as George Cadbury (Bournville, Birmingham), Joseph Rowntree (New Earswick, York), William Lever (Port Sunlight, Liverpool),[4] and Utopians such as Robert Owen (New Lanark, near Glasgow), and Titus Salt (Saltaire, near Bradford), who all experimented with the planned integration of factories and living accommodation. However, they created factories predominantly from just one industry which were interwoven with housing and services; these were not industrial estates. Howard's ideas were different from the philanthropists in that they advocated planned industrial areas zoned apart from housing. This idea, although it had enlightened overtures in terms of the evident environmental improvements, did not deviate from existing property developers' practice where zoning was used to preserve land values by excluding 'low-rent' developments (see Goodman, 1972, p. 187).

These early planned town and suburban developments were financed by private subscription, usually from the prospective occupants. The Tenant Co-operators Limited were such a company who developed housing in Hampstead, north London. At the time interest paid to investors was limited to a maximum of 5%, while return on capital was running at about 5.5%. The profit was distributed as a dividend on capital, like the Co-operative Retail Societies (Rose, 1985, p. 45). In

---

[4] An industrial estate was later developed adjacent to Port Sunlight in the early 1930s called Bromborough Port.

common with Trafford Park, which was developed by a limited company especially created for the task (Farnie, 1980, p. 120), these developments did not achieve a good return on investment. For example, no dividend was paid at Letchworth (the first garden city, 50 km north of London) for the first ten years (Rose, 1985, p. 47), and at Trafford Park for the first twelve years (PEP, 1939, p. 103). In both cases this was primarily due to huge initial infrastructure costs. Later developments cut costs by forming accretions to existing developments and by splitting sites so as to achieve an early flow of revenue. For example, costs were saved at Trafford Park by selling land serviced with infrastructure to industrialists who could build their own factory units (Farnie, 1980, p. 126).

The dramatic industrial restructuring, foreshadowed at the turn of the century, dominated the interwar period. Hall (1975, pp. 84–85) divides this into three parts related to empirical changes: first, the slowing of the rate of population increase choking off demand for industrial goods. Second, technological changes weakening demand for staple goods. Third, competition from other industrializing economies relating to the collapse of 'free-trade'. Massey (1985, p. 345) suggests a deeper causal explanation in terms of the reorganization of the structure of a manufacturing industry that has previously been based upon a colonial trading system, and the actions of the British state. The decline of the heavy industries in the North based upon exports were part and parcel of the declining position of Britain in the world economy. At the same time a new 'spatial division of labour' was emerging. These industries were based upon a domestic market. The 'new' industries that developed were organized on the principles of mass production and were primarily located in the Midlands and South East.

These new forms of the organization of production required more space; they also benefited those companies who invested in new technology rather than property. Slough Trading Estate, established in 1920 situated 40 km west of London, was able to satisfy these demands and grew rapidly. It was ideally located for access to the new mass market, and there was space enough to facilitate the establishment of large-scale production lines with minimal outlay (in rented factory units).

The development of a trading estate at Slough was seemingly a chance occurrence. Originally it was owned and developed by the War Department and operated as a transport depot. The development of infrastructure, a problem in previous estates, was thus by-passed at Slough as much of this was already on site (Slough, 1978, p. 2). The company was able to start up by selling the assets of the transport depot, then by renting the existing premises. There was thus an immediate flow of income. It was not until 1928 that factory units had to be built. Later the estate company was able to develop premises itself, and by 1930 there were 8,000 employed at Slough (Slough, 1978, p. 4). In later years the Slough company went on to develop another estate in Birmingham and to manage another, on behalf of the government, in Swansea.

Although perhaps the best known of the trading estates established in this period—and without doubt the most successful—Slough was not alone. Wolton's (1938) survey of trading estates details 26 estates in all: the majority of which were located on the arterial road network to the north and west of London: particularly the A4 (the Great West Road), A40 and A406 (the North Circular Road). Hobsbawm (1969, p. 219) observed that the development of 'new' industry at this time had generally spread

> "along the Great West Road out of London, while emigrants from Wales and the north moved to Coventry and Slough. Industrially Britain was turning into two nations".

Whilst, all of this growth cannot be attributed solely to the emergence of industrial estates, they must have had a considerable impact.

Although few details are available as to the origins or size of these estates, aside from Wolton's survey, most were built by 4 major trading estate developers: for example, Allnatt estates had 10 developments to their name, including Park Royal, another well known early estate. Other major developers were Commercial Structures (3 estates), Percy Bilton (5 estates) and Laing Estates (7 estates) (Wolton 1938). These developments were, as with Slough, built speculatively. However, unlike Slough, factory units were built for sale rather than rent. Chamberlin (1938, p. 74) suggests that there was a degree of functional grouping of firms on these estates. Whether this was as a result of agglomeration economies or representative of local specialization is not clear.

Some clear points emerge from this early period of estate development. First, the similarities of industrial and residential 'estate' development, particularly the idea of zoning. Second, the close relationship with changes in industrial organization, particularly large scale activities. This is evident both in the production of buildings and the occupants of them. Third, related to this is the locational change, taking advantage of new communications network developments. Finally, the changing relationship between the developer of industrial premises and the occupant. There is evidence of the loosening of ties of property ownership and a shift to leasing and renting. In part this change of priorities was necessitated if profits from producers were to be reinvested in new techniques.

1929–1951: Keynesian Economic Policies and Intervention

The economic depression of the late twenties and early thirties bought into sharp focus the geographical dimensions of the restructuring of industry. The contemporary researcher is struck by the similarities with the monetarist and neoliberal policies of the 1980s that characterized the Thatcher administration. A 'noninterventionist' government was keen not to be seen to be 'interfering' with the market. The period around 1930 was a watershed for state–society relationships. The new roles that local government had taken on prior to this period were being tested, attempts were even being made to extend them particularly in areas suffering from the effects of a new round of industrial restructuring and deindustrialization.

The derating of industrial property in 1929 was an early attempt to cut the costs incurred by industrialists.[5] In order to attract new firms, some local authorities (Kirkby, Jarrow and Liverpool) sought private acts to develop and prepare sites for industry. Two 'garden suburb extension' developments (Speke, Liverpool, 1929 and Wythenshaw, Manchester, 1930) are of interest as they were originally planned with self-contained employment opportunities (and industrial estates) and were developed by local councils (Ravetz, 1986, p. 29). Local authorities were more generally enabled by the 1931 Local Authority (Publicity) Act and the 1936 Health Resorts and Watering Places Act to promote themselves and their locale.

It is difficult to grasp the novelty and significance of these developments when in the 1990s the role of the state in industrial development is so widespread. In the 1930s this role was novel and ground breaking. It is notable that the use of these new Acts had to be brought to wider attention by writers such as Fogarty (1947) in *Plan Your Own Industries*. Fogarty also advocated the establishment of industrial development councils. King (1986, p. 4) notes how the Tees District Development Board, founded in 1926, eventually helped to establish the Team Valley Industrial Estate. Camina (1974), in her study of local authority promotion of industry, notes that by 1939 some 69 boroughs and 285 metropolitan boroughs and urban districts in England and Wales had set up development organizations. There was still a catch for local authorities intent on industrial promotion: aside from the private acts individual gain from any development carried out with public monies was *ultra vires*. Nevertheless, some local authorities used this legislation to engage in industrial promotion (see Ward 1988, p. 209, and Ward, 1990).

It is important to consider the size of the industrial population in this period. There were approximately 140,000 factories by the mid 1930s. Of these, some 519 employed more than 1,000 each, while some 30,000 establishments employed 25 persons or less (Hobsbawm, 1969, p. 216). Industrial estates, numbering 40 or so and concentrated around London, accounted for a small proportion of buildings and a slightly greater proportion of total employment. Industrial buildings were at this time predominantly owner-occupied (Cadman, 1984, p. 68), and in 'traditional' urban locations. In contrast to housing development where there was a substantial amount of legislation aimed at relocation and

---

[5]This amounted to a 75% rebate on rates, or property taxes.

redevelopment the state had not had a significant influence on the location of industry.

With the postwar economy in recession and civil unrest running at a significant pitch there was pressure on central government to intervene. The crucial step was to undertake another restructuring of state–society relations. The Liberals' extension of franchise had created tensions which threatened the continuation of capitalist relations. The management of democracy, through divide-and-rule tactics, was followed by the Liberal Lloyd George. The 'historical compromise' arrived at was the incorporation of working class representation into the political form of the Labour party, and the eradication of other radical movements (Hall, 1984, p. 43). This still left open the problem of how the state would actually manage the economy. The key here was Keynes's advocacy of macro-economic demand management, proposing intervention but within the framework of a 'minimal state'.

Parsons (1986) details the convolutions experienced by the government in achieving state influence over the location of industry whilst still preaching noninterventionism.[6] Unemployment had been considered by policy makers as a social, rather than an economic issue up to this time (Parsons, 1986, p. 6). The 1934 Unemployment Act established several nongovernmental bodies to administer assistance. This was a key manoeuvre to distance the state from the regional problem by intervening, but not appearing to be directly involved (Parsons, 1982, p. 12).[7] First, investigators, then commissioners were contracted to examine the problem. One of the inspectors, Wallace, who had been a former member of the Tees Development Board, recommended the establishment of a Trading Estate at Team Valley (Tyne and Wear) along the lines of Slough and Trafford Park (King, 1986, p. 4).

The progenitor of regional economic policy — the 1934 Special Areas Act in which the Special Areas that were to receive assistance were designated — significantly cut across the departmental boundaries of the Treasury and Ministry of Works. However, commissioners were given few powers in the Special Areas, and that finance that was made available could not be used in the assistance of profit-making concerns. There was a hope that, like the development boards, these areas might somehow simply

---

[6] Many of these new consumer orientated industries already (after 1931) benefitted from state protection (such as through trade barriers), or state technological investment. This was also linked to production and distribution of electricity, via the national 'Grid'. (Hobsbawm, 1969, pp. 218–219). The improvement of the arterial roads out of London was another example of state infrastructure investment further weakening 'traditional' locational factors.

[7] Whilst this act was passing through parliament a series of articles was published in *The Times* newspaper entitled "Places without a future", highlighting economic and social conditions in a North East pit village. The final part was published on the day of the debate and proved to be the focal point of the subsequent debate (Parsons, 1986, p. 12).

attract an industrial estate and industrial regeneration would follow. Recognizing that such a hope was not likely to come to fruition, as well as the ideological opposition to state intervention of the administration, one of the commissioners—Stewart—in his second report pushed for more powers: in particular to establish and find

> "one or two more trading estate companies, which would be companies not operating for a profit, and these companies should acquire suitable sites in the Special Areas and equip them with all requisite facilities" (HMSO, 1936, p. 13).

After having this and other 'radical' suggestions regarding the relocation of industry blocked Stewart resigned. However, the proposals for Trading Estates were mentioned in the manifesto of the coalition government which came to power in 1935. Ward (1988, p. 216) notes that

> "the Government wanted very large and visible estates with maximum publicity value, even though this might not be the best solution to the alleviation of local unemployment".

The 1936 Special Areas (Reconstruction) Act provided the legislation necessary to create estates at Team Valley (Newcastle), Treforest (Pontypridd, South Wales), and Hillingdon (Glasgow). It is significant that much attention was paid to the design of the Team Valley estate. The architect, Holford, emphasized the necessity of three-fold expansion space for individual factory units, good circulation for traffic, and standardized designs for factory units (Holford, 1939). Whilst some of the ideas were borrowed from Slough, which itself had originally been laid out by the then War Department, Team Valley was the first comprehensively planned and purpose-built industrial estate. Such attention to comprehensive site-planning was not in evidence at either of the other two comprehensively developed government estates at Treforest and Hillingdon.

Further battles between the Treasury and the new estate companies (each with a responsibility for a Special Area) eventually led to the establishment of several other estates, all of a smaller size (Percival, 1975).[8] In Wales these smaller developments were called 'group sites'. Parsons considers the process of establishing the Special Areas as demonstrating

> "both the flexibility of the state towards containment of local interests, and potential political and social disturbance, and also a pragmatic and accommodating attitude towards the idea of regulation in a capitalist society" (Parsons, 1986, pp. 2–3).

In all not only was intervention in the economic sphere legitimized but the foundations for a centralist regional policy were also laid.

---

[8] Many of the smaller estates were built on, or converted from, ex-Royal Ordinance Factories, or War Department Army Camps. There is an interesting parallel here with the immediate postwar housing crisis and the squatting, and eventual legal housing, in converted camps (see Ward, 1983, p. 21).

The Royal Commission on the Geographical Distribution of Industry and Population (chaired by Barlow) that reported in 1940 was set up in 1937 as a result of Stewart's recommendations. The Commission found that, as Stewart had suggested, industry was over-concentrated and that this was a result of the existence of a favourable industrial structure in some locales. This was a significant formal acknowledgement of the relationship between the 'regional problem' and industrial structure (Hall, 1975, p. 93). Significantly, the Commission split on its recommendations. The moderate majority voted for controls on new industry just around London whilst the radicals called for control of the location of industry over the whole country.[9]

The Report of the Committee on Land Utilization in Rural Areas (chaired by Scott) added its call for reform by recommending that planning control be applied to rural areas as well as urban ones in order to both contain urban growth and to preserve agricultural land. Together with the Report of the Expert Committee on Compensation and Betterment, chaired by Uthwatt, that also reported in 1942, these three reports provided the basis for the introduction of a comprehensive town and country planning system.

The way had already been made for the political step towards postwar state intervention when Keynesian style demand-management policies had been passed during preparation for war. Whilst Keynes was not a supporter of the strong state, the 1940 Emergency Powers Act had provision for a Ministry of Labour which had powers to direct workers to jobs, as well as prescribing wages and conditions (Harris, 1984, p. 56).

The end of the war had fuelled speculators hopes of development, which had caused a revival of the market. There was also considerable demand for reconstruction and the beginnings of peacetime production. Cadman and Catalano (1983, p. 4) estimate that three and a quarter million properties were destroyed in the war, of which a quarter of a million were factories. Demand was clearly evident, but the state structured the priorities. Subsequent legislation should be seen in this light.

The postwar Labour administration embarked upon a programme of nationalization of key sectors of social and economic provision. This was not such a major break with prewar conditions, more of a tidying-up of the existing municipally controlled utilities, and others in post-war organizational disorder (Harris, 1984, p. 84). Significantly, this policy shifted power and resources away from local and towards central Government.

The 1945 Distribution of Industry Act was heavily influenced, in spirit if not in practice, by the radical version of the Barlow report. Although a

---

[9]The minority were perhaps not so radical as they seemed. Whilst they were suggesting a clean break with the 'hands-off' approach of the state and industry, they had also been informed *in camera* of the vulnerability urban industry to the potential bombing in wartime (Hall, 1975, p. 97). Seen in such light it was probably a strategic move.

national body for the relocation of industry was not created a system of legislation was, a key part of the Act was the use of Industrial Development Certificates (IDC). IDC's were initially required for all developments in excess of 929 square metres or expansion in excess of 10%, but this was later relaxed. The Act also created positive measures, in the form of grants for firms moving to the newly designated Development Areas which superseded and expanded upon the Special Areas of the 1936 Act.

The 1947 Town and Country Planning Act nationalized the right to develop land, thus facilitating the introduction of a comprehensive planning system. The general shortages of materials and the need for reconstruction after the war made the introduction of building licences, restricting construction to those areas that the state considered most needy, less controversial than they would have been previously. The potential bonanza of development for developers, investors and the construction industry did not materialize until the early fifties due to the imposition of a Development Charge (a 100% tax on gains from the sale of development land). The development that did take place was in infill sites in the inner city areas and on those properties where the greatest profit could be extracted. Thus, the development that took place was primarily for offices and retailing rather than industry.

The 1953 Town and Country Planning Act abolished the Development Charge which had generally been regarded as a failure (Goodchild and Munton, 1985, p. 29), and in 1954, as the postwar shortages eased, building licences were also removed. Marriott (1967, p. 11), writing primarily about office development in this period, rather evocatively considered this Act to be the

". . . starting pistol that signified the great property boom".

Whilst little information is available regarding existing private industrial estates, some details are available as to how the state-assisted estates fared in this period. The new industrial estates had experienced an initial boom in the pre-war period, partly as a result of the increase in production in preparation for war, and partly as a result of many firms fleeing occupied Europe. This was followed by a slump in the immediate postwar period; in part due to former occupants and employees taking part in the war, and also due to plants being temporarily commandeered to accommodate relocating 'strategic' industries. Most of these strategic firms moved away from the government estates at the end of the war (Percival, 1975).

The shortage of building materials meant that little new industrial development took place in the immediate postwar period, despite a considerable demand from the demobilized forces personnel. A new government estate was opened at Hirwaun (South Wales) which was a converted Royal Ordnance Factory complex. New industry had to make do with the premises that were available. Percival (1975) notes how, in

1953, materials were so short that industrial buildings were even being dismantled in East Anglia and transported to Wales. Partly as a result of these shortages, and partly due to the changes in both the 1952 fire regulations and 1958 thermal insulation regulations different building materials and styles emerged. Prefabricated buildings and timber huts with felt and board roofs were replaced by those with concrete frames and asbestos roofs (Brett, 1984, p. 11).

It is appropriate to highlight changes in the construction industry at this point. The initial construction of the Government-sponsored estates was held up by a materials shortage in 1937 (Percival, 1975, p. 20). This period was a traumatic one for the construction industry which was itself undergoing restructuring. The specialized firms which had previously dominated the market were being replaced by larger construction companies with subsidiaries for (predominantly housing) estate development. In the industrial sector, the new trading estates were an opportunity for empire building; for example, Wimpey's first major land clearance contract was the Team Valley Trading Estate (King, 1986, p. 12).

More generally, these specialized building firms had localized markets (Clarke, 1980, p. 39). With the exception of the trading estate most factories were built by contractors working for manufacturers who had already bought their land. There was little speculative development outside of the residential market (Rose, 1985, p. 143). It can be concluded that much of the speculative development that did take place would have been located on industrial estates. The amount of industry located on industrial estates increased rapidly in the postwar period.

The postwar construction market ceased to be localized, becoming fragmented into separate specialist contractors such as plant owners and builders, who had set up on their own account (often demobilized service people) (Clarke, 1980, p. 39). As the construction industry had a small capital base it was not able to participate in many schemes that increasingly required a high gearing of initial capital (Ive, 1980, p. 3). Those building companies that did fund developments achieved it by 'rolling-up'[10] construction costs in the period of construction (Cadman and Austin-Crowe, 1983, p. 205). Changes were also taking place in the internal use of space. Materials handling technology had also changed. The fork-lift truck had been developed in the USA during the war period. In the short postwar period to 1960, developments made possible lifts of first 3 metres then 6 metres, later this was to rise to 20 metres. Clearly, this made possible new building designs which saved floorspace (Brett, 1984).

---

[10] Rolling-up construction costs is an arrangement where debts are allowed to accumulate at the current rate of borrowing, in the hope that they will be recouped on a final sale of the property (Fraser, 1984, p. 9).

These changes increased the cost of construction, making it more difficult for a firm simply to set up new premises. Up until this period rented accommodation was not popular with industrialists due to the insecurity of tenure; however, the 1954 Landlord and Tenant Act gave occupants of premises far more security (Scarrett, 1983, p. 44). This was to aid the redirection of investment into machinery, make firms more 'footloose' or flexible in their location. The corollary was the growth in popularity of rented accommodation, much of which could be found on industrial estates.

Such industrial development that did occur was left to a few specialist developers who had been pre-eminent in the interwar period. The development that did occur was predominantly the expansion of estates which had been established in the interwar period, and the reuse of ex-War Department property. The advanced factory programme was in abeyance from 1954–1958 (although minor modifications in the areas eligible of assistance were made between 1958 and 1960) there was a move away from full-scale industrial estate development by the state as an integral part of regional policy. An exception was the New Towns Act (1948) that involved the establishment of some new estates as part of the new towns programme. However, the materials shortages of the late fifties and early sixties slowed down this programme.

The structure of the development industry also changed quite dramatically in the interwar period. The availability of mortgages, modified by the new building societies legislation, facilitated expansion of home loans and private housing (Boddy, 1979). This factor further fuelled suburbanization which had already been encouraged by the shorter working week and wage increases. Growing consumerism went hand in hand with restructuring of the retail and distribution industry. New outlets were sought in the suburbs. These new retailers aimed to be flexible and this was achieved by concentrating less capital in buildings. These factors were drawn together by an emergent agent in the development sector: the estate agent. The estate agent commonly worked as an intermediary, matching a specialist local knowledge of location with the need for a retail site in a specific market (Ambrose, 1986, p. 13). The property connection was achieved by leases from life assurance companies who, due to their increased savings ratios, were in need of new investment outlets (Marriott, 1967, p. 10).

Due to the uncertainty faced by smaller firms with regard to leasing arrangements for industrial premises, the market for speculative premises was mainly confined to the office and retail markets. Nevertheless, it is still important to analyse the postwar property market for the actors involved and the restructuring that was characteristic of the period. The boom was possible because of the depressed land values, construction markets, and the restructuring of agents that had occurred in the interwar period.

TABLE 4.1. *Bank of England Minimum Lending Rates 1932–1981 (CSO, 1987, 1992)*

Year	Interest rate (%)
1932	2
1939	2
1951	2.5
1961	6
1971	6
1981	12
1991	12

In the immediate postwar period, property companies emerged as a force in their own right. On one hand apart from the landed gentry in the production of the built environment, on the other, from the relatively underfunded construction industry (Smyth, 1985, p. 110). Even so, they were a small group, by 1964 there were only 100 property companies listed on the stock exchange (Cadman and Catalano, 1983, p. 6). Typically these companies, comprising 2 or 3 persons, had few financial resources of their own. Financing of development was arranged by 'dual funding'. Short term development finance to cover the construction period was obtained from a merchant or clearing bank secured against overdraft facilities, or loans against the assets of the developer (Boddy, 1979, p. 18). Commonly, an insurance company would provide a long-term mortgage secured against the site or the completed asset. (Cadman and Catalano, 1983, p. 203). Little capital was required 'up front'. As Boddy (1979) notes, there was no interest payable until completion of the buildings. Thus, there was little risk involved for either party; in any case interest rates were relatively low in this period (see Table. 4.1). It is significant that, in this period, it was possible to differentiate clearly between the developers who had short-term interests in property, and those with a long-term interest i.e. the property was leased rather than sold-on after development (Cadman and Austin-Crowe, 1983, p. 245). It is worth noting that a shift of power had occurred, and the role of the landowner in initiating development had been diminished.

The jump in the rate of inflation in the early sixties created funding difficulties for developers, through what is known technically as an adverse 'reverse yield gap'[11] for investors (Cadman, 1986, p. 206). The solution to this was for the lender to invest in the property directly in order to maintain security on the investment. Similarly, developers sought to bridge their

---

[11] A 'yield gap' refers to a situation where ordinary shares perform better than Government securities (gilts). An adverse yield gap is where interest on Government securities is higher than on ordinary shares (Fraser, 1984).

funding gap by 'sale and leaseback' agreements with bankers.[12] Both shifts foreshadowed greater direct involvement in the property sector by financial institutions. A further impact of increased inflation is that investors insisted on security and the upkeep of the property; this was achieved by the writing-in of a 'Fully Repairing and Insuring' lease (FRI)[13] (Smyth, 1985, p. 132). Furthermore, inflation meant that the rather generous rental reviews[14] were reduced in stages to 21, then 14 and 7 years (see Smyth, 1985, p. 152; Cadman and Catalano, 1983, p. 5).

It is helpful here to take a wider and longer term view of what was happening in the investment sector. Before 1960 investment in land and property accounted for 10% or less of funds' total assets (Property Advisory Group, 1975). Housing had become a private ownership sector, and following the imposition of the rent acts the sector decline from 36% to 20% in the eight years to 1964 (Boddy, 1979, p. 154). Investors were diversifying and spreading their risk into commercial property. Office development suffered mixed fortunes with intense government regulation in the mid sixties, particularly in and around London. The retail sector was booming with new local authority contacts to redevelop whole city centres; hotel development was also encouraged through capital allowances on developments. Consequently, only a limited amount of available funds were devoted to industrials (Sim, 1983, p. 106).

A key innovation of this period that was to be developed later was the establishment of the role of the state in both economic management and land use planning. In the former case both the economic restructuring of interwar industry and postwar modernization implied the adoption of mass-production techniques and the need for new large production spaces. The combination of land use planning regulation and state assistance facilitated the establishment of new sites for industrial production away from the former sites which had often been located in the inner city. In the core economy, the South East, private developers fulfilled this need, in the peripheral economy it was performed by the state. At this time owner-occupation was the dominant tenure for industrialists. This could, potentially be a poor utilization of productive resources for firms. A shift in tenure in hand with the increasing dominance of developers over construction, and the emergence of the financial institutions as actors in the property sector were significant trends that were to mature in the 1960s.

---

[12] 'Sale and leaseback'. This is where a property company sells land to a funder in return for a loan to finance the building and an agreement to lease the completed development back to the development company; the property company repays the funder the return on the interest from the rental stream gained from subletting the building to occupiers.

[13] A FRI lease basically means that the tenant has full responsibility for upkeep of the premises, keeping it in good condition, decorated and repaired.

[14] Rental review. The period between when the rental paid by the tenant can be altered, later upward-only reviews became the norm.

The net result would be the emergence of a new form of investment property: industrials.

1960–1975: Local Government Initiatives

A dramatic state infrastructure investment programme was initiated in the early sixties. The beginning of a national motorway network and the 'pruning' of the rail network not only encouraged the modal split of transport in favour of the roads, but also the diversity in the location of industry. Bale (1974b, 1977) has equated the development of postwar private industrial estates with the development of the motorway network (see Fig. 4.2). Whilst these developments lent implicit support to the diffusion of industrial development, explicit encouragement came by way of local government. Boddy (1983, p. 38) argues that the state assumed a new role in the sixties—mainly local—of redeveloping and planning. The original need for development—postwar reconstruction—was perceived to have been met.

The 1960 Local Employment Act marked a revival of regional policy, but this time in a weakened form focusing upon local 'pockets of high unemployment' in a nation otherwise experiencing low unemployment (see Table. 4.2). The new extended Development Areas (now called Development Districts) were designated or removed from time-to-time depending upon the local unemployment rate.[15] The 1960 Act also reorganized and reintroduced the advance factory building programme. The smaller trading estate companies were merged into three national management bodies: English Industrial Estates Corporation, Scottish Industrial Estates Corporation and the Welsh Industrial Estates Corporation.

In the early sixties, as before in the 1930s, central government distanced itself from the economic dimension of the problem by shifting responsibility on to local authorities; which whilst they gained new powers also had their budgets reduced. Under the 1963 Local Authorities (Land) Act local authorities were given powers to acquire and develop land and buildings, and to make loans to developers utilizing local authority sites for employment purposes. Although such powers had already been granted to some local authorities under private Acts, the 1963 Act was important in extending these general and permissive powers; previously the central state had constrained them closely. In the same year local councils acquired further power via the Local Government (Financial Provisions)

---

[15]This was set at 4.5%.

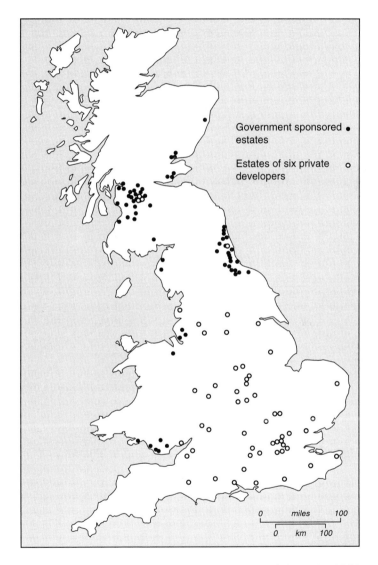

Fig. 4.1. The distribution of industrial estates in 1970 (after Bale 1974b).

TABLE 4.2. *United Kingdom Average Unemployment Rates 1950–1990 (CSO, 1992)*

Year	Unemployment rate (%)
1950	1.4
1955	1.0
1960	1.5
1965	1.4
1970	2.4
1975	3.6
1980	6.2
1985	11.9
1990	6.0

Act whereby they were able to spend the product of an additional penny on the local rate bill on any item that was deemed to be in the interests of the area and its inhabitants: this 'loophole' was widely exploited in later years to support economic development at a local scale. The limited evidence available suggests that few local authorities took advantage of these powers at this time (Boddy, 1983, p. 37).

The role of local government was to be undermined shortly after by the shift to a corporatist style of state management. Corporatist stability in this period was maintained by a pact between unions, employers and the Government. A virtuous relationship was established between these three parties that supported mass production and mass consumption and underpinned it with a substantive welfare state (Thompson, 1984a, p. 106). This strategy was focused on new mechanisms of economic negotiation and representation: the National Economic Development Office (1962), the National Plan (1965), the National board from prices and incomes (1965), and the Industrial Reorganization Commission (1966).

There were important spatial and structural aspects of this re-structuring of state–society relations revolving around a regional tier of government. This shift undermined the legitimacy of local government; so much so that a Royal Commission, chaired by Redcliffe-Maud, was set up in 1966 to question the need for local government at all (Byrne, 1985, p. 49). The continuation of Keynesian macro-economic management of the economy in this period of growth led to further pressure on local government in the form of financial constraints.

The DC had only been engaged in a limited amount of factory building prior to 1960, exclusively in North Wales; however, the 1960 Act undermined the role of the DC. In 1964 a limited programme of small factory unit building was established in rural areas, Minay (1986, p. 7) suggests that the DC programme was only used to expand the extent of the areas receiving (regional) assistance. The units built, ranged from 232 to 1,400 square metres in size.[16] As with regional industrial policy before, it was hoped that a small investment in one or two factory units would stimulate further development in the surrounding localities. These 'Trigger Areas' were in Mid-Wales, the Eastern Scottish Borders, and South East Lindsey (Lincolnshire) (Tricker and Martin, 1984, p. 509).

Following the results of the 1971 Census an Inter-Departmental Group on Rural Depopulation was set up and its conclusion was that the DC should engage in an extensive factory-building programme (Tricker and Martin, 1985, p. 294). Whereas previous policy had concerned 'traditional' rural industries, the attention was now focused on any small industry. The five year programme, initiated in 1975, aimed to create 1,500 jobs per annum in the newly designated Special Investment Areas which covered the remoter rural areas. Additionally, the Development Commission introduced joint schemes funded by local authorities, grants for the conversion of redundant premises and pump-priming grants for local enterprise trusts (Williams, 1984).

Other significant legislation included the 1965 New Towns Act which paved the way for the 'second generation' of new towns each with their accompanying industrial estate developments. The 1966 Industrial Development Act further expanded the Development Districts (now renamed Special Development Areas). A new tier of assistance, the Development Area, was added in 1967. The 1970 Local Employment Act initiated a third tier of aid, the Intermediate Areas, and a new programme of advance factory units. No specific legislation in these three Acts referred to the establishment of industrial estates; consequently local authority action was invariably a prerequisite for any new development of state funded advance factory units. According to Camina (1974, p. 89) it was not until the early 1970s that the powers of the 1963 Act were extensively used.

Some significant changes arose from a further reorganization of other public agencies. The Development Agencies Act of 1975 hived off the Scottish and Welsh Industrial Estates Companies to the newly created Scottish and Welsh Development Boards. The English Industrial Estates Corporation remained directly responsible to the Department of Industry with the slump of the early seventies over and new areas to service, the English Industrial Estates Corporation identified a new market for premises concentrating on the construction of units of below 232 metres square (Czartoryski, 1975). Later, in 1977, they also developed units on inner city sites (King, 1986, p. 29).

---

[16] Of 203 units built between 1959–1976 the average size was 419 square metres (Tricker and Martin, 1984, p. 506). From 1966 EIEC were responsible for the DC factory building programme in the assisted areas, from its formation in 1968 CoSIRA was responsible for factory building plus various advice, management and marketing activities outside of the assisted areas.

The expansion of the assisted areas caused local authorities to 'jockey' for position and compete in terms of 'attractiveness' to industrialists (Forester, 1979). Local Authority action was further broadened by the Town and Country Planning Act 1971 and the Local Government Act 1972. Powers for purchasing land for and the erection of buildings for relocating industry were granted under the former. In the latter, local authorities were enabled to acquire equity for land development and to form companies, to give rent-free periods, and to spend the product of 2p in the pound on local rates 'in the interests of the area'.

In 1972 36% of local authorities had sites available on industrial estates whilst a further 42% simply had industrial land for sale, much of which was probably located on already established industrial estates (Camina, 1974). This is not to suggest that local authorities were able to operate in total autonomy; there was significant tension between the central and local government. Whilst local agencies appeared to have greater control after 1963, financial provisions were closely administered by the Treasury. It is significant that local control was further reduced by the Regional Economic Planning Councils and Boards (established in 1964), and the Industrial Development Executive created by the 1972 Industry Act. Camina (1974, p. 89) suggests that there was a significant division of labour between local and central government at this time as regards economic development; central government as the promoter and local government as the provider.

The local authority role was strengthened, for a while, by the Community Land Act (CLA). The CLA was operational from 1975–1979 and allowed authorities to acquire, compulsorily if necessary, land for industrial activity and to fund infrastructure works prior to selling the leasehold interests to the private sector. Although over half of the sites acquired were located in the assisted areas, most were small later being disposed of to individual industrialists or developers (Boddy, 1983). The take-up of the scheme was patchy and the Act, although apparently a local initiative, remained under strong government control. The significance of the Act for understanding later development was not in what was carried out when it was on the statute book, but in that it,

> "undoubtedly encouraged a wide range of authorities towards more active involvement in the industrial field and more sophisticated development practices." (Boddy, 1983, p. 37).

By the mid-seventies many local authorities were taking on a quite different role to which they had previously taken on as land use planning bodies; local economic development. Significantly, a new type of officer had been emerging within local authorities to deal with this new role: industrial promotion. Usually located in the planning office, a special section was increasingly offered as the first point of contact for incoming industrialists and developers, as well as being in part responsible for the promotion of the area. This change is indicative of wider changes in the role of planning departments in local economic development (see Mills and Young, 1986; Totterdill, 1989).

Action also came from central government in the wake of the infamous 'u-turn' of the Conservative government. This came in the form of the 1972 Industry Act. IDC's were ended for Development Areas and Special Development Areas, and investment grants were made available for plant machinery and buildings. New funds were also available from the European Economic Community from the time of Britain's accession in 1973. The main support here came via the European Regional Development Fund (ERDF), established in 1975, where a contribution to infrastructure provision by local authorities was possible.

The restrictions on the development of prime office markets in the mid-sixties (due to Office Development Permits) were to some extent offset by the scope available in the retail sector. However, the changes of the 1965 Finance Act affected property developers precipitating a spate of consolidations and take-overs in the property development sector.[17] Between 1964 and 1970 sixty property companies disappeared (Property Advisory Group, 1980, p. 8); the net effect was that a small number of companies came to dominate the market.

The continued growth of the assets of the occupational pension funds, as it had previously done with the insurance funds, led to renewed interest in property investment. Further restructuring occurred due to inflation which was increasingly undermining the fixed rates that funds were giving, in effect cutting their share of the profits. These conditions effectively ended the practice of 'dual funding'. Investment via mortgage debentures and 'sale and leaseback' schemes became more popular. There is a significant difference between these two types of investment. Mortgage debenture is indirect investment in the development company, but 'sale and leaseback' is a direct form of investment in a particular scheme (Boddy, 1979). Not surprisingly, the funds' interest in property jumped from 15 to 19% (pension funds), and 13 to 23% (insurance companies) of portfolios between 1963 and 1969 (Debenham *et al.*, 1982).

There are two clear trends to be noted here: first, the growth of funds and their investment in property; second, a more direct interest in particular properties, which eventually led to a greater control being exerted over the design, location and tenants of those properties. The expansion of the commercial property sector overall and the new security

---

[17] The 1965 Act introduced Capital Gains Tax at 30% and a Corporation Tax which was set at a level of 52% for developers. Significantly, financial institutions were not liable for either corporation or capital gains tax, thus the market was left wide open for them. Thus direct investment and development in property began. However, at this stage (1966–1970) no insurance company had a major share in a property company (Franklin, 1976, p. 1127).

of tenure for industrialists fed a growth of a new market for rented industrial property that the institutions were beginning to appreciate. However, the market was relatively under researched and the identification of prime or 'blue chip' investments was largely 'hit-and-miss'. Grant (1970) noted an increasing number of developers and building companies entering into the development of industrial estates, the fruits of which were "springing up all over the country".

Certainly, the information contained in the 1970 *Financial Times* survey of industrial property supports this. The majority of the development was taking place in the South East, while in other areas such as Scotland, public development of industrial estates by both local and central government was more common. The survey suggests that industrial estates were a relatively new phenomena in the North West and the Bristol regions. The importance (actual or perceived) of the newly-developed motorway network was considered to be significant in the location of industrial estates in all parts of the country.

Institutional interest in industrial property had some profound implications. First, the density of the development on any particular site was determined by the yield obtained there;[18] low density sites were just not viable for developers. Second, in design terms a standardized building suitable for both warehousing and industrial development was required to spread the development risk. Third, the length of leases was reduced to 21 years, reflecting the rapid turnover of occupants in buildings, and reviews were set at 7 years to accommodate inflation rates. These criteria only emerged after some difficulty in the property and investment markets.

As well as changes in the types of buildings required by funds and users, there were also new developments in construction technology. Together these changed the form and appearance of industrial buildings. The modern industrial estate came into being. The low pitch asbestos roof and brick construction that had been popular in the early sixties was superseded first by saw-tooth profiles then, later, by flat roofs with curved features made possible by the use of plastic-coated profile steel cladding (Brett, 1984, p. 11). Increasing labour costs were offset by the reduced cost of the shallow or flat pitch roof 'portal frame' building. These changes were not only confined to the private sector. Indeed, shortages of steel and the over-supply of units induced the English Industrial Estates Company to introduce a standardized unit of modular construction (King, 1986, p. 28). As with the private sector, such units were considered easier to let and cheaper to build, thus reducing risks all round.

---

[18] The good locations were determined by the yield available on the property. Yields were important more generally as they offered a means of comparison between different sectors of the property market. Furthermore, they have a distinctly spatial dimension (see Flanagan *et al.*, 1980)

Contributors to the *Financial Times* survey referred to the new character of the industrial property market, and to the fact that many mistakes had been made in the recent past due to a lack of knowledge of the sector. The argument put forward—rather hopefully in the light of later events—was that the amateurs had been shaken out, and that market research was now the rule.

Although it is an under-researched area, some idea can be gained of the extent of industrial units owned by producers from a survey of 632 new firms, new branches of existing firms and existing firms relocating carried out in 1968–1989 by the Department of Industry. The survey indicated that 34% of all industrial hereditaments are leased or rented, though this figure was slightly higher for assisted areas (DTI, 1973, p. 651). However, only 59% of those properties that were owner-occupied had been specifically built by, or for the current occupants; 27% of the hereditaments were built specifically for previous occupants, and 14% had been speculatively built.

There was clearly a trend towards firms renting accommodation. The changes in the structure of the development market are important. Whilst interest rates were low, development of premises by the individual firm was not too problematic. However, increasing rates of interest, as occurred in the 1970s, create funding problems. A second reason may be the complexity of the task of development. Turner-Samuels (1970) notes that a considerable risk is taken in large property development projects such as industrial estates due in part to the belief that whilst land was an appreciating asset, buildings were not. There is also risk involved in estimating whether the development will achieve the predicted value in the first place. Turner-Samuels (1970) suggests that this risk accounts for the increased popularity of the 'package deal' style of development, where everything is handled by a developer. Increasingly, this scheme has been extended to creating property that, although purpose built, is not purchased but rented. The influence of the revision of tenure in the 1954 Landlord and Tenant Act must also be taken into consideration.

Another reason is the changing economic climate and the balance of internal investment in the manufacturing firm (Wainman and Brown, 1978). In recessionary periods it makes financial sense to lease property, as little capital is tied up in property and greater sums directed into value creating areas; for example, product development. There is no estimate of the proportion of properties located on industrial estates, but clearly it was a growing trend especially with regard to smaller units. Thus, it must be concluded that property developers were having a greater influence on the location of not just industrial estates, as Bale (1974b) suggests, but all industrial property. When considering the growing popularity of rented industrial property and industrial estates, the role of the state must also be considered as practically all of its industrial property is leased or rented.

The 1960s were an interesting time for industrial building. The agents that were to influence it most in later years were just making an entry into the market, in a rather haphazard and tentative manner. Much private development was in the form of industrial estates in the south east of the country. In the rest of the county industrial estates were developed by a combination of local government intervention in the servicing of land and infrastructure and private contractors providing buildings. The investors and developers of industrial property had made the first inroads into influencing the location and form of industrial development.

However, it was not a smooth transition and by 1971 the industrial property boom was drawing to a close (Smyth, 1983, p. 198). The two problems faced by private developers were first, finding new funds and second, the rising cost of old finance; both made new development problematic. However, this was only a shadow of a cataclysm that affected the property market in the early 1970s.

The corporatist phase of state–society relations was at once closest and most fraught in the mid 1970's. The tensions that gave rise to the three-day week, and the eventual downfall of the Conservative administration in 1974, were temporally resolved through the period of the Social Contract (Thompson, 1984a, p. 107). The actions of the outgoing Conservative administration were a factor in triggering the property market crash of 1973.[19] There were two key elements; a freeze on office rental growth and an imposition of a tax for developers on the first letting of a property.

The property market crash of 1973 has been well documented.[20] Investors lost confidence in property generally as a safe investment. Little

---

[19] Very briefly, the lack of confidence in the paper values of property caused banks to call in their loans leaving developers with very highly geared investments and huge reverse yield gaps. Those developers who did not have their own capital and could not sell (in such a situation nobody will buy) were left to sink, or rather the banks that loaned the money were. The prospect of several merchant banks owing their creditors was enough for the Bank of England to launch its £1,200 million 'lifeboat operation' to bail-out the banks.

The lack of confidence was compounded in the office market by the rental freeze, introduced in an attempt to curb speculation and the introduction of the Development Gains Tax (DGT). This tax was an extension of the Capital Gains Tax introduced in the 1965 Finance Act (see Footnote 16). The DGT was payable on the first letting of a property. The DGT was superseded in 1976 Development Land Tax Act by the Development Land Tax (DLT). The DLT was introduced initially for a short period to cover the introduction of the CLA. However, the change of administration and the abolition of the CLA kept the DLT on the statute books for a considerable period. The subject of taxation is a considerable complex one and companies are variously liable depending on how they structure developments and their other activities. Although an important topic, taxation has been ignored by industrial geographers, not least because of its complexity. This topic is dealt with generally by Goodchild and Munton (1985, Chapter 2) and in more detail for industrial development by Darlow (1983, Chapter 9).

[20] See Ambrose and Colenutt (1975), Property Advisory Group (1975, 1980), Cadman and Catalano (1983), Plender (1982), Boddy (1979), McRae and Cairncross (1984).

development took place in the period following the crash. But, most significantly, what did take place was a 'mopping up' of the £2,000 million of unsold property in all sectors of the commercial market by the remaining developers and funders. The number of property companies was reduced from 129 to 98 over the period 1970–1978. Of the 31 lost 10 collapsed and 21 were taken over (Property Advisory Group, 1975). Like the restructuring that followed the introduction of the 1965 Finance Act, the result was a concentration of control into fewer 'hands'. In this case the only 'hands' that had finance were the pension funds and the insurance companies.

The collapse of the Bretton–Woods system of fixed exchange rates in 1972 and the oil price increase enforced by the Organization of Oil Producing Countries in 1973 bought the economic boom of the sixties to an end. The oil price rise in particular led to a balance of payments deficit and heavy overseas borrowing, which in turn gave rise to a deflation of sterling. Thus, the Government was caught between a commitment to the Social Contract and substantial borrowing commitments. In order to maintain public expenditure borrowing would be required, interest rates would rise, and expenditure would again be put under pressure (Thompson, 1984b, p. 287). The 1975 budget announced public expenditure cuts and the beginning of the end for Keynesianism. In 1976 the Labour administration sought a loan from the International Monetary Fund. One significant condition attached to this loan was the introduction of a limit on the money supply (Thompson, 1984b, p. 286). Not surprisingly the Social Contract was abandoned in 1977. The downward pressure on public expenditure, and strong monetary supply controls effectively cemented the break from Keynesian 'demand' management. The foundations of 'supply-led', or monetarist, policies pursued with vigour by the incoming Conservative administration of 1979 were laid.

This period, 1960–1975, was a crucial one in terms of the development of industrial estates. There are three key elements. First, the modernization of industrial production techniques and the requirements of new spaces creating a demand for new buildings; rising interest rates adding caution to investment plans coupled with improvements in the security of tenure; both gave rise to an increase in demand for rented industrial property. Second, the restructuring of the property sector, through the action of taxation, easy loans that led to the market crash, and later high interest rates all contributed to a dramatic restructuring of the property development sector. Third, the key agents, the pension funds and insurance companies whose reserves had been swelled in the prosperous 1960s and benefited from state changes in pensions policies in the 1970s. These agents came, by the end of the period to be in a dominant position in property investment and, to a lesser, extent development.

The inter-relationship between these three elements gave rise to a new form of industrial development; the industrial estate. However, there was a crucial spatial dimension in the development and tenure of these properties. Those in the south were generally privately funded. In the rest of the country a combination of local authority, central government and private investment was used. As a consequence two major industrial property landlords emerged: the state and the pension funds. It was the needs of these agents that began to drive the newly emerging industrial property market. Just as the commercial property market for investment came into being in the 1960s, a submarket, the industrial property investment market, was beginning to emerge by the mid-1970s.

1976–1987: Monetarism

The incoming Conservative administration carried through explicitly what in many respects the Labour administration had done covertly. This policy came to be known as the 'Medium term financial strategy' (Thompson, 1984b, p. 276). The two key elements in this strategy were: first, the reduction of state involvement in the economy through decreases in state expenditure and lower taxation. Second, that the labour market be left to 'regulate itself'. Thus, in contrast to the postwar consensus to achieve full employment the control of inflation became the major objective and unemployment a minor one.

Six major areas of policy change that affected the role played by the state in the property market since 1979 can be identified: taxation, regional policy, urban policy, central government agencies, local government, and planning legislation. Whilst they can be dealt with separately they all represent different facets of the restructuring of capital–state–civil society relationships.

A key first step taken by the incoming administration was the freeing of exchange controls in 1979, which opened up investment opportunities for institutional investors in the world property market (Greater London Council, 1986, p. 26). Whether these funds would have invested in British property if the exchange controls had not been lifted is uncertain. More crucial has been the restructuring of the nature of state intervention in the property sector.

Direct measures were taken to reduce taxation for developers. The Development Land Tax was reduced to 60% in 1979 and eventually abolished in 1985 leaving the Capital Gains Tax as the only remaining tax on development. Capital Gains Tax was itself reduced in the 1988 budget. Another significant step was made in 1980, by extending the Industrial

Buildings Allowances (IBA) to small workshops.[21] The practical effect of the IBA scheme is to allow the development of small industrial buildings the cost of which is off set against taxable income. This scheme encouraged a significant amount of activity, although it was not locationally targeted. There is no evidence as to the extent or location of the IBA investment, but it is likely that it followed existing investment patterns focusing on the south and east of the country.

1979 was a significant breakpoint in state regional development initiatives. A key point was the gradual redrawing of the assisted area boundaries to cut the working population covered by the policy from 47% in 1979 to 28% in 1982, and later to 15% in 1984. Industrial Development Certificates were first abolished in all Assisted Areas and eased elsewhere; in 1981 they were abolished altogether. The reform of policy reduced the amount of state financial support for the assisted areas (see Table 4.3), whilst at the same time reaffirming rhetorical support, as set out in the 1983 White Paper on Regional Industrial Development:

> "Although an economic case for regional industrial policy may still be made, it is not self-evident. The Government believe that the case for continuing the policy is now principally a social one with the aim of reducing . . . regional imbalances in employment opportunities" (HMSO, 1983, p. 4).

This strategy was consolidated in the 1984 Act whereby a further reduction was made to the regional policy budget. Assisted Areas were also further reduced and Special Development Areas deleted. The last vestiges of regional industrial planning were also removed with the abolition of the Regional Economic Development Councils in 1980.

Instead of Regional Policy the Conservative administration 'targeted' the Inner Cities for receipt of assistance. Policies implemented have been in the form of Enterprise Zones (EZ) (1980) and Freeports (1984). These initiatives, together with the Urban Development Corporations (UDCs) (from, 1979 onwards), were later consolidated under the banner of 'Action for Cities'. A common theme in these initiatives has been the reduction or

---

[21] The IBA was aimed at Corporation Taxpayers, and personal investors on high rates of income taxation (DoI, 1982, p. 1). IBA for all industrial buildings was introduced in 1944. Initially it was set at 10%, increasing to 30% in 1970, 40% in 1972, 50% in 1974, and 75% in 1981 . This latter change detracted from the Small Workshops IBA (DoI, 1982, p. 1). The IBA was later reduced to 50% in 1984, and 25% in 1985. For the purposes of the small workshops IBA, a small workshop was defined as below 232 square metres from 1980–83, this was later redefined as a unit of less than 116 square metres for the period 1983–5 when the scheme ended (DoI, 1982, p. 5). Initially the guidelines were strictly drawn as indicated in Section 7 of the 1968 Capital Allowances Act, referring to manufacturing activities. However, with the problems of letting these units and the rather vague nature of defining activities of small firms this was eased. It was thus no longer applied to individual units, but in terms of the dominant activity for whole schemes.

TABLE 4.3. *Regional Policy Expenditure 1982–90 in England.*

Year	Regional policy expenditure (£million)
1982–3	365.2
1983–4	296.5
1984–5	293.4
1985–6	242.4
1986–7	349.7
1987–8	271.6
1988–9	317.9
1989–90	264.5

Source: HMSO (1991).

removal of taxation and other rules and regulations. In the case of UDCs the control of the area is taken away from local authority control and vested with an unelected body accountable to central government.

The English Industrial Estates Corporation, charged with industrial property development on behalf of the state, has also undergone some dramatic changes in its scope of activities since the 1981 English Industrial Estates Corporation Act: its name was changed to English Estates (EE) and it was given the additional role of building factory units for the Development Commission. More significantly for the future the Act also allowed EE to build and manage factories *outside* the assisted areas. Ostensibly, this facilitated a role in the inner cities in line with the new emphasis on urban policy. A common theme in urban policy since the 1978 Inner Urban Areas Act introduced by the Labour Government has been the idea of 'partnership'. This has manifest itself with regard to EE as a means of subsidising its activities. King (1986, p. 31) reports that some £20 million was attracted from Legal and General Assurance, the National Coal Board Pension Fund, and Barclays and Midland Banks, predominantly for the establishment of a subsidiary—Beehive Workshops—to develop and manage small factory units.

The 1985 Industrial Development Act pushed English Estates further along the road as a self-funding organization further revising its financing arangments. These new arrangements allowed the reinvestment of rental income into new projects rather than returning it to the Treasury. In other words it encouraged English Estates to make profits. In line with monetarist policy there had been a questioning of the role of the English Estates in terms of efficiency and the possibility of it 'stifling competition'. Two reports were commissioned on these topics in 1984 and 1986 (quoted in Fothergill *et al.*, 1987), neither of which suggested immediate changes. Significantly, in answer to a question in Parliament, it emerged that wholesale privatization had been considered, then rejected (Butcher,

1986, p. 4). Nevertheless, English Estates has clearly become a more 'market orientated' organization in terms of their stricter adherence to a 'market' rate of return required on investment. The development of Science Parks and office developments outside the Assisted Areas had not been characteristic of English Estates activity previously.[22]

The public expenditure cuts of the in-coming Conservative administration in 1979, coupled with renewed economic recession created uncertainty and later an abandonment of the ambitious DC rural factory programme of 1975. In 1984 the area covered by the DC was reduced as Rural Development Areas (RDA) replaced the Special Investment Areas.[23] Along with the RDA's came the more comprehensive Rural Development Programmes (RDP's). These rolling five year programmes were an attempt to coordinate the variety of agencies active in rural areas. The funding (approximately £24m in 1985/6) was intended to be 'pump-priming' and not to cover the full costs of development, the co-funding comes exclusively from public and voluntary bodies; some 100% funding of factory building does remain. Another significant change that affected the Development Commission factory programme was that, in 1981, English Estates took over the entire factory programme, leaving the Council for Small Industries in Rural Areas (CoSIRA) to concentrate on advice and marketing assistance for small firms. CoSIRA's duties were eventually transferred to the Commission in 1987. The Development Commission also operated a refurbishment grant which encourages the re-use and conversion of existing rural infrastructure. In effect this was an attempt to re-use property from a previous period of 'industrialization' (agriculture).

The Development Commission's role was consolidated and updated in the 1983 Miscellaneous Financial Provisions Act further allowing it to make grants to bodies, such as local authorities, promoting industrial development in England. Due to letting problems of the larger units previously built, new developments were predominantly of a smaller size: between 45 to 90 square metres. Interestingly, reference is made in the guidelines for the Rural Development Programmes to the importance of the provision of a 'hierarchy' of industrial premises in a local area (Development Commission, 1984, p. 25). Whilst not explicitly supporting industrial estates, the economies of scale required to develop land in rural and remote areas imply such development. A major criticism of these new

---

[22] There was a further merging of agencies responsible for the provision of industrial units in 1993; the new Urban Regeneration Agency became responsible for the development of industrial buildings under the Urban Programme a well as EE's former activities.
[23] The Rural Development Areas reduced the areas eligible for assistance by 5%, and the population covered by 10%, significantly towns over 10,000 population were not included in these areas.

programmes by practitioners has been the complexity of the preparation and the lack of resources devoted to them (Green, 1986, p. 19). The Rural Development Areas were revised once again in 1990.[24]

A major consequence of the Development Commission's programme in the 1980s was the proliferation of industrial estates of only three or four units. Such development relied heavily upon the local authorities, and the resources of the European Regional Development Fund to provide funds to enable basic servicing of industrial sites. The redrawing of the UK regional development programme Assisted Area boundaries in 1983 had an apparently unforseen knock-on effect. There are considerable areas that fall into the RDA's, yet outside the Assisted Areas. Being outside the Assisted Areas debars them from European assistance, which itself was used to 'lever' Development Commission resources in the form of advance factory units. The indications are that this further modified the character of rural industrial development in the RDA's not falling within the Assisted Areas.

By 1978 the number of local authorities developing industrial estates had grown from the 36% of 1972 to 53%. These industrial sites were characteristically acquired freehold by the local authority, serviced in phases with infrastructure, and individual plots were then offered to industrialists or, in RDAs, to the DC (Boddy 1983, p. 36). Local government assistance, such as that enabled by legislation of the early 1960s, in the form of new and refurbished property and sites has been curtailed under expenditure limitations introduced under the 1980 Local Government, Planning and Land Act and the 1982 Finance Act. The measures of the latter became known as 'rate-capping'. Basically, local authorities were given progressively less leeway to spend money as they saw fit. The boldest act of intent by the Conservative administration to draw back control over the style and mode of state intervention was evidenced by the abolition of the metropolitan tier of local government (see Duncan and Goodwin, 1988). These agencies had been particularly active in the field of industrial promotion (Armstrong and Fildes, 1989; Totterdill, 1989). Ironically, many of the enticements given to industrialists by local authorities and curtailed after 'rate-capping' such as rent-free periods and rate 'holidays' were now being offered by central government agencies in specific areas such as Enterprise Zones.[25] This emphasizes the aspect of shifting power and control, and the relation of the state to both civil society and capital. Instead of localized collective provision, local authorities have

[24]The Development Commission was subsequently renamed the Rural Development Commission for England.
[25]The final extension of central government power over local authorities was the 1989 Local Government and Housing Act. This act coming on top of the severe financial limitations of the Community Charge further curtailed local economic development activities. In many respects it marked the end of an era of pro-active local economic development (see Hayton, 1990).

been encouraged to enter into partnerships with the private sector,[26] ostensibly to act as 'pump-primers', but clearly at the cost of both subsidizing private sector developers and underwriting the risk of ventures to private developers.[27]

Legislation in the form of *Lifting the Burden* has reduced the need for compliance to planning and safety legislation for smaller businesses (see DTI, 1988 for an overview). The proposal for Simplified Planning Zones would be to do away with detailed planning applications and only requires conformity to a broad land use category. In the meantime the Uses Classes Order (1972) has been reissued with a new classification of industry. Particularly relevant is the new 'B1 business class' that allows both office and industrial uses of land without the need to seek change of use (DoE, 1987). Understandably, this change was particularly heavily lobbied for by developers as it facilitates development of very flexible buildings that can accommodate the whole range of occupants from offices, through research, to light industrial (Henneberry, 1985). Developers holding onto buildings in the hope of a future rise in value have been helped by the concession recommended to local authorities by the Department of the Environment, namely that they do not charge rates on empty property.[28]

The actual amount of industrial floorspace grew over this period (see Table 4.4); however, this headline figure disguises a decline in manufacturing floorspace, and increase in warehousing floorspace[29] and a substantial increase in vacant and redundant property (see Table 4.5). Fothergill *et al.* (1987, p. 117) estimate that the public sector accounted for just 5.9% of the total industrial floorspace in 1984. However, the public sector contributed 42% of new buildings in that year.

Cadman (1984, p. 77) estimates that by the early 1980s the pension funds and insurance companies controlled some 83% of all property investment. Moreover, they were searching for new investments (not just property) at an increasing rate. The total assets of the sector estimated at

---

[26] There have been a stream of advice notes (circulars) from the Secretary of State to local authorities on this point. One of the first was 71/77 which urged local authorities to be more flexible and to involve themselves in the promotion of industry. This was in part the extension of the CLA. More significant have been the changes since the Conservatives came to power. Circular 22/80, and later 16/84 urged local authorities to speed up the planning process for industry. A more direct erosion of local authority planning control came with circulars 1/85 and 14/85, that warned planners not to be obstructive to economic development by refusing planning permission. This trend was formalised in the *Lifting the Burden* legislation (HMSO, 1985) which offered the prospect of simplified planning zones and revision of the UCO.

[27] This has been particularly evident in sale and leaseback schemes where the local authority guarantees to pay the rent roll from completion if any units are vacant.

[28] Circular 34/78, and The 1980 Local Government and Land Act.

[29] For a commentary on the growth of warehousing in England, and its relationship to the restructuring of distribution activities see McKinnon (1986). A notable feature of this growth has been a trend towards larger units (regional distribution centres) and a relocation at motorway intersections (see McKinnon and Pratt, 1985, 1986).

TABLE 4.4. *Floorspace in England (Manufacturing and Warehousing) 1975–85 (Millions of Square Metres) Source: DoE (various)*

Year	Manufacturing	Warehousing
1975	229.5	95.2
1976	231.7	99.0
1977	232.6	101.8
1978	232.2	104.5
1979	233.4	107.6
1980	233.9	111.2
1981	234.5	115.7
1982	232.5	120.1
1983	228.9	124.5
1984	225.7	128.3
1985	222.2	131.9

TABLE 4.5. *Vacant Floorspace (Manufacturing and Warehousing) in England and Wales 1975–85 (Millions of Square Metres). King and Co (various)*

Year	Manufacturing	Warehousing
1975	3.3	3.1
1976	3.9	3.0
1977	3.5	2.7
1978	3.4	2.5
1979	3.0	2.0
1980	5.8	3.8
1981	8.9	4.7
1982	10.2	6.1
1983	9.9	5.9
1984	9.5	6.5
1985	8.7	6.5

£150,000 million (Philipp, 1985, p. 13); the largest fund, the Mineworkers pension fund, has assets of £5,730 million (Philipp, 1985, p. 133); Postel, another of the largest funds, has to find a home for £3 million of new investment finance per day (James 1983, p. 13). The following gives some indication of the total property assets held: the institutions assets grew from £27,400m to £57,491m[30] between 1980–1988 (CSO, 1991a)[31]; over

---

[30] All figures are constant 1980 prices unless otherwise stated.

[31] The collation of data and other information on the property development and investment sector is notoriously difficult (see Pratt, 1994). As much of this data has such a high market value it is collected and only selectively released by private research organisations, usually chartered surveyors. The best source of information on the activities of financial institutions is the annual report of the Investment Property Databank (1989) and occasional reports of Debenham, Tewson and Chinnocks (1982, 1989a, and 1989b). Some relevant financial information, in an aggregate form, is also to be found in the both the CSO Financial Statistics and the quarterly Business Monitor MQ5. Commentaries on these trends can be found, most recently, in Healey and Nabarro (1990), Phillip (1983), plus the commercially produced *Healey and Baker Quarterly Investment Report*.

the same period corporate property sector assets grew from £7,000m to £23,200m (Debenham *et al.*, 1989a, p. 11). To explain this it is worth noting that between 1983 and 1988 new orders for industrial and commercial property increased year on year after having previously been stable (DoE, 1989). This property boom has led to the re-emergence of the private property company. This expansion has been funded by a huge injection of bank lending to property companies which grew by a massive 540% over the period 1981–8; surpassing even the level of outstanding loans in the 1973–4 period (CSO, 1991b). Over the same period the net annual investment by financial institutions has declined; particularly those of pension funds. What little investment by institutions that did take place in this period can almost solely be accounted for by retail developments (Investment Property Databank, 1989, p. 9).

Two trends were noteworthy in the 1980s. First, the two larger Property Unit Trusts (PUTs) were sold off; mainly to the institutions. Hence, despite the lack of development activity the institutions' assets did continue to grow. By 1989 the total assets held by the institutions totalled £63,817m (£42,487m insurance companies, £20,228m pension funds and £1,102m PUTs) (CSO, 1991a). Second, the events of October 1988 ('Black Monday') led to disinvestment in equities and investment in other media, thus strengthening the institutional sector's interest in property which had already been bolstered by the reduced availability of gilts as a result of monetarist policies. Conversely, the corporate property sector lost interest in property development due to both the difficult in justifying self-financing of development through equity issues and high interest rates causing conventional borrowing to be increasingly expensive.

Looking more closely at the institutions, one of the key characteristics of the period is the concentration of power. A 1984 survey indicated that 59% of pension schemes were managed by merchant and clearing banks. Furthermore, half of all externally managed funds of the pension funds were managed by fewer than 12 merchant and clearing banks (Greater London Council, 1986, p. 29). With regard to the property holdings of the institutions further concentration is evident. It is estimated that some 60–65% of the institutional sector's UK property holdings were controlled by just 37 of the larger institutional funds (each holding assets in excess of £1,000m) (Debenham *et al.*, 1989a, p. 16). These larger funds currently dedicated on average 11–12% of their investment portfolios by value into property. It should be noted that this figure was both lower for the smaller funds and has been, on average, much higher in the past: for example, 30% for the larger funds in 1981 (Debenham *et al.*, 1982, p. 11).

Table 4.6 shows the portfolio mix of financial institutional investors. Overall, the period 1980–7 has seem a decrease in the proportion of funds dedicated to industry, and an increase in retail investments. This distribution represents the spread of risk for these different properties.[32] It can

TABLE 4.6. *Property Asset Mix (Capital Values) by Type of Institutional Investor*
(1980–87)

| | Institutional type | | Investment medium | | | |
| | Retail | | Office | | Industrial | |
	1980	1987	1980	1987	1980	1987
Pension fund	19.5	44.3	59.7	41.2	20.1	13.9
Insurance Co.	26.8	29.1	58.2	60.8	13.3	7.9
PUT	34.6	47.1	38.3	38.3	27.1	17.2
All Institutions	25.3	34.9	57.2	53.4	16.3	9.6

Source: Investment Property Databank (1989) Figs 3.11 and 3.10.

be estimated that the value of industrial property held by institutions in 1981 was £3,809m and it grew to £4,531m in 1987. However, even these figures are misleading in that they represent a static situation and fail to do justice to the increasingly dynamic nature of the property investment market in the 1980s. The institutions 'turn over' their investments to maintain balanced and up-to-date portfolios. Despite being considered to be a long-term investment approximately 10% of all investment property is annually 'turned over' compared with 45% of gilts and 14% of equities (Debenham, Tewson and Chinnocks 1989a: 15). Prior to 1980 less that 2% of property was annually 'turned over' by institutions. Thus, not only is a substantial share of property directly developed and owned by institutions, but also an increasing proportion of all property is passing through institutional portfolios at one time or another.

A separate industrial property sector emerged in the early 1960s in the context of more general restructuring in the whole commercial property sector. The further segmentation of the sector in the 1980s would at first seem to be a logical development. Hi-tech and retail warehouse developments, which are manifestations of reorganization at both ends of the

---

[32] The relationship between rental income, yield and market price for property is represented by the equation: Rental Yield (%) = (Current Net Rental x 100) / Market Price. Basically the yield is an indicator of risk, the higher the yield the better the return on investment, but the lower the yield the more secure the return. Investors will seek to assemble a portfolio of investments. Institutional investors are renowned for their conservative attitudes and preferences for secure, low yielding property. The equation above is a crude representation as, in practice, yields may be 'rolled up' into a whole company's yield on current income that takes account of the costs of borrowing and other company activities. Thus an acceptable yield for any particular company may be related to a global internal rate of return rather than a narrowly defined one. As a guide to the relative attractiveness of particular types of property for investment, major chartered surveyors and analysts regularly produce tables of yields. Industrial media are regularly poorer (higher yields) than other media such as offices. There is also a spatial element to yields. Properties otherwise the same, if in a different location, will attract quite different yields (see Pratt, 1983).

production process (new product development and new consumption patterns), became the key foci of investment invariably in the form of industrial estate and science park developments (McIntosh, 1986, p. 125). On closer inspection this new subsector owes its existence more to pressures within the property investment sector for new outlets for investment than to simple restructuring of industrial production.

Two points account for the growth of investment-led development in this subsector. First, the nature of hi-tech property development. Basically, even when the higher quality of building is discounted, the developer is creating a property with a higher percentage of office space. Office space commands a far higher rental, and industrial land (upon which such developments are invariably located) is cheaper than at more traditional inner urban office locations. These conditions allowed developers to make a bigger return on investments. Furthermore, the premium attached to science park locations has led, in Cambridge for example, to rentals outstripping even neighbouring urban office levels (Evans and Plumb, 1984). Second, there was considerable pressure on financial institutions with expanding funds to acquire new property in order to simply balance existing portfolios (Plender, 1983). Clearly, those sectors of the market with more favourable yields are key targets for investment, whether or not there is a 'real' demand for them. It is interesting to note that the science park 'boom' was only possible due to a change in land use zoning regulations in 1987 (the Use Classes Order), referred to above, that effectively allowed office development on land previously zoned (and valued) for industrial activity.

The segmentation of the property investment market has not only taken place according to the type of user, but also by the size of the property. This is a general bias against smaller properties as they imply more clients for landlords/developers/investors, which means in turn more rents to collect, greater administrative overheads, and, due to the greater failure rate of small firms, greater financial risks (Coopers and Lybrand Associates/ Drivers Jonas, 1980). As noted above the development of smaller units was temporarily boosted by the introduction of the 100% Industrial Building Allowance (1981–1985).

There is also a spatial aspect to market segmentation. Localities that are remote from London and the M4 and M11 motorway corridor are considered to be of a greater risk by investors. A consequence of this is that little institutional investment occurs in the economically peripheral localities. Table 4.7 gives an indication of the spatial distribution of the amount of institutional portfolio investments, when compared with the actual distribution of industrial floorspace the disparities become clear. The greatest disparities are to be found in Wales, the North, and the Midlands. Two caveats should be added at this point. First, that floorspace figures are very difficult to interpret given their poor statistical definition and the

TABLE 4.7. *Regional Disparities in Institutional Property Investment (1986)*

Region	Investment (%)	Floorspace (%)	Ratio
Wales	0.6	4.3	0.13
North	6.6	34.5	0.19
Midlands (E & W)	7.2	23.0	0.31
East Anglia	3.8	4.5	0.84
South West	4.8	7.6	0.63
Rest of South East	45.9	15.7	2.90
London	31.0	10.2	3.00

Source: adapted from McNamara (1990, p. 99). Note, the columns do not add up to 100 due to rounding errors.

disregard for 'marketability'. This is particularly the case in the older industrial regions where, for example, large areas of multi-storey properties are vacant. Second, the use of standard regions for such comparisons conceals more than it reveals, intraregional disparities are significant but not revealed in such an analysis. For example, the property market hardly exists in Cornwall, but is very active in Avon. Both are subsumed under the 'South West' region.

Property development that does occur in remoter areas and less favoured subsectors can only do so, if at all, at considerable risk to developers. It is in these localities and subsectors of the property market that state intervention has occurred to provide accommodation in conditions of market failure (see Adams, 1990). However, public sector developers are still bound by requirements to achieve an internal rate of return on developments, albeit commonly at the rate of 1% below that normally expected in the private sector.

The poor performance of the industrial property market has been blamed upon the excess of supply (King and Co., 1986). It is argued that the vacant property is either in the wrong place, is the wrong design, or is in poor condition: in 1989 just 22% of all vacant buildings were new (King and Co., 1989). The response from King and Co, based on their survey information (see Table 4.5 above), has been to urge demolition. Clearly, there is a conflict of interest here. Limited investment in older properties can easily refurbish them and prolong their useful life, as well as providing accommodation at relatively cheap rentals (Green and Foley, 1982; Green *et al.*, 1985). However, the rate of return on the investment for the developer is likely to be both poor and high risk due to the nature of the tenants, and the non-prime location; furthermore, rentals are likely to be low. Thus, new small unit developments are not likely to be attractive to the institutional investor, but they may be attractive for the small private developer or investor.

The 1980 report by Coopers and Lybrand Associates/Drivers Jonas, highlighted some of the issues surrounding the development and re-development of premises for small businesses. The conclusion was that institutional developers and investors were unlikely to be interested in such developments. This is an issue that lies at the core of a polarization of the industrial property market into a 'prime' and 'nonprime' market that developed in the seventies. However, there are indications that this market structure is itself now becoming segmented.

The 'prime' market consists of the well-located (near a motorway junction with access to an airport and preferably London), well developed (constructed to institutional standards), and well occupied units (by a well-known transnational or public limited company). However, shortage of potential investments in this category has led funds to reassess what have been termed 'secondary' markets.[33] Basically, these are units in less favourable locations, with older or lower quality building specifications, or with less reliable tenants: the prime units of ten years ago. Market research and performance monitoring has made investors more confident in their assessment of the scale of risk in such investments. As before, the 'non-prime,' or what are now termed 'third-tier' developments (McIntosh, 1986, p. 130), are the remaining developments. These developments will yield very attractive returns on investment but at a greater risk.

A fragmentation of the industrial property has occurred in the late 1980s: prime and secondary; hi-tech, and warehousing. Each of these sub-sectors has a different spatial pattern in terms of the yield on investment property. The expectation of good yields in hi-tech property and the expectation of growth of specialist research and development companies has spawned a new form of industrial estate: the business park and the science park. These developments are characterized by the lower density of development, flexible internal layout and, above all, high rentals. Like industrial estates since the mid-1970s these developments have been supply rather than demand driven. In the south east and west the main provider has been the private sector, in the north the public sector.[34]

At the other end of the spectrum developers have developed new legal instruments in order to protect themselves from greater exposure to risk. Grant and Partners (1982, p. 2) note that leases on premises were modified in the early 1980s; a five year review period was became the norm and three year reviews occurred more regularly. Furthermore, rental payments were written into leases so that they became a prior charge on bankruptcy. This is a clear indication of a shift towards insulation against risk by developers.

---

[33] There is an analogy here with the 'junk bonds' popular in the equity markets of the early 1990s; high risk investments that are spread between portfolios.
[34] For further discussion of the development of science parks and 'hi-tech' developments see the discussion in Massey *et al.* (1992), Chapter 7; and Pratt (1993).

More recent evidence highlights the trend to shorter and more flexible leases to give landlord and tenant more flexibility; relocation for the tenant, refurbishment for the owner (McKenna, 1986, pp. 178–179).

The major shift in the provision of industrial property that occurred in the post-1975 period was the increased control and interest by investors in the final product; particularly by the financial institutions. The role of the state in industrial property provision was still significant; in some localities it was exclusive. The provision of EE and DC units declined in the mid-1980s as funds were withdrawn. Likewise local authority provision declined after 1982. The impact of decline in local authority provision is unlikely to be felt until the early 1990s due the stock of land already prepared.

The limited information available on industrial tenure suggests that owner occupation was continuing to be less common; a sample survey carried out for the Department of the Environment (McIntosh and Keddie, 1979, p. 17) of 501 establishments in urban areas indicates that half were renting property compared with just over a third in the DTI survey of 1973. The 1979 survey indicated two issues: first, that two thirds of all firms renting or leasing accommodation did so from private landlords, second, that the smaller the firm the less likely it was to be an owner-occupier. However, McIntosh and Keddie's (1979 p. 18) survey indicates that a majority of those surveyed wanted to become owner-occupiers. Firms engaged in manufacturing and with more than 50 employees were more likely to want to own their own property.

There are indications that rising land values have been as much to blame for the shift away from owner occupation as the need to invest in production or the power of the financial institutions. Healey and Baker (1990) note that despite impressive growth in land values between 1977 and 1990 of 14.4% per annum that the depression of 1989 was forcing highly geared developers out of the market; this was making it possible again for owner-occupation of industrial property.

Conclusion

The aim of this chapter has been to explain the emergence of the industrial estate in Britain by reference to the restructuring of relations both with and between the state and capital. In contrast to the idealist conception of industrial estates and industrial location discussed in Chapter 2 it was argued that the development of industrial estates could be related to specific changes in the structure of ownership and provision of industrial premises.

The development of the first private industrial estates was facilitated by the emergence of private property development companies. Long term ownership of industrial property by developers was not common. Essentially, the developer was acting as an intermediary for the industrialist. The existence of such intermediaries was clearly important in enabling the restructuring of production in the interwar period in the proximity of the conurbations. These new buildings on new sites facilitated new mass production techniques that would not have been possible on former inner-urban locations.

Further restructuring within the commercial property development sector that took place in the late 1960s and 1970s which gave rise to the merging and dominance of investor rather than developer interests was particularly significant. The requirement for all investment media to 'perform' against market criteria led to greater influence being exerted over the design, form, and location of development activity; as well as a segmentation of the industrial market by type and location of premises. In contrast to the earlier period there was an increasing potential for conflict in terms of the users' and the owners' requirements of premises. It is significant that the majority of new industrial estate developments took place in this period. By the late 1980s the form had become ubiquitous.

The role of property in urban–rural shift of manufacturing industry documented by Fothergill and his colleagues can now be questioned. That the shift took place is not in dispute; the explanation is. Lack of expansion space in inner urban areas is not a sufficient explanation. Reference is required to the nature of the ownership and provision of property. Inner-urban sites were, in effect, being revalued the 1960s through a combination of planning control, redevelopment and social and economic change in the use of cities; in growing city centres higher yields were possible from office and retail activities, alternatively in depressed parts of inner cities, yields were high and too risky to invest in. Likewise peripheral rural localities could only achieve derisory yields. The main locations that would produce acceptable yields were green field sites predominantly in the emergent motorway corridors that provided good access to large markets. The relocation of industry to such locations in the 1960s and 1970s needs to be explained by consideration of the restructuring of the property development and investment sector and the role of the state in terms of planning and infrastructure provision. The empirical result may be an apparent lack of space, or rather that appropriate expansion space is too expensive. However, an explanation of both why such space is so costly and other sites are cheaper, and why developers could afford new developments in the outer urban and rural fringe areas would seem to be required. The recent development of science parks is only the latest phase in the revaluation of segments of the green field industrial land market. This shift owes as much to changes in investment patterns of financial institutions and changes in planning legislation regarding land use zoning as much as any 'objective need' for 'hi-tech' industrial property, offices on industrial sites or science parks.[35]

This increasing dominance of industrial property provision by a few actors would not have been so significant if it were not for the fact that there was a corresponding shift in the tenure of industrial property from owner occupation to rental. This must be related to the decline in manufacturing more generally and to the increasing cost of property. In effect property would, if it were owned, become a proportionately greater burden for a firm. The costs and risks of development in periods of high interest rates made development more difficult for industrialists, just as it had done for the private property companies. High interest rates and increased competition in productive activities caused industrialists to re-invest surpluses into production innovation and modernization rather than property. This twin squeeze had the effect of making industrialists more reliant than ever on property providers for industrial premises.

The public sector has also played a very significant role in creating this new form of industrial property. The changing role of the state in British society is crucial in this explanation. The development of the first industrial estates were the first evidence of a new interventionist role of the state. Whilst the Keynesian style policies would seem to be sympathetic to intervention in the built environment their main effect was at the macro scale. At the local scale it was only with the weakening of Keynesian fiscal controls on local government that the great growth occurred in property provision, significantly in tandem with the emergence of a new spirit of local economic planning. It was ironic that the emergence of local economic planning was itself a response by local labour controlled councils to the failure of labour policies in the national realm. In the early 1980s these policies increasingly came into conflict with those of both central government and its quangos (DC and EE) which were adopting monetarist and neoliberal forms of regulation. The abolition of the metropolitan counties and the 1989 Local Government and Housing Act bought that period to a close, and with it, a significant period of the restructuring of the industrial built environment.[36]

The net result is a tendency in the current geography and form of industrial development to be influenced more by the forms of provision of that property than by its users. Those firms operating in the core sectors of the economy such as high technology, and those located in the Cambridge, London, Bristol crescent are perhaps better served by this shift than those in peripheral sectors and locations. This is more by a chance coincidence of interests of property developers and investors and potential occupants of

---

[35] See discussion in Pratt (1993); Pratt, D. (1994); Henneberry (1994).
[36] The major development of science parks took place, significantly, in the mid-1980s; this boom also now appears to be on the wane (see Pratt, 1993).

those premises. If there was a divergence of interest from property investment then many potential occupiers could be left 'high and dry'. The key issue is that any mismatch will manifest itself in a spatially disaggregated pattern of property production.

It would be wrong to conclude that the shifts summarized above are determinate ones. What this chapter has set out are the changing conditions within which individual property developers, investors and industrialists operate. The exact form, location, tenure and nature of provision of industrial property cannot be simply read off from such an analysis. The following chapters explore how the industrial estate development process has operated in one locality: Cornwall.

5

The Origins of the Industrial Built Environment in Cornwall

Introduction

The aim of this chapter is to provide the context for a local analysis of the role of the industrial built environment in economic development. Cornwall provides an unusual, but very clear, example of such a process. Cornwall's main period of industrialization was associated with tin and copper mining which had its heyday in the mid-nineteenth century; kaolin (china clay) extraction continues to be important to this day, albeit with drastically reduced employment. This mode of industrialization and deindustrialization is now a familiar pattern in the North East of England and South Wales. In Cornwall it all happened earlier and because of the nature of the materials mined, coupled with the nature of ownership, little subsidiary manufacturing activity was developed. The legacy of decline was consequently much harsher; the result being a particularly dispersed settlement pattern, a long term out-migration of population and a very specialized — but obsolete — industrial built environment.

The focus of this chapter is the period from the Second World War until the late 1980s. This period neatly covers the total re-production of the industrial built environment, infrastructure and economic structure of Cornwall. Because of the absolute lack of appropriate industrial buildings, or prepared — serviced — land, a key element in this restructuring has been the industrial estate. Whilst Cornwall is an extreme case a similar pattern was widespread in the UK in this period. It is one thing to describe these macro-scale changes, as noted in the previous chapter, it is another to explain the micro-scale changes. This and the following two chapters explore such a micro-scale example: Cornwall. Before considering the detail of this development it will be useful to make a few preparatory comments about the structure of the Cornish economy in the interwar period.

TABLE 5.1. *Employment Structure of Cornwall Compared with England and Wales (1931)*

SIC	Cornwall Employment	%	England and Wales %
0	2628	27	6
1	93	1	7
2	862	9	5
3	497	5	8
4	652	7	19
5	681	7	5
6	1689	18	18
7	781	8	7
8	497	5	7
9	1236	13	19

Source: Census of population (10% sample). Note: industrial classification modified to correspond with SIC (1980). Broadly the SIC classification is as follows: Agriculture, forestry and fishing (0); energy and water supply (1); extraction of minerals (2); metal goods and engineering (3); other manufacturing (4); construction (5); distribution, hotel and catering (6); transport and communications (7); banking, finance and insurance (8); and other services, including armed forces (9).

The Interwar Legacy

The most immediately striking feature of the employment structure (see Table 5.1) is the great emphasis upon primary activities and the relative lack of manufacturing activities. Not surprisingly extractive industries are well represented in the industrial structure. What manufacturing activities there are were confined to one subsector—mining engineering and equipment—and to a couple of companies. According to a survey carried out as late as 1948 there were just 20 firms who employed more that 200 people in Cornwall (Cornwall County Council, 1952, p. 69), in 1931 the median size of companies was just nine persons (University College of the South West, 1947, p. 81).

For a county with such a poor economic base, suffering long term industrial decline in the mining industry and high unemployment it is surprising that it was not designated as a Development Area along with the North East and South Wales in the 1930s. Whilst political factors must have been crucial, the County Council attributed this anomaly to the fact that

"the West Cornwall area was not considered a sufficiently large economic unit to merit classification as a Development Area, but the comparatively high, but localised, unemployment following the war was considered sufficiently severe to justify special action....in the Camborne–Redruth area through the efforts of the local authority in conjunction with the Board of Trade and the County Planning Committee" (Cornwall County Council, 1952, p. 84).

This special action was limited to the identification of suitable sites for industry. Fogarty (1945) in his survey of industrial development initiatives in the UK notes that, compared with other areas suffering similar economic plight, little seems to have been done in the prewar period to attract industry to Cornwall. Influence on the Government was not mobilized in the county's favour to restructure the local industrial base as it had been, for example, in North East England.

Like other depressed areas in the UK, Cornwall had infrastructure development problems. Historically, these can be related to an over dependence on the rail network for links with the rest of England, and a rather disparate road network (see Figure 5.1). In particular, Caesar (1949, p. 210) notes congestion in town centres and the lack of a crossing of the lower Tamar as problematic. The 'gateway to Cornwall' was still Launceston, and the spinal route was merely a trunk road. Other basic infrastructure was also missing; this was a legacy of an earlier period of industrialization based upon mining. A postwar survey of the region referred to the lack of adequate electricity grid coverage in the county in the early thirties—a common problem in remoter areas of Britain at the time (University College of the South West, 1947, p. 191). Caesar (1949, p. 211) later also noted the lack of water and sewage facilities; a problem that continues to create difficulties in contemporary Cornwall.

Caesar (1949, p. 216) indicated that the most significant issue at the time was the shortage of

"... modern factory premises, [and] first class industrial sites".

As noted in the previous chapter this was not a unique problem; but given the absolute lack of industrial infrastructure relevant to 'modern' manufacturing in Cornwall this must have been considered to be an issue of overwhelming importance both in facilitating indigenous economic activities and in the attraction of migrant firms. Caesar (1949, p. 216) also suggested that the lack of suitable premises was a key factor in explaining the lack of both interwar and wartime dispersal of industry to Cornwall. The situation did not appear to have improved in the immediate postwar period either;

"there is no vacant modern factory space, wartime factory buildings having been allocated to firms that were operating in Camborne-Redruth in the prewar years, industrial facilities are not good." (Board of Trade, 1945, quoted in Caesar, 1949, p. 217).

Generally, the lack of infrastructure investment both in the late nineteenth and early twentieth centuries, as a result of the ownership and the organization of mining production activities and the continued economic

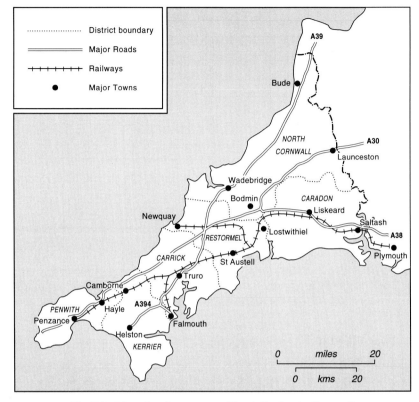

Fig. 5.1. Map of major towns and local districts in Cornwall.

depression,[1] created an economy in Cornwall which was characterized as rural and peripheral. It is for these reasons that Cornwall did not benefit from the economic development experienced in the South East of England over this period. Furthermore, it put the County in an unfavourable position as regards future economic development: effectively reproducing under-development.

It is not surprising that out-migration generally, and rural depopulation in particular, continued to be the rule for the young coupled with low

---

[1]Economic depression related to loss of 'export' markets and competition for 'home' markets (Hudson and Williams, 1986, p. 4). In Cornwall the loss of the world market hit the mining industry. It may be argued that a similar process (this time related to transport and infrastructure rather than tariff barriers) has also acted at a national scale. Over a similar period the incursion of the South West regional and the national market into the locality adversely affected firms' survival chances (Spooner, 1972, p. 200).

TABLE 5.2. *Employment Structure in Cornwall and England and Wales 1951, and 1961*

SIC	1951 Cornwall Number	%	E & W %	1961 Cornwall Number	%	E & W %
0	2653	20	5	1950	15	4
1	258	2	8	301	2	5
2	603	5	6	732	6	7
3	741	6	14	754	6	17
4	687	5	16	440	3	15
5	900	7	6	963	8	7
6	2825	22	18	3242	25	20
7	1042	8	7	1049	8	9
8	533	4	5	808	6	8
9	2807	22	16	2511	20	10

Source: Census of population (10% sample).

participation rates for women,[2] and a high percentage of retired persons. At one and the same time, these factors alleviated the unemployment problem and disguised its full extent.

Postwar Planning

An immediate consequence of the 1947 Town and Country Planning Act was the preparation and publication of the *County Development Plan* (Cornwall County Council, 1952). Industrial policies, as expressed in the document, reflected pre-war attitudes

> "...rigid control over siting by site reservation is not justified except in the case of large projects or 'obnoxious industries'..." (p. 85).

Allocation of land for industrial activities in smaller towns was considered

> "...not [to be] an urgent requirement." (p. 85).

In Cornwall, as in England and Wales more generally, agriculture was the favoured land use in rural areas (p. 239). In all but the case of new roads, infrastructure concerns were also muted in the Development Plan. Instead, the emphasis was on the 'market-led' solution,

> "although certain areas have been allocated in the Plan for industry, generally their development will be carried out by private enterprise" (p. 229).

Even by 1951 the Cornish economy did not appear to be performing too well under market conditions, as Table 5.2 shows. Both farming and

---

[2]Both general, and specifically female, activity rates have been persistently low in Cornwall compared with the rest of the country. 30% of the population were economically active in 1948 compared with 42% nationally. For females the activity rate was 27%, for males 73% (Cornwall County Council, 1952, p. 63).

fishing were still in decline as was manufacturing, a trend that was to continue into the 1960s. Employment in manufacturing was of course in decline in England and Wales as a whole, but the decline was relatively greater in Cornwall which also, proportionally, had a smaller base. Perhaps this accounts for the fact that—in practice—planning policies appeared to be different from those stated above. The County Planning Officer commented that the policy for industry was one of encouraging existing industry, attracting new ones, and reducing the effects of peripherality by improving transportation and the electricity supply (Heck, 1964, p. 455).

Whilst, as noted above, the development of industrial sites was not the policy of the county council; it was carried out in a piecemeal fashion by local districts with county approval, albeit constrained by the *ultra vires* nature of developing land for industry at that time. Derelict mining land was reclaimed for what was to become Cornwall's first industrial estate at Camborne[7][3] by Camborne–Redruth Urban District Council in 1947.[4] Such was the shortage of sites for new industry that the first firm occupied the recently vacated council offices adjacent to the site. In 1949 the new powers of compulsory purchase were used by the Truro City Council to acquire land [13]. This was considered necessary to relieve pressure on land use in the town, and to improve circulation on the site which had previously been used by the War Department.[5] Launceston Borough Council also acquired land from the War Department [40] in 1951, this time complete with some existing buildings, in order to establish an industrial estate.

The importance of action by the urban districts in the provision of infrastructure, rather than simply waiting for the 'market' to supply developed land, seems to have been formally recognized by the county planning authority who set up the Industrial Development Sub-Committee in 1956 to deal with these and associated problems (Heck, 1964, p. 455). The local unemployment rate had reached a post-war low of 2% in 1954; nevertheless, a strong seasonal component was evident in many locations, particularly those dependent on tourism. Rising unemployment in the Camborne–Redruth area made it eligible for assistance under the 1958 Distribution of Industrial Finance Act (see Fig. 5.3). There is evidence that at least one firm was attracted to the Camborne [7] site on

---

[3]As an aid to identification industrial estates mentioned in the text have also been numbered: these correspond to Fig. 5.2.
[4]The history of industrial development has been gathered from a detailed analysis of the archive minutes of the 'Development Plans and General Purposes sub-committee' of Cornwall County Council, and the County Development Plan (Cornwall County Council, 1952). Detailed reference to sources can be found in Pratt (1989).
[5]The significance of ex-War Department sites (storage dumps, transport depots and, most importantly, airfields) cannot be underestimated in the structuring of the location of industrial development in Cornwall (and much of the UK) in the post-war years.

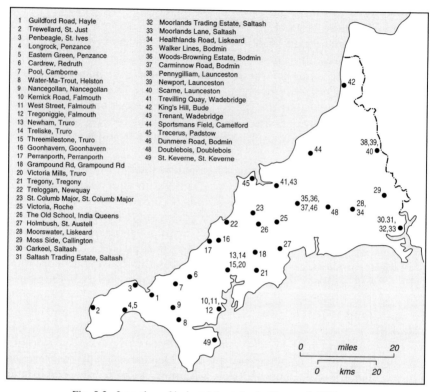

1 Guildford Road, Hayle	32 Moorlands Trading Estate, Saltash
2 Trewellard, St. Just	33 Moorlands Lane, Saltash
3 Penbeagle, St. Ives	34 Healthlands Road, Liskeard
4 Longrock, Penzance	35 Walker Lines, Bodmin
5 Eastern Green, Penzance	36 Woods-Browning Estate, Bodmin
6 Cardrew, Redruth	37 Carminnow Road, Bodmin
7 Pool, Camborne	38 Pennygilliam, Launceston
8 Water-Ma-Trout, Helston	39 Newport, Launceston
9 Nancegollan, Nancegollan	40 Scarne, Launceston
10 Kernick Road, Falmouth	41 Trevilling Quay, Wadebridge
11 West Street, Falmouth	42 King's Hill, Bude
12 Tregoniggie, Falmouth	43 Trenant, Wadebridge
13 Newham, Truro	44 Sportsmans Field, Camelford
14 Treliske, Truro	45 Trecerus, Padstow
15 Threemilestone, Truro	46 Dunmere Road, Bodmin
16 Goonhavern, Goonhavern	48 Doublebois, Doublebois
17 Perranporth, Perranporth	49 St. Keverne, St. Keverne
18 Grampound Rd, Grampound Rd	
20 Victoria Mills, Truro	
21 Tregony, Tregony	
22 Treloggan, Newquay	
23 St. Columb Major, St. Columb Major	
25 Victoria, Roche	
26 The Old School, India Queens	
27 Holmbush, St. Austell	
28 Moorswater, Liskeard	
29 Moss Side, Callington	
30 Carkeel, Saltash	
31 Saltash Trading Estate, Saltash	

Fig. 5.2. Location of industrial estates in Cornwall 1984.

the strength of this in legislation in 1959 (Weber, 1964, p. 621). However, it was in the wake of the legislation of the early sixties that most new development occurred.

Assisted Area Status Confirmed

The 1960s marked a turning point for infrastructure investment and state intervention in Cornwall. The persistent high unemployment, made Cornwall eligible for regional assistance under the 1960 Local Employment Act (see Fig. 5.3).[6] This together with the three acts of 1963—the Local Authority (Land) Act, the Finance Act, and the revised Local Employment Act—paved the way for a more active development policy in

---

[6] The unemployment level in Cornwall was two and a half percent above the national average which was then two percent. The Bodmin area was excluded in 1962 as unemployment fell in that locality.

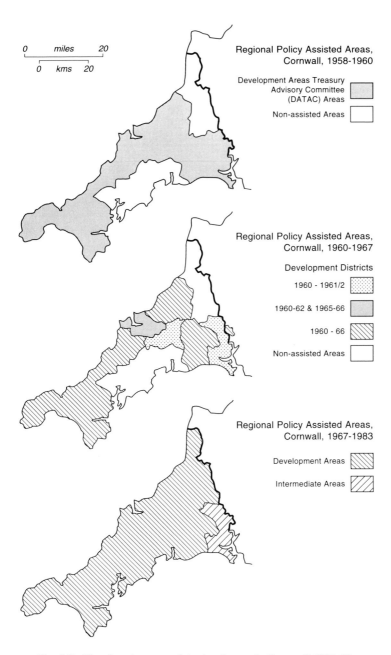

Fig. 5.3. The changing map of Assisted areas in Cornwall 1958–83.

Cornwall. Investment in infrastructure of other kinds was also demon-strated by the completion of the Tamar Bridge by the Ministry of Transport in 1961. This development gave a significant boost to the south and east of Cornwall, both making Plymouth accessible to SE Cornwall, and creating the possibility of firms setting up in SE Cornwall who were still able to draw upon Plymouth as a local market for goods produced. The only contrary tendency was the 1963 'Beeching' cuts in the rail network which reduced accessibility to the remoter rural areas, particularly in the north of the county.

Contrary to the national trend in local authority economic development which Camina (1974, p. 89) and Boddy (1983, p. 37) suggest were little used prior to the 1970s, there was substantial use of these new powers in Cornwall, particularly by the Urban Districts of Penzance, Camborne–Redruth and Liskeard (Heck, 1964, p. 456). Given the fact that the Board of Trade did not have a programme of establishing industrial estates, it is difficult to see how the Advance Factory Unit (AFU) programme could have been implemented in Cornwall were it not for the ability of local authorities to acquire and service new land for industrial development. Some developments occurred on sites with a previous non-agricultural use, mainly ex-War Department sites. In other cases local authorities resorted to placing compulsory purchase orders on sites to release them for industrial development.

Not all local authorities responded in the same way in providing infrastructure. Some simply serviced land, upon which it was hoped that units could be built by private developers or industrialists. When this was not forthcoming (the usual case), other means were used. AFUs were acquired for Camborne [7] in 1963 and 1964; local authorities also built their own units. In other situations sites were acquired with buildings intact. For example, in Launceston [38] an old school was used for industrial activities.

The new development of industrial land at this time was significant overall, but characterized by the small scale of individual developments: the average size was less than 4 ha. The exception was the expansion (22.6 ha) of the estate at Camborne [7] in 1962. A similar scale development (14.6 ha) was suggested by a private developer at Saltash [33]; however permission was only forthcoming, after an inquiry, for a considerably smaller plot (2 ha). This was the first privately developed estate in the county. Commonly, private factory units were developed on or directly adjacent to land already developed by the local authority. Despite the local authority dominance over the initial layout and infrastructure of industrial estates, it is significant that in most cases there was little or no attention to design and layout features of the estates. In particular, no reference was made to the need for, or provision of, communal services. Other sites were also being considered by local authorities, but the problems of finding readily available sites caused difficulties in locations such as Gunnislake, Newquay, Bodmin and Bude. Further problems were experienced in Penzance, where the only site available had poor sewage and water provision.

In the 1960s the Cornish economy was still over reliant on a few large companies. Thirty percent of employment being in just two firms: Holman's and English China Clays, Lovering and Pochin (ECLP) (AIC 1965, p. 58). One of these, ECLP, had stabilized after its wartime decline; nevertheless it was now, by virtue of a modification to the Standard Industrial Classification, in receipt of Government assistance via the Regional Employment Premium (Spooner, 1971, p. 11).

A consultant's report published in 1965 noted that the regional development policies seemed to be having an effect in attracting industry (AIC, 1965, p. 68). Spooner's (1971, 1972) research provides a more systematic insight; of the 247 firms employing 30 or more persons in both Devon and Cornwall in 1967, he found that some 94 had located there since 1939. Most of these migrants went to Cornwall, and nearly all dated from the post-1960s; two-thirds of which were branch plants. Although he does acknowledge the significance of 'noneconomic motives' for firm movement, Spooner's research indicates that at an intraregional level, site provision by local authorities was not just the prime locational factor but, ". . . taken as given by many firms" (Spooner, 1971, p. 239). Despite this upturn in the fortunes of the Cornish economy the more general national decline in employment in manufacturing industry suggests that this growth was merely a 'holding operation (see Table 5.2 above.[7]) This state of affairs was compounded by the reversal in population and migration trends that was just becoming apparent to planners.

Population had been, until the 1960s, declining due to substantial outmigration. However, a reversal of this trend became evident from the 1961 census. The population gain since that date — amounting to 10% and 11% respectively in the decades 1961–71 and 1971–81 — primarily benefitted the central and south east of the county, specifically the districts of Kerrier, Carrick and Restormel. The anatomy of the population change is complex. The strong out-migration, predominantly amongst the younger cohorts, continued, but in-migration of the older, but still economically active, increased. Research in West Cornwall indicates that in-migrants were better educated and of higher socio-economic status than the indigenous population. Moreover, a dominant reason for migration was overwhelmingly environmental or social (Perry *et al.*, 1986). Clearly, a social and political restructuring was in the making.

---

[7]A Department of Trade and Industry analysis of assisted firm movement to Cornwall from 1966–85 revealed a survival rate of 64% and 66% respectively for firms new to manufacturing and transfers from outside the county. The figure for branch plants is a little lower at 52% (Cornwall County Council, 1986, p. 8).

Expansion of Government Support

The Industrial Development Act of 1966 made most of Cornwall eligible for assistance, the rest being added in 1970 when the intermediate areas were designated (see Fig. 5.3 above). In this period many AFUs were started in Cornwall, and most of the urban industrial estates now established were developed (see Fig. 5.4).

The size of sites initially serviced was, in most cases, small. This can be explained in terms of the relatively low take-up of sites, and the restrictions on servicing or releasing more land than is indicated in the town plan requirements as noted in the case of Saltash. In this case the designation of an Intermediate Area appears to have attracted developers, and pressurized planners into releasing more land. It must be considered whether this was a result of the very restrained land release policy in neighbouring Plymouth. In any case land was in short supply at both Saltash and Plymouth. The major development was secured at considerable cost by the developers who acquired a whole farm and an exWar Department site (21 ha) at Saltash [30] in order to achieve a moderately size development (10 ha).

The inclusion of Callington in the Assisted Areas scheme stimulated activity—initially from the district authority—to release land. The difficulties of a land sale—which involved the bankruptcy of the vendor—led to the County Council becoming directly involved [29]. This pattern was repeated in another case—Hayle [1]—where there were also problems relating to the purchase of the site. In effect the County Council became involved as a last resort.

The involvement of the County in Guildford Road Industrial Estate [1] underlined the both the difficulty of, and desperate need to, release land for industrial development. For example, the *West Cornwall Study* (Barrington, 1970) noted the problems of land availability at a variety of sites. The common difficulties were a lack of flat drained sites in the major population centres (apart from Camborne–Redruth); namely Truro, Penzance, Falmouth, Helston, and Hayle. The same report—echoing the comments of Caesar and the Board of Trade in the wartime period (see above)—also mentions the lack of industrial buildings suitable for modern industry. Apart from the few AFUs the remaining buildings were

"... purpose built mainly on industrial estates and occupied by firms for whom they were built" (Barrington, 1970, p. 51).

Five of the industrial estates established or expanded in the early 1960s received AFUs: Penzance [4, and 5], Camborne [7], Falmouth [12], and Camelford [44]. Additionally, two of the newer estates, Bude [42] and Helston [8], also received units. The public sector factory units built in this period were quite large (the average unit size was 1,392 square metres). This was consistent with the national policy of AFU provision at that time.

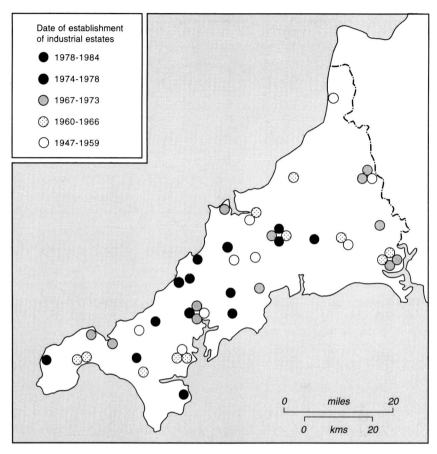

Fig. 5.4. Dates of establishment of industrial estates.

The units were 'off the shelf' rather than designed for the locality. Thus, it was of little surprise that local authorities, such as Falmouth and Truro, voiced their concern about what they considered as the excessive size of the units. This argument was reinforced by the long periods of vacancy of existing large units, which certainly demonstrated the inappropriateness of regional policy instruments which were primarily targeted on large migrant firms and not small firms: the sort commonest in Cornwall.[8] Not surprisingly, the local authority-developed units at Saltash and Bodmin

---

[8]To give an indication of how 'small' small is, the Bolton Committee reporting in 1971 considered a small firm to be one of below 200 persons. However, such a firm would be regarded as large in Cornwall; 55% of all those employed in Cornwall work in firms of fewer than 20 persons, and a further 22% are self-employed.

TABLE 5.3. Employment in Cornwall and England and Wales 1971 and 1981

| | 1971 | | | 1981 | | |
| | Cornwall | | E & W | Cornwall | | E & W |
SIC	Number	%	%	Number	%	%
0	1535	11	3	1208	8	3
1	247	2	3	229	2	4
2	860	6	6	824	6	4
3	1074	8	13	772	5	15
4	864	6	13	937	6	7
5	1319	9	7	1253	8	2
6	3373	24	18	3678	25	23
7	816	6	7	672	5	2
8	1099	8	11	978	7	9
9	2716	20	18	4241	29	32

Source: Census of population (10% sample).

were considerably smaller in scale than those provided by central government agencies. Furthermore, privately-funded units at Liskeard [28] and
Bodmin [36] were generally smaller in scale than public developments.
The exception to the rule was Saltash [31] where the activities of the
private sector—in one of the few nonpublic sector serviced sites in the
county—reinforced the local authority call for smaller units even in larger
settlements; larger units were built at Saltash and they were very slow to
let.

Turning now to the wider context of the development of industrial
estates, it is worth noting changes in the economic structure. The decline in
agriculture and fishing, and the extractive industries continued, but
between 1961 and 1971 manufacturing seems to have undergone a
transformation (see Table 5.3). In England and Wales as a whole this
sector declined, as it had done previously in Cornwall, but by 1971 there
were signs of growth. Changes also occurred in the patterns of population
and migration too. Between 1961 and 1966 43% of the increase in
manufacturing jobs was accounted for by in-migrant firms to the county.
In tourism-related activities, the proportion was as high as 60% (Barrington, 1970, p. 36). This state of affairs was characterized as a "labour
supply problem" by the South West Economic Planning Council's regional strategy. In order to alleviate such problems, the strategy proposed
the creation of a growth pole at Plymouth (SWEPC, 1967, pp. 92 and 101)
for the south and east of the county, and what it termed a "focal area" for
West Cornwall incorporating Truro, Camborne–Redruth and Falmouth.

In pursuance of this 'growth pole' strategy discussions were set in
motion between Camborne–Redruth Urban District Council, the County
Council, and the Greater London Council with the aim of dispersal of
population from London to facilitate the creation of a 'critical mass' of

TABLE 5.4. *Persons Unemployed as a Percentage of the Workforce in Cornwall and Great Britain (1974–84)*

Year Month	Unemployment (%)		Year Month	Unemployment (%)	
	Cornwall	G. Britain		Cornwall	G. Britain
1974 June	3.3	2.3	1980 June	8.9	6.7
1974 December	n.a	n.a.	1980 December	14.0	9.1
1975 June	6.5	3.6	1981 June	13.3	10.9
1975 December	10.9	5.0	1981 December	16.6	12.0
1976 June	9.6	5.5	1982 June	15.3	12.6
1976 December	n.a	n.a.	1982 December	17.5	13.1
1977 June	10.6	6.0	1983 June	13.7	12.3
1977 December	12.2	6.0	1983 December	16.4	12.7
1978 June	9.6	5.9	1984 June	14.6	12.4
1978 December	11.1	5.6	1984 December	19.2	13.2
1979 June	8.9	5.4			
1979 December	10.9	5.5			

Source: Department of Employment (various). n.a. data not available.

population in a locality within Cornwall (Barrington, 1970, p. 3). Whilst this scheme did not come to fruition, a smaller one developed later in Bodmin did. A new estate of 21 ha (13 ha of which were usable) was developed there in 1966; again, it was a War Department site complete with buildings and roads. Purchase of the site by the local authority had been under negotiation since 1962.

More generally, significant changes have occurred in terms of population movement, particularly notable is the shift from urban to rural areas. The population structure was in this period, as it remains today, generally deficient in those of working age and over-represented in those of retirement age compared with the national rate. Districts to the west of the county displayed a marked bias towards the older age groups (Barrington, 1970, p. 12).

In the 1960s net in-migration was strongest in the managerial and self-employed groups (Cornwall County Council, 1981, p. 9). Thus, most of the net gain in the economically active population was male. Clearly, this presented problems for job creation, particularly in a period of recession. After the turbulence of the 1960s, there is evidence to suggest that the economy of Cornwall was stabilizing; in 1974 unemployment had almost fallen to the national level (see Table 5.4). Unfortunately, this was not to last. By 1977 St Ives had a winter unemployment level of 33%, one of the highest in the entire country.

Expansion into the Remoter Areas

As noted in the previous chapter, 1974 proved to be an important date with regard to the changing policy of the Development Commission. The recognition of the changing migration patterns by the Treasury committee applied particularly to Cornwall. Whilst there was a net increase of population year on year it was achieved by large flows both in *and* out of the county. Migration gains split equally with respect to males and females, a greater proportion of noneconomically active women were entering the county than leaving it (Cornwall County Council, 1981, p. 8)

From 1975, the newly established European Regional Development Fund was available for infrastructure schemes in Cornwall, the level of grants was £5 million per annum in this period (Cornwall County Council, 1985). There was also an increase in the activity of UK government agencies in the field of job creation. Whilst two thirds of UK Regional Development Grants over £25,000 went to one company (ECLP) between 1975 and 1980, the remainder was used in the construction of factory units and the servicing of industrial land (Cornwall County Council, 1986, p. 8).

The English Estates AFU programme was by now well established; additions were made to Falmouth [10], and Wadebridge [43] received its first AFUs, as did the new estates established at Redruth [6], Liskeard [34], Hayle [1], Truro [15], Newquay [22] and Callington [29]. The average size of units fell from 1977 onwards. As previously stated, local authorities had been petitioning for such a reduction for some time, the force of their argument was reinforced by the fact that previously built large factory units had remained vacant. English Estates changed its policy over new unit sizes from 1975 onwards. The delay in the implementation of this new policy in Cornwall may be attributed to some extent to the time-lag taken to plan, acquire land, approve and construct units. Nevertheless, the legacy of 'oversized units' has caused difficulties with regard to current lettings. Three large units were constructed after 1976, but they were built especially for 'named' incoming firms.

The Development Commission's (DC) factory programme also commenced in this period. Understandably, these units were smaller than the standard English Estates units of the time. The first units completed in Cornwall were, perhaps ironically as it is more strictly an urban area, at Truro. Others followed on existing estates at Bude [42], Camelford [44], Helston [8], St Columb Major [23], and St Ives [3]. Few of the new DC estates were really in remote areas, the exception was Goonhavern [16]. There are two reasons for this. The main problem was the acquisition of land; this also added to the time scale of the project (for example at Gunnislake, or Looe). Another reason may have been the greater risk incurred in such investments.

Finding suitable land for industrial development was not only a problem in 'rural' areas. There were significant shortages of land in the Truro, Camborne–Redruth and the Falmouth triangle. After difficulties in servicing the land with sewage facilities and opposition from local residents, Kerrier District Council developed a prestige site near Camborne [6] (11.7

TABLE 5.5. *Site Area Developed on Industrial Estates 1974–84*

| | Site area (ha) | |
Year	Occupied	Unoccupied
1974	43	no data
1976	116	295
1984	251	376

Source: Minutes of Cornwall County Council.

TABLE 5.6 *Regional Grants from the DTI, ERDF*

Year	Regional Selective Assistance ERDF	Regional Development Grant	European Regional Development Fund
1981–82	1.49m	6.5	5.3
1982–83	0.39m	4.5	3.7
1983–84	1.90m	2.3	6.1
1984–85	0.50m	2.3	10.3
1985–86	1.55m	2.22	3.6
1986–87	0.61m	5.63	11.9
1987–88	0.82m	1.81	11.6

Source: Cornwall County Council 1988.

ha). Meanwhile, Carrick were beginning an ambitious scheme using the Derelict Land Grant to reclaim previously mined land on a site at Carrick Downs (west of Truro). Despite the difficulties in locating sites for new estates[9] there was a significant expansion of serviced industrial land on estates in this period (see Table 5.5).

Whilst the information collated in Table 5.5 suggests that it is an under estimate, an Estates Times (1978) survey carried out in 1978 suggests that 105 ha of land had planning permission for industrial development in Cornwall. Of this some 45 ha were in local authority hands, 8 ha owned by EE, and 52 ha in private ownership. Even this breakdown of owners may present a rather deceptive picture. What is really significant is not that land which is available, but that land which is serviced. Even so it is not clear whether this land is actually available, i.e. immediately for sale. In the private sector land may be retained simply for its potential development value.

A further complicating factor was the economic recession of the late 1970s which hit Cornwall particularly badly; in 1978 Wheal Jane and Mount Wellington mines closed, and 700 jobs were lost in one locality where unemployment jumped overnight to 40% (Turner, 1978, p. 477).

---

[9]There have long been problems of finding a site for Development Commission units in Gunnislake and Looe. Both took nearly 10 years to locate and service.

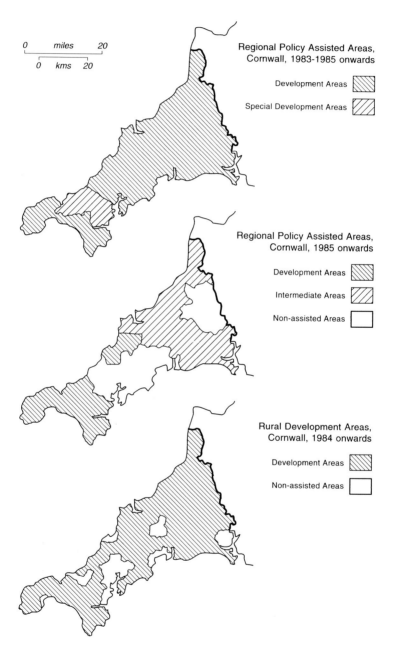

Fig. 5.5. The changing map of assisted areas in Cornwall 1983–1985.

Later these mines were reopened and, along with South Crofty, Delabole and Geevor taken over by Rio Tinto Zinc. However, worse was to come.

1980s Recession

The recession hit Cornwall very badly in the early 1980s. In addition to the mining closures, British Shipbuilders (the county's third largest employer) announced the closure of operations at Falmouth in 1979. The 1,400 redundancies, combined with multiplier effects, increased unemployment from 15% (which was twice the national average) to 30% (*Financial Times*, 1979).

Not surprisingly, unemployment in the County was particularly bad, a situation that was exacerbated by seasonal fluctuations (see Table 5.4 above). The revision of regional policy that followed the election of the Conservative government in 1979 was heralded as one that would 'roll back' the map of the Assisted Areas. So severe were the Cornish problems considered to be that even under a regime of reductions to Assisted Area coverage Cornwall received additional status achieving it's greatest spatial extent ever (see Fig. 5.4). The local grant-in-aid support from the DTI declined dramatically in the 1980s (see Table 5.6), this was exacerbated further by the reforms heralded as the 'Enterprise Initiative' (1988). The immediate impact was the removal of mandatory Regional Development Grants for the Development Areas, these were replaced by investment and innovation grants for firms smaller than 25 persons, Regional Selective Assistance continues to be available for both the Development and Intermediate Areas. Support from the European Commission via the ERDF has strengthened in the 1980s. The average annual grant aid to Cornwall amounted to £7.5 million between 1981–87, however, the vast majority of this was spent on road improvement; typically just 2% was spent on laying out industrial estates (Cornwall County Council, 1988).

Cornwall experienced a period of dramatic job losses in its indigenous employment. A significant departure in terms of industrial infrastructure was the closure of Rank Toshiba at Camborne [7] in 1981.[10] The company had occupied the first, and the largest, AFU in the County (8,361 square metres): symbolically, in 1984 the building was demolished making way for four workshop units with a total floorspace of just 929 square metres.

A further 1,000 redundancies were announced by ECLP during the five year period up to 1985 (Dalton, 1987, p. 75). The company are the county's largest employer with 7,000 employees. Significant problems were also experienced by cutbacks at Compair–Holman, Cornwall's second largest employer, located in Camborne. Finally, there were 650 redundancies as a result of the tin crisis in 1985. Despite a £25 million

---

[10]The irony here was that Rank relocated to Plymouth.

Department of Trade and Industry loan, Rio Tinto Zinc sold their stake in Cornwall to a local management team, making another 250 redundant in 1988 (Cornelius and Smith, 1988).

Despite these dramatic job losses the Cornish economy actually grew in the period 1971–81, and between 1981–84. However, the structure of this employment has changed. Table 5.3 (above) indicates growth in service sector activities. Although Division 4 (other manufacturing) declined slightly, one might have expected greater decline compared with figures for England and Wales.

English Estates' (EE) developments were more limited in the 1980s. Problems with funding (particularly due to the commitment to very large schemes in other parts of the country) and threatened reorganization, coupled with its new role as DC's factory builder, have seen them standardizing developments to more profitable locations, and larger units. Large terraces of small units were constructed in the early 1980s Falmouth [10], and Redruth [6], both in partnership with Coal Board Investment Nominees (CIN). Others have been built at Newquay [22], Penzance [4] and Bodmin [37].

By 1984 about 13% of the whole of the DC's national industrial property portfolio was located in Cornwall. Whilst the areas afforded aid (Special Investment Areas) under the DC's policies were reduced, the new designation, Rural Development Areas, still covered much of the county (Figure 5.5 above). New developments have taken place in truly rural areas such as St Keverne [49], Nancegollan [9], Roche [25], Tregony [21], Grampound Road [18], and St Just [2]. A significant addition to development has been at Bude [42], where a DC funded a terrace of smaller units in the early 1980s. Other additions have been made at St. Columb Major [23], Liskeard [34], St. Ives [3], Goonhavern [16], Wadebridge [43] and Callington [29].

The joint funding arrangements with local authorities, introduced in 1981, yielded small units (46 square metres) at Helston [8], Wadebridge [43], and India Queens [26]. This latter scheme was interesting as the first phase was the conversion of an old school by the County Council and the DC in partnership. Local authority developments were confined to a terrace of workshops constructed by Carrick at Truro [15]. These were of far better design than the previous prefabricated units that were basically adapted household garages.

The potential for the conversion of existing buildings in Cornwall is limited due to the lack of a stock of suitable buildings in the first place. Additionally there are problems associated with conversion costs, which sometimes may exceed the cost of a new building. The first private sector-initiated conversion was carried out in the shell of an old agricultural building near Truro [20] in the mid-1980s. It was not until the end of the 1980s that several other developments took place: a conversion of some

TABLE 5.7. *Cumulative Total of Occupied Establishments on Industrial Estates in Cornwall*

Year	Number of firms
1973	150
1977	264
1981	96
1984	654

Source: Shaw and Williams (1982), extensive survey.

TABLE 5.8. *Industrial Estate Size Characteristics, 1984*

	Median	Range	Total
Estate floorspace (m²)	7,088	334–79,378	519,930
Estate site area (ha.)	4.8	0.1–40.2	376
Number of plots	16	3–69	947
Number of units	14	2–66	800
Plot size (ha.)	0.2	0.01–0.6	—
Unit size (m²)	232	60–1,000	—

Source: Extensive survey.

china clay drying sheds near St Austell, a former railway station at Lostwithiel, former Compair–Holman factory units in Camborne, and old dock buildings at Falmouth.

As noted in Chapter 4, nationally, there was a resurgence of private sector interest in small-scale development in the early 1980s following both the introduction of 100% Industrial Building Allowances (IBA), and—in rural areas—the introduction of DC partnership conversion schemes. Small terraces of units have been built as a result of IBA schemes in less marginal locations at Callington [29], Truro [13], St Austell [27] and two new estate developments have been established in Bodmin, and St. Mawgan (near Helston). In the late 1980s individual units were built under the IBA scheme at Perranporth [17] and Doublebois [48]. As may be expected, no significant pension fund involvement has yet materialized in Cornwall outside Saltash, Truro and the partnership deals with English Estates and CIN noted above.

The Form and Extent of Industrial Estate Development in 1984

Forty six industrial estates had been developed by 1984; most of the occupants of these estates had located there in the period 1981–84 (see Table 5.7). An extensive survey of these developments—as detailed, later, in Chapter 7—revealed that these developments accounted for some

519,930 square metres of floorspace and 376 hectares of land[11] (Table 5.8). This industrial development was not evenly distributed; in fact it would have been surprising if this had been the case.

There was a considerable variation in the size and characteristics of industrial estates; Table 5.8 shows that both the industrial estates and the individual land plots and industrial units located on them were quite small.[12] Figure 5.6 gives some indication of the actual layout of both a small and a medium sized estate. Figure 5.7 shows the overall spatial distribution of industrial floorspace located on industrial estates; this pattern corresponds quite closely with that of population concentrations.[13]

Nature of Development

The variation in the scale and incidence of development, may give the impression that these were the only aspects of heterogeneity of industrial estates. This is clearly not the case as other variation exists in terms of the quality of buildings, the physical density of their development.[14] and the estates' environmental characteristics. As well as the survey of the size, location and occupation of industrial buildings already referred to, an extensive survey of the quality of industrial estates, and the individual buildings developed on them, was also carried out.[15]

Three components of building design were chosen to illustrate aspects of building quality; height of access door, material used in construction, and the overall quality of the development and general state of repair. These particular criteria were selected as they were indicative of both institutional funding criteria, and current market norms.[16] In terms of building

---

[11]The site area referred to here, is the total net site area. The net site area refers to the total of industrial hereditaments comprising an industrial estate. Common areas such as roads and landscaping are not included in these measurements.

[12]By comparison Lever's (1968) study suggests that 40 ha was a common estate size in the UK during the 1960s (there are no comparable figures for the 1980s). Only four estates achieve Holford's minimum recommended size (20 ha), and only eight fall within the United Nations' (1962b, p. 25) recommended size range (12–20 ha).

[13]The exception is St Austell, a major population centre, which has only one industrial estate. This may be accounted for by the location of the county's largest employer there, but not located on the industrial estate. It might be reasonable to expect that there would be a proportionately less of a need for industrial accommodation due to this fact.

[14]The physical density of development is defined as the coverage of the site by buildings. It is distinguished from the issue of employment density, the number of persons working from a site or building.

[15]The technique used to collect this information was very simple; it involved a site survey of all of the industrial estates and buildings whereby every building structure was classified into categories referring to building quality.

[16]For example, access doors of 4.9 metres and higher were considered to be indicative of an institutionally acceptable unit. Those with doors of 2.5 metres and lower were considered to be not only indicative of poor quality but also quite possibly giving rise to difficulties in use. It would be quite difficult to drive a small truck or transit van through such a low door in order to load or unload the vehicle.

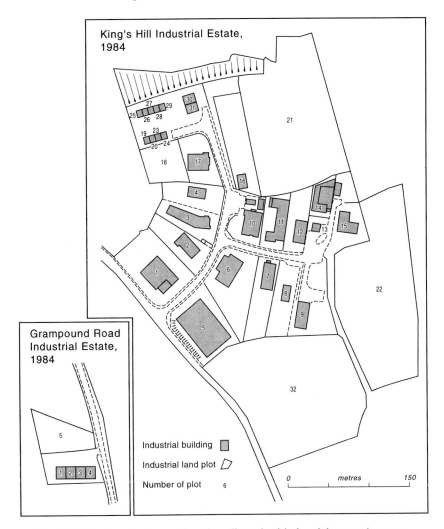

Fig. 5.6. Site layout of a small and medium sized industrial estate (to same scale).

materials, those favoured by the institutions are brick, and combinations of brick and metal cladding. Nonstandard, or poor quality materials, included wood, asbestos and combinations of brick, asbestos and wood. One quarter of all units—in terms of both number and floorspace—were found to be constructed of nonstandard or poor quality materials. In general, these buildings were larger than the median and concentrated on industrial estates in the larger population centres.

The overall condition of buildings was derived from a subjective

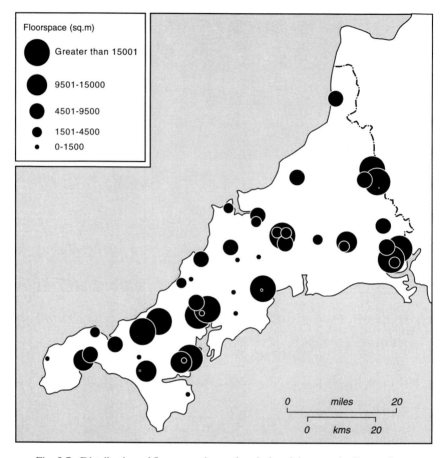

Fig. 5.7. Distribution of floorspace located on industrial estates in Cornwall.

measure relating to the overall state of repair of the building. Some 17% were judged to be of poor quality, i.e. quite obviously in need of immediate repair work. These were mainly smaller units clustered on the older industrial estates. The proportion of these poor quality units that were vacant corresponded to the average, however, a higher proportion than average of poor quality units were found to be in owner occupation.

The east–west trend in building quality, that may be expected if yields or rentals were the simple determinant of the quality of development, was not evident. The actual picture is more complex. Higher quality developments are to be found in larger population centres where—presumably—risks are lowest and larger developments can be sustained. Poorer quality buildings can be found scattered over a wide range of estates, but their general pattern relates most closely to the concentration of small units and older estates. This factor can itself be related to the longer term trend away from the custom-built owner-occupied unit, towards the 'flexible' rented or leased industrial unit characteristic of the emergence of developer-led industrial property construction and development of recent years.

Ownership

As has already been suggested in previous chapters the ownership and origin of the development of industrial buildings and estates may be significant in explaining their form and location. Overall, 49% of the buildings (63% of the floorspace, median size 465 square metres) were owner-occupied. Of these 53% (60% of the floorspace, median 566 square metres) were custom-built for the present occupant. Owner-occupied building tend to be much larger than the median building, but they are a small proportion of the whole. Just 28% of all occupied buildings (43% of the floorspace) was both owner-occupied and custom-built for the present occupant. Of the custom-built premises themselves, 85% were in owner occupation, leaving 15% (or 5% of the total) as leased property. This would seem to indicate how little control most firms have had over the location and design of their premises. This can turn into real restrictions on the potential choice of premises by industrialists.

There is an under representation in the quality of the owner occupied buildings with respect to main access door size, this might be expected as one would hardly buy an industrial unit if access were difficult. A low representation of owner occupants is found in the good material and good condition categories. These nonstandard design features all indicate that the occupants might have difficulty selling on their properties as investments, thus possibly constraining their future activities.

Some interesting comments can be made if the degree of owner occupation is considered at the individual estate level. First, that the degree of owner occupation of buildings was not evenly distributed. Just four estates were totally in owner occupation and some eleven estates were completely nonowner occupied;[17] moreover, in all these cases there is just one owner. The fact that most estates are under multiple ownership and tenure would tend to reduce the direct impact of any one developer on the total estate form and emphasizes the importance of the initial servicing and layout of the estate. Even with total control over the estate, there is a less than resolute approach by developers to site development, as already noted.

Vacancy

Some 18% of the total number and 11% of the floorspace located on industrial estates was found to be vacant (see Table 5.9). The median unit

---

[17]Vacant property is not classified as in owner occupation.

TABLE 5.9. *Utilization of Buildings on Estates*

Utilization	% Total numbers	Floorspace Total(%)	Floorspace Median(m^2)
Vacant building	17.9	10.8	186
Unoccupied site	15.3	33.5	4,000
Manufacturing	62.4	65.7	232
Retailing	2.6	3.4	290
Warehousing	18.7	21.3	444
Other services	16.4	9.6	232

Source: Extensive survey.

size of vacant property is approximately half that of the all property on estates. Sixty percent of these units are in private ownership, a little above average. Considerable variation can be noted between estates; eleven estates have no vacant property, but on others there is a considerable range. At St Just, Trewellard [2], the estate, which was totally vacant, has just two units on it and is in a very remote location near Land's End. Vacancy data although useful, gives no indication of how long units have been empty. For example, the units on the estate at St Just have been occupied within the past two years, but some at Falmouth [12] have been vacant for more than 10 years.

Some interesting patterns can be noted with respect to building quality. Those buildings made from poor materials have better than average occupancy, and those in good overall condition a worse than average. This is possibly evidence that rentals are a greater influence on occupancy than 'good' design.

An important issue with respect to any future development, and its location and form, relates to the vacancy of sites. Some 15% of sites are vacant. However, it is the size and amount of plots that are most revealing, the median vacant plot size is much greater than for occupied plots (see, for example Fig. 5.6). Considerable variation exists in the proportion of vacant estates, the median is 35%. In total, 33% of the site area on estates is vacant, of which 66% (72% of site area) is in the ownership of private sector developers.

There is also considerable variation in site coverage, from 8 to 85%, although the median is 22%. If the degree of physical development of the estates is considered then significant variation (19–100%) can be noted. Whilst this is indicative of the immaturity of most estates, it should be treated with caution. Even those estates that are relatively full may still develop more as space is often available on sites adjacent to existing development, and planning permission is likely to be forthcoming if applied for, for example at St Keverne [21], Tregony [49]. Even those estates that have apparently reached or nearly reached, their size limit may be in the process of *in situ* redevelopment, particularly if they are old, for example those estates at Truro [12] and Camborne [47]. Both factors are likely to have adverse implications for the appearance of estates environmentally, as well as the working environment of the occupants. The overall quality of landscaping found on estates is heterogenous, minimal efforts have been made in the majority of cases to improve many estate's appearance beyond that of a building site.

All of the factors discussed above would seem to indicate that a lack of attention is paid to the day-to-day requirements of the occupants of industrial estates. This can be interpreted as a result of developers shifting risks and costs to occupants of estates and their workers. Even those who own their property on estates are still prone to the adverse environmental elements of the estate as a whole. Surveys of the industrial users would seem to back up this observation (Shaw and Williams, 1985, pp. 236–237).

Conclusion

The aim of this chapter has been to stress the local context and composition of Cornwall and its industrial development. This forms a framework within which the institutional processes, detailed in the previous chapter, operate.

A key point emphasized in the first section is the influence of the early economic development of the county on the lack of development of the built environment and infrastructure, compared with other localities in the UK. This was related to patterns of ownership and control, and the development of particular labour and social processes (see also Chapter 7). The lack of infrastructure and out-migration helped in the continued reproduction of unequal growth of the county compared with the nation. In the latter, as noted in the previous chapter, the benefits of infrastructure provision (and the new industrial estates) facilitated the development of 'footloose industries' in the 1930s.

In the immediate postwar period when many areas were undergoing reconstruction, Cornwall was, with a declining population and a limited manufacturing base and infrastructure, in a difficult position. The petty-capitalism combined with the poor industrial base, reinforced the reproduction of uneven social and economic development. Changing population movements in the sixties gave rise to a net population increase, this had two consequences; the modification of the social structure and the need to create more jobs. Both the Employment Acts and Regional Policy legislation of the early and mid sixties was eagerly seized by local authorities to rectify the infrastructure problems. The in-migration of firms in the late sixties led to both a further modification of the industrial base and the pattern of ownership.

It was not until the early sixties that expansion and development of industrial estates began, mainly led by local authority development. The central state provided for the interests of large-scale capitalist interests. This policy was strengthened in the late sixties with the expansion of Regional Policy. There was a long struggle between the local authorities and central government over the scale of provision of industrial units, with the local authorities resorting to building their own small units. By the early eighties the election of a government with sympathies for petty-capitalist enterprise had reinforced this.

Over the period as a whole, a dramatic restructuring of industrial location can be noted. In the beginning most industry was located in, or close to, towns with existing accommodation. By the end of the period most industry was located on state serviced and state provided premises let to the occupant. The role of the private sector in the provision of industrial buildings has been limited to a few urban locations. Even then, the financial interest has been predominantly local rather than national.

6

The Social Relations of Property Development in Cornwall

Introduction: The Nature of Property Development Activity

The aim of this chapter is to focus on the process of industrial property development in Cornwall. It draws upon a series of intensive interviews with property developers concerning their activities. This analysis is profoundly shaped by the critical realist methodology developed earlier in this book in three ways. First, as already been noted in Chapters 2 and 3, through focusing on the significance of the property development process in the explanation of the form and location of industrial development. Second, by characterizing the process of industrial development as being neither reducible to 'structures' (large corporations, the state, the built environment, or the property development industry) nor to 'agents' (industrialists, developers, or planners). Third, through the specific methodology used in the research reported here.

In relation to the first point, Chapter 4 highlighted how the relationships between owners and users of industrial property have empirically changed—moved apart and multiplied—in the UK in the postwar period. Local authorities, central government, regional development agencies, private sector developers, and institutional investors, have all become significant actors in the industrial property development process. Consequently the individual owner-occupier industrialist became less numerous, and a less powerful actor. Whilst the description of these new actors, and the changing structural conditions under which they have emerged or acted, is a useful and necessary task it still leaves open the issue of the development process itself. As I shall demonstrate, a key question that needs to be explored is how we make sense of the tangle of inter-relationships that constitute property development. It is by answering this question that we will be able to explain the emergence of particular forms of the built environment in particular places and at particular times. This will achieve our objective; an explanation of the emergence of the particular industrial built environment in Cornwall in the postwar years.

The second way in which critical realism shapes this analysis concerns conceptualization of the development process. Building upon the principles developed in Chapter 3 we will avoid the characterization of the property development process in an idealistic, voluntaristic or rationalistic manner. In this sense we will be 'working against the grain' of previous research which, due to its particular conceptualization of the property development process tends to reduce the complexity and variety of the social relations of building production to neat—but unrepresentative—formulae.

Take one example—the costs of development. These costs can be objectively stated and expressed in simple arithmetic form: as a yield calculation. Yield calculations represent a particular means of valuing development. This type of calculation is the bread and butter of surveyors and valuers; it is primarily a guide to investment returns. It is not the objective here to dispute the arithmetic validity of such a calculation, rather to contextualize it. Yields are part of the language of property development but they are not exhaustive of its processes—the social relations of building production—as such they do not provide the best means of access to its explanation. The point is that costs have different significances to different property actors in different situations. Development can have other—broader—objectives aside from the achievement of a particular yield. It is in this sense that a simple yield calculation has the effect of reducing a whole plethora of social relations to the same 'bottom line'—at the expense of obscuring the variety of social processes.

In this chapter some of the richness of the social processes of property development are recovered by considering the different organizational forms that facilitate what are at face value similar activities. As we will see both in this and the following chapter the outcomes of the process, as well as the ways of going about it, are all subtly different. A crucial element in understanding the social relations of building production is the notion of risk. Risk is represented in the property world by yield: the greater the risk the higher yield that is required to compensate. In the context of the argument outlined above we need to consider risk as a relationship. Risk is a very important relationship as it represents the day-to-day working out of power within and between developers and occupants of buildings. In order to develop, developers need to bring together people and resources into a particular relationship. However, all of the actors bring to the relationship at any one time different resources. Resources can best be considered as either finance, experience, or organization; as we shall see these elements are intermeshed. The risk of the development is not equally shared between the different actors. In order to engage in the development relationship some actors may well have to take on extra risks. This is a micro-scale process of uneven production. It is the combination of a multitude of such relationships that constitute 'uneven development'. We have already seen in Chapter 4 how the structuration of the property market led to a distribution of risk between developers and industrialists. Within the—necessarily—restricted focus of this chapter it will be argued that the distribution of risk structures the provision of building form.

The issue of methodology is a central, though not immediately apparent, component of this analysis. In Chapter 3 the need for intensive research, based on in-depth interviews was discussed along with issues relating to the analysis of such interviews. In practice the first major problem associated with collecting information on the activities of property developers is actually identifying who the developers are; as discussed below not all developers would call themselves a 'property developer'. A whole variety of property professionals seemed to be possible contenders: planners, builders, investors, property developers, and industrialists. In order to clarify the situation the act of development (entailing the assembly of materials, skill and finance) was considered to be a defining feature; hence anyone involved in these activities in relation to buildings located on industrial estates was included in the potential interview population.

Thus, the starting point was the identification of the end result of the process: industrial buildings. The Cornwall County Council Industrial Development register of vacant property was analyzed for an indication of the property professionals active within the county. This list was supplemented by information collected whilst undertaking a survey of all the buildings on industrial estates in the county (see Chapter 5 and 7), and by carrying out a review of advertisements in the property pages of local and regional newspapers. A final cross-check was made by questioning a wide range of property actors. In all, twenty developers and three local authorities were identified as active in the industrial development process.

The interview schedule was developed around the key concept areas identified in Chapter 3: involvement in development and other activities, firm organization, finance, the local market, past construction activities, leases, and general inter-relationships with other property actors. For reasons of clarity the questions were ordered so that they corresponded to the logical order of the development process: the 'property pipeline'. Whilst it is accepted that this is a misleading conceptualization it seemed to be the most widely used by developers themselves in their discussion of the development process. Each interview lasted, on average, one hour and the interviews were tape recorded with the interviewee's permission. They were transcribed and analyzed later as outlined in Chapter 3.

Only two developers were unable to be interviewed during the period in which the research was to be conducted. Information on these agents was,

D1: established in the early 1970s, mainly involved in building contracting for local authorities and one large manufacturing firm. At the time of interview no further industrials were being developed, the main development activity was residentials. Development carried out by this developer was self-funded and developed under the IBA. 4 units, 606 m^2.

D2: this developer's activities were mainly concerned with up-market residentials, though they had previously done some subcontracted development of industrials for local authorities. The involvement in development of industrials arose when a tenant vacated the building of a subsidiary company. The subsequent development was carried out under the IBA. 5 units, 1476 m^2.

D3: this developer had attempted to develop a small industrial estate. The incentive to develop was the need for new premises for the existing business (garden equipment). The aim was to 'get a free plot' out of the development. 1 unit, 232 m^2.

D4: the developer was based in Devon, activities were split between industrials and offices. The Cornish development was only considered viable due to the IBA and the potential to 'sell-on' the units to an institutional investor. A local authority bought the headlease on the development. 10 units, 1037 m^2.

D5: a small family business, active since the late 1960s, primarily concerned with housing development. Began developing industrials in the early 1980s, the buildings were unconventional being timber framed (as the houses developed by this company are). Subsequent units built in the mid 1980s on the same site were of more conventional design. 8 units, 845 m^2.

D6: mainly concerned with building and construction activities. In the early 1970s they developed exclusively industrials, later mainly residentials and some retail (the latter on the site originally developed for industrials). The initial units were speculative, many have lain empty for some time. 12 units, 6674 m^2.

D7: primarily involved in design and build work of industrials and leisure facilities, they are the franchisees for a building frame company. They have developed since the mid-1970s but only in prime areas. They developed units to 'sell-on' to tenants or small investors. They have developed some IBA units. Current holding: 9 units, 756 m^2.

D8: primarily a landowner who sold a lease in the early 1970s to a builder to develop a small industrial estate. After the bankruptcy of the landowner the developer regained control of the estate. The developer's lack of experience in developing and managing such a scheme and lack of new finance caused many problems. Other company involvement is a franchise for a car sales company. 19 units, 3251 m^2.

D9: developers who needed a site for their own business (food packaging). Recently brought premises and converted them, received funding from the DC (redundant building grant). Subsequently decided to subdivide the remaining (large) building for letting as small units. Funding from a bank loan. 6 units, 1,115 m^2.

D10: primarily a residential builder and developer. Got involved in industrials in the early 1970s to offset profits in residentials. Developed buildings and opened up an estate. They also own a golf club were they employ workers 'between jobs'. 12 units, 4,345 m^2.

Fig. 6.1. Thumbnail sketches of developers interviewed.

D11: a regional developer, based in Devon, part of a group of companies including specialist building contractors. The development arm is independent of other parts of the group. Developed units since the late 1970s, since the early 1980s exclusively industrials. They have sold on developments to financial institutions, but are finding this difficult, hence they retain industrial buildings. 8 units, 1,561 m^2.

D12: a small firm manufacturing scientific instruments that relocated to Cornwall in the early 1970s. Using a loan from the local authority they developed their own unit. Aiming to expand, they sought to develop a new unit for their use on the same site. Financial difficulties led to letting of the original building, using their own personnel to build the new unit, which beside housing them is let to other companies. 3 units, 669 m^2.

D13: the major national public sector developer, active since the early 1970s in Cornwall. Pension fund investment in some small terraced units, using the IBA. Prior to the 1980s there was little local control over the size of units built. They use local building contractors to construct their units. 215 units, 61,490 m^2.

D14: a company whose main activity is food distribution throughout the region, they also own a builders' merchants. They own many depots and sites in the region which they are redeveloping. In Cornwall a conversion of old buildings was subdivided into small units. 36 units, 4,013 m^2.

D15: primarily a building contractor who has recently moved into industrial and residential development. All contracting work is done 'in-house'. Initial objective was to develop a units for their own business. Subsequently they have built, under contract, units on the (new) estate, and developed their own units. 4 units, 687 m^2.

D16: was a builder, mainly residential conversions for 15 years, recently sold this company and now is a developer-investor of industrial conversions. Self-supporting from own funds. Administrative work carried out by family members, building work subcontracted. 3 units, 1,858 m^2.

D17: a timber frame residential building company and an antique dealer involved in a conversion and subdivision of a large property. Initially the property had been leased for storage for the antique business, when this fell on hard times the development took off. Used a Redundant building grant to convert, subcontracted conversion to the building company. The scheme is financed by a (third-party) private investor. 15 units, 1,301 m^2.

D18: a conversion of a modern building through subdivision, the second such development in the same town. The first unit was sold on. The company is only three years old. The finance is internally derived, all conversion work is subcontracted. 8 units, 2,137 m^2.

D19: a local authority, mainly servicing sites, initial development to open up an early estate of one unit, the rest of the estate was then sold off in the early 1970s. 1 unit, 2,043 m^2.

D20: a local authority that carried out building conversions (after the initial developer was declared bankrupt) and built very small workshop units in the 1970s. They have also recently developed new units on the same estate. 16 units, 1,366 m^2.

D21: a local authority, aside from servicing sites developed in the 1970s. Very small, poor quality units, on two estates. 22 units, 1,022 m^2.

Fig. 6.1. *Cont'd.*

however, in part obtained from other agents cognizant of their operations. It might be considered that the point of contact within an agency may colour responses, but this implies the (fallacious) assumption that an agency has but one viewpoint. The people interviewed were those who normally took decisions on a day-to-day basis regarding development. In many cases the interviewee was the sole owner of the company; in the case of larger companies the industrial projects manager was contacted. The interviews were conducted over a three month period in late 1985.

Thumbnail sketches of the developers interviewed are listed in Fig. 6.1. Each developer was coded to maintain anonymity. Before proceeding to the detailed analysis some general points can be made. The scale of development activity is primarily small, many of the developers had only been active on one site and their activity usually been funded from internal sources. Many developers seemed to have reached the 'natural limits' (in terms of scale) of self-financed developments; they were unable, or unwilling, to sell-on their developments. This is perhaps a contributory reason for the variety of building style and quality found on industrial estates. Many developers were involved in other activities apart from property development, often it was this activity that was the stimulus, or provided the funding, for the subsequent property development. The industrial estates themselves were primarily serviced and laid out by local authoritities.

Why do Developers Develop Property?

Most previous explanations of the development of industrial buildings draw upon notions of supply and demand. This section explores the validity of such an explanation. The initial question that needs to be addressed is, 'what is supply and demand?' First, consider the responses of developers to a question concerning assessment of demand for industrial premises.

Most developers made reference to ". . . gut feelings"; others to ". . . knowing the area", and some to a combination of both in respect of development. Developers prided themselves in the possession of local knowledge, commenting that they saw no use in an agent's services (or wanted to save money by marketing the unit themselves). However, some changed their minds when letting became difficult. Those acting over larger areas employed the services of several local estate agents in order to obtain knowledge of local markets. References were made by some to ". . . watching the units on the market"; ". . . talking to tenants"; and ". . . driving around industrial estates". Others chose to develop after some-body else had shown an interest and withdrawn from the scheme. For example, D11—a larger developer—had withdrawn from a site because of the inability to find funding "we had a scheme lined up with pre-lets, but as a group we didn't want £450,000 more industrials, and we couldn't have sold it on. So, it was cheaper for us to do nothing".

However, D2—a smaller developer—took on a development in a similar location for similar, though fewer units. Instead of looking for outside funding they used their own funds as well as utilizing tax relief. Another option commonly adopted was to consult other property professionals and the local authority. The other stimulus for development is for developers to be actually involved in the market by looking for the units themselves, then realizing that nothing is either appropriate or available, to take steps to develop it themselves.

The more systematic developers replicated the estate agents activities of keeping records of interested parties. Sometimes this was done in conjunction with local authorities and estate agents. D13 was the most sophisticated, quantifying enquiries and letting over the past two years in the locale where development was proposed. Additionally, vacant property on the market was considered. Others did this intuitively. It would seem that inquiries were not necessarily a significant indicator of demand prior to development being carried out. Instead the internal relationships of development (relating to the production of the building) were often more crucial than the external ones (lettings). D13, said that

"in the end market research means nothing. When the buildings go up, often the original enquiries evaporate",

but new ones come along. One way of hedging the risks, as D11 did, is by putting a speculative advertisement in the local newspaper, or by erecting a signboard to 'test' the demand. For the smaller or more localized developer the consensus was that if there was no obvious oversupply in the area (vacant) premises, then they could not fail, as long as they were only thinking of building a few units at a time (or on a let and build basis). Judgements were qualitative as well as quantitative. In areas of apparent oversupply new units were built and let quickly if the building quality or rental levels were different to those already available. Invariably, rentals were the most critical element. Thus, vacancy figures on their own were not considered by developers to be sufficient to estimate a potential market. Most developers confessed to acting on a 'gut feeling', even in some cases where the immediate evidence (of firms requiring premises) would appear to indicate otherwise.

Given the general speculative character of development sketched out above, it might be considered that marketing would be a crucial part of the development process. Whilst most units are included on local authority property availability lists, there was surprisingly little overt marketing of units. This tends to reinforce the nature of the localized market. It has already been noted that many developers do not use agents to market property; those who market property do so over a local area. Developers were often alert to the opportunity of writing editorials for free newspapers, others advertized in local papers. Such activity reinforces the local trawl for tenants.

It is clear from the above that 'demand' is neither a clear nor unambiguous sign for developers' activities. In fact it may seem that developers were apparently acting *in spite of* demand. Not developing when there was 'demand', or developing when there was not. Again, this is an example of a single 'market' indicator being taken for all of the social relations of property development. The market is not exhaustive of these social relations: the developers' activities reported here would seem to reinforce this view. This state of affairs effectively creates an unequal power relationship between the providers and the users of premises. The balance of power regarding when, where and what to develop clearly lies in the first instance with the developer. The following section explores the process of property development in more detail.

Risk and Development

Discussion of the objective of property development is at once both a simple and a complex issue. Simple in the sense that the objective is to achieve a return on an investment in a building development. Complex in that there are many ways of costing and assessing development. Put simply, this means that development can not be simply or universally reduced to a single 'motive': economic or behavioural. In order to comprehend property development activity the relationships between the developers' activities—as developers—and the rest of their business and personal activities, have to be considered. The concept of risk is useful here.

In common property parlance 'risk' is interchangeable with yield: it represents a narrowly defined investment decision. In its broadest sense investment potential depends on the state of international and national investment markets across all sectors, and the amount of investment required by investors at any one time. From an investor's point of view, the yield on any investment has to be compatible with a successful portfolio management that achieves both a balance of investments an absolute rate of return in excess of inflation. In this context, if industrial properties are not yielding sufficiently there is little incentive to invest, unless the portfolio is unbalanced, even if there is apparent demand from potential occupants. Furthermore, even if industrials as a whole are attractive, investment properties in Cornwall may not be achieving appropriate yields. It is worth considering this latter point in more detail.

In Cornwall, the low average rental level and nominal growth in rental values makes industrial property relatively unattractive. This is compounded by the risk of letting difficulties (a reflection of the industrial structure and economic health of the locale, as well as past, and existing provision of industrial property, in terms of quality, quantity, price and location). What it comes down to is the willingness of investors to take risks. In low risk environments such as retailing investors—especially conservative financial institutions—will accept low yields because investments are considered to be secure. Valuers and investors are famous for their listing of the three most important characteristics of property as location, location and location. This apparent obsession with location hides what are—*de facto*—further crucial elements: the quality of buildings and the quality of tenants. The interplay between these three elements is represented by relative levels of risk. There is a lower risk either of vacancy or slow rental growth on an established science park, compared with a site comprised of a few industrial buildings. Likewise, risks are higher if either of these were located in West Cornwall rather than Berkshire. This does suggest that the concept of risk is rather broader that it might have at first seemed to be.

One further characteristic of the larger investors and developers was the scale of development; generally, they were only interested in substantive 'blocks' of investment. For example, Cornish developers felt that funders would only consider investments of more than £1,000,000 in a site: there are very few sites of such a size available in Cornwall. There was not sufficient population within a given area to support such a scale of investment. Others felt that the institutions ". . . are not prepared to get off their backsides in London" (D4) and hence were unlikely to be interested in Cornwall.

It is not surprising to note that, in general, pension and insurance funds are not interested in investments in Cornwall as the investment risk is greater there. In the case of industrial developments only one such investment has taken place in Cornwall, and that was in 1979. There are consequences for developers in the County, as the following example demonstrates—

> "I've had a pension fund interested in my buildings, but they'd only buy it at below cost, and with a guarantee over leases" (D15).

The material discussed above may give the impression that no industrial property development apart from that for owner occupation should occur in Cornwall. This is clearly not the case for all developers. Thus, it is necessary to explore the means by which industrial property development is made possible. In the discussion of the structures of property provision the subtle shifting—or division—of potential risks can be noted. This is, in effect, the means by which the re-production of the local property market takes place. An important point to acknowledge when considering property development and investment is that not all investors are pension funds looking for a particular return on investments. There are smaller investors, or even developer–investors who may be prepared to take such a risk (which may be offset by other advantages such as the securing of an 'insurance policy' or industrial premises), in the hope of favourable returns.

Two types of risk should be considered; those incurred by the developer, and those by the investor. It may be argued that because of the ways in which costs can be modified by developers, the yield from the development can be modified. The result is that the element of risk is borne by the developer, rather than the investor. As detailed below, the longer the time period, the greater the exposure to risk of higher interest rates on loaned capital. The extent to which risks can be sustained varies in relation to the source of finance, temporal changes in interest rates, and possibly more significantly, the initial motive of the developer. If the motive of the developer is to sell-on the completed development, then there is always a risk that this may take longer than expected, or may not materialize at all. In the latter case it might be expected that the response would be not even to contemplate the deal.

It has been assumed so far that all developers calculate yields in the same way. However, it was noted in Chapter 4 that there were several ways to calculate yields. The most commonly used was residual valuation. In some cases a rather crude 'cash-flow' method was also used. In these instances little attempt was made to set out formally the costs of the development.

> "They were not built on the lines of an investment valuation, as long as overheads were covered" (D1).

Even in cases where a formal valuation was arrived at *post hoc*, initially,

> "the valuation was worked out on the back of an envelope" (D2).

In such instances the objective of development is important: in the case of D1, a pension fund and for D2 to 'tidy up' a plot of unused land. Another factor is the source of funds. In all the cash-flow situations, the funds were internally generated equity from the development company.

This point is important because this affects the activities of developers as subsequent landlords: they are not so desperate to find tenants;

> "I had nothing to lose if the units were empty, there's appreciation in bricks and mortar" (D1).

Whilst tenants were required in the long term, the bricks and mortar were retaining their value, or so the developers thought,

> "... any property holds its value, you could bulldoze most developments after ten years and start again" (D10).

Whilst these developers were seemingly able to bear no yield, others are able to bear lower rates. The investor who uses tax allowances can make the poorest yield attractive (albeit for one year only) in such a way. Using the Industrial Building Allowance (see below) yields of 20% could be achieved on what would otherwise be a 10% yielding property. However, this apparent bargain is deceptive; the long term benefits of the property are fixed to rental growth, and in Cornwall this has been low. But as has already been noted a constant stream of rental return is not crucial to all developers.

Another way to reduce risk, confined to large-scale investors, is by negotiating headleases with local authorities. In such an arrangement the local authority takes the responsibility for getting tenants, or paying for the units, if they are not let. In the words of the developer, it is just necessary to

". . . sit back and collect the rents" (D4).

It would seem that developers fall into two categories: those tied to market yields; and those able to accept lower yields by using the premises, or absorbing the benefits elsewhere in the company. However as was noted above, this results in the developer holding a greater proportion of the risk. To investigate this point further it is necessary to consider exactly how developers go about costing their developments.

Accounting for Development

Whilst there is a general relationship between the particular building cost, rental level and yield at which a scheme may, or may not, appear to be able to 'work', what is interesting is that there are a variety of ways by which this cost figure can be arrived at, depending on the organization of the company. Costs can be divided into four components: development finance, construction costs, land costs, and the nature and degree of state subsidies related to these activities.

Development finance

So far, it has been assumed that the capital for development is equally available to all, but this is not the case. Before a developer gets a loan for development, proof of the security of the loan will be required. The exact nature of such proof will depend upon the institution that the loan is made through. As noted in Chapter 4 the requirements of these institutions are variable in time, dependant upon their other commitments. The larger the scheme, and the smaller the equity of a company, then the larger the loan required and the greater the risk suffered by the lending institution. The developer may be able to compensate for a lack of capital by taking a greater risk. The opportunity to undertake risk is not equally available to all, or equally assessed by all, the individual circumstances of the developer will determine what risks can be taken. This is an example of a situation being both enabling and constraining.

An element of self-funding (equity capital) was used by all developers to various extents. In some cases it was in the form of savings, or more often in the form of assets such as buildings (in the case of construction companies), and plant and machinery (in the case of production companies). The former case is worthy of more analysis, as it further highlights the inter-relationships of companies' activities. Some smaller developers, such as D1, have used residential developments to provide capital security, against which industrial development is later funded. In this way residential development is, due to the low capital outlay, often used as a 'stepping stone' for prospective industrial developers. Alternatively, investment shifted between sectors can be used as a means of spreading the risk of development (see D11).

A range of sources are used to fund developments, from the simple bank overdraft to the formal loan from a local bank, to a loan from a merchant bank. The more formal the loan and the longer the term the more risk is involved, hence the higher the cost to the developer. For many developers personal equity—savings—backed by simple overdraft provision was sufficient to carry out the development. Overdraft facilities were obtained from local branches of clearing banks which offered lower rates of interest compared with more specialist finance houses.

A close correspondence can be noted between the developers in the groups who used 'overdraft' and 'overdraft and loan', and those with a capacity to carry out large capitalization developments; these developers have considerable securities, and are thus able to arrange loans with little difficulty.

> "Most of our projects are self-supporting, we usually pay for them in two years, though we borrow for five . . . we can arrange for a £30,000 loan, with £1,000,000 to back it up in twelve hours, others have to arrange mortgages etc" (D16).

A smaller number of developers utilized short-term bridging loans. According to the literature such loans are the most commonly used source of finance in commercial property development (Cadman and Catalano, 1983). Because of the large sums involved, they tend to attract high interest rates. This sort of loan is commonly used if the development is to be sold-on after completion. If there is a delay in construction or selling-on then costs, mainly in the form of interest charges, would rise quickly.

Overall, smaller developers also suffer additional punitive charges. Local branches of clearing banks have lending limits above which the application is referred upwards in the organization. This may be problematic as the application will go to a manager beyond the influence of the developer. D4 recounted how no bank in the Devon or Cornwall had a high enough lending limit to authorize a loan. The way round it for him was to use a contact in a bank in a large city with a higher credit authorization limit. Otherwise, the loan would have to have been made via a merchant bank whom, it was claimed, may charge 3.5% over base rate, plus a 1 or 2% arrangement fee.

The final group of developers were those using long-term loans or mortgages. These loans are by far the most expensive: as much again over (short-term) base rates as merchant bank loans are, for example at the time of the survey (1985) base rates stood at 12.5%, merchant banks were lending at 13.0%, and the mortgage rate was 14.5%. Understandably, long-term loans such as these are the most prone to interest rate changes and charges. Clearly, the developer is taking on a substantial risk to develop under such conditions. D9 lamented the situation,

> "interest rates were terrible, they went from 9 to 15% in a year (1984–5), we almost went under".

In the second year D9 had rescheduled a proportion of his loan on a fixed interest payment of 14%. Many of the developers were involved with local government development; often as contractors. The advantage here is that local government is able to negotiate lower rates of interest. Local authorities are able to help local business by making loans available at favourable rates, making it possible for them to take on longer term loans. In the case of D12, who was mainly involved in production not property development activities, a mortgage was arranged through the local authority —

> "we realised that we could get a mortgage cheaper than we were originally paying rent [in South East England] . . . the loan was at 10.5% in 1970, but it was fixed, at that time the banks were not into loaning venture capital".

Relationships between actors are governed by economic power, which can affect access to resources. In general, the more capital that a developer has, the less they are either forced to borrow, or the lower the rate of interest that can be negotiated with the bank. Those with least resources are forced back onto greater dependency on their own resources. What they do borrow is usually at high rates of interest. This conclusion would be echoed by Barrett and Whiting (1983, p. 16) who suggested that those with the least bargaining power end up bearing the most risk in a development.

Construction costs

Boddy and Barrett (1980) indicate that building costs represent the largest single element in the overall development of an industrial building. Construction costs comprise; profits, labour, and materials. In one respect these may seem to be beyond the developer's control. This section details how control may be regained through the modification of cost margins and the sources of both labour and materials used, but at another 'cost': risk.

Developers variously reported that costs of £1.20 to £2.50 per square metre for recently completed schemes for units of between 100 and 200 square metres. How can such variation be accounted for? The most obvious way of ensuring lower costs is to use competitive tendering. One alternative is to restructure the development relationships and to adopt a 'cost-plus' system where the developer 'shares' the profit with the builder. When this is done within different sections of the same company one 'layer' of profit is removed. This method is indicative of cost saving; primarily it enables the developer to have direct control over cost elements, rather than leaving them to the market. Skilled work processes are commonly subcontracted to other companies in the construction industry. Such specialist sub-contracting is usually used for industrial building frames, foundations, plastering and electrical installation. The greater the number of these activities that can be carried out 'in-house' the greater the potential for cost reduction, and the greater the level of control achieved over the costs of the development.

Developers made comments concerning the costings of their develop-ments, "the company originally owning the unit [industrial building] couldn't make the development into small units due to a 'head office loading' [administration] that increased costs" (D9);

> "...on involving the public sector your costs go through the roof [due to administrative costs]. The only option is a builder developer using his [sic] own income and labour" (D21).

The case of the developer with the cheapest costs—D15—would seem to bear out this pattern; they do not use subcontractors at all, all activities are contained 'in house'. The degree to which costs are actually saved in such cases or simply absorbed into other parts of the company is debatable. This is not to say that such a development is unviable; it is an example of the financially weaker developer bearing a greater proportion of the risk by utilizing these organizational means of cost 'reduction'. In many cases—one might say characteristically—this risk extends into personal life too.[1] In the case of D16 the developer's immediate family had been 'employed' to carry out administrative duties—a classic one-person business scenario—absorbing costs through the domestication of labour. D10 was proud of this fact;

> "it's a small family outfit . . . we have a high absorbed-labour element".

Developers that reduce costs in such a manner can operate in places, or at times, when others cannot.

---

[1] Considering that such developers are effectively 'small firms' this pattern of organization and operation is not at all unusual. One would expect the notion of 'risk'—the uneven re-production of the social relations of firms and markets—to be as valid an analytical category here as in property development.

In some cases risks are enabling, rather than constraining, in terms of the development coming about in the first place. An interesting example is D12, where the business (manufacturing measuring instruments) fell on hard times; labour had been transferred from the production to construction activities and hence 'costs' had been reduced to very low levels. Here 'costs' are not exactly meaningful, but the organization of the firm is. The costs of using a trained and technical workforce on construction activities is debatable in pure accounting terms. However, the sentiment expressed by management was that

"... you can't lay-off half a person, it was either that or use them in a productive manner".

This pattern of transferring workers within the company's different activities to balance the accounts is also the case with construction firms which transfer construction workers to development, when construction activity is in decline (D1, D5).

There is an even more subtle division in the way in which sub-contracting and direct labour are used. This is a classic practice within the construction sector. Employees are self-employed, which has the effect of lowering costs by removing the employer's responsibility for employees, and reducing the company's liability in slack periods. Workers are only paid when actually on-site

"I found employing people a liability: it won't work in my system. In slack periods it gobbles up profits. The last major project I did the foreman got more than I did" (D16).

Of those developers at the lower end of the scale many used their own subsidiary building company. In effect there was a cross-subsidization of activities with in the boundaries of 'the firm'.[2]

Clearly, costs are not a fixed item, they depend upon the organization of a company's activities, and the resources, informally and sectorally can be drawn upon. Larger operations were concerned with investment income and tended to work with fairly high cost structures, reducing overheads and liabilities through subcontracting. This is essentially a low risk activity. This limited their spatial and temporal scope of activity.

Smaller companies find it necessary to use informal labour, or casualize existing labour in order to compete on cost terms. However, this strategy incurs greater risks as it may involve the internalization of much of the capitalization. The consequence is that it allows the company more flexibility in that it may increase both the spatial and temporal limits of its

---

[2]Perhaps a way of characterizing this is as organizational flexibility. However, the analysis that is being developed here deconstructs the concept of flexibility and stresses the nuances of power and organization implied. It is worth emphasizing the benefit of the sort of conceptualization employed in this book, it is clearly sensitive to this complex web of relationships that cross what are apparent boundaries between and within firms, as well as between the public realm (of formal business activity) and the private realm (of family employment and use of personal funds).

operation. Both of these types of activity are underpinned by differential use of, and access to, funding by different developers. Less powerful developers use their organizational individuality (such as D15) in order to negotiate profits in a different manner to more conventional investors. As such, this form of the organization of activities reproduces inequalities. Those developers with the least power have to expose themselves to greater risks—often of personal bankruptcy—in order to be able to develop property.

Land development costs

Few developers serviced land for industrial use, they relied upon local authorities to do it for them. This may at first seem puzzling, given that land costs are considered to be low in Cornwall compared with other parts of the country. One may expect this to be an advantage. However, when one considers the additional and necessary costs of servicing land the situation is less attractive. For example, in 1984 serviced industrial land cost between £8,000 and £10,000 per hectare in Cornwall; unserviced land was less expensive. The costs of unserviced land are crucial in the viability of a scheme; if it cost £6,000 per hectare to provide the land with roads, storm and foul drainage, electricity and telephones, then the unserviced land could not—realistically—be marketed at much more than £4,000 per hectare. If it was to cost £8,000 per hectare to service the land then, technically, the unserviced land would have to have a negative value if development were to be able to proceed in profit. Calculations concerning the relative costs of land and servicing sites may be critical in determining whether development can occur in a locality.

The South West Water Authority (SWWA) place an additional connection charge for providing the necessary infrastructure to new industrial estates in areas that are not already served with adequate water. This, in effect, adds an additional premium to the cost of servicing a site, further affecting its viability for development. In areas of the country that have existing development, infrastructure costs may be significantly lower, making land development more viable. Parts of the country where land prices are higher tend not to suffer from such problems as servicing costs only represent a minor proportion of the total land cost. Thus, in such cases infrastructure is not the absolute constraint that it can be in localities such as Cornwall.

The problem of servicing land may be alleviated to some extent by the economies of scale of developing a larger plot. One strategy that can be adopted by a developer is to purchase a large plot, to service a proportion of it and then sell it and use the profits accrued to service the remainder. However, this option is not open to all developers. First, the absolute cost may be a problem for smaller developers. Second, the interest charges on the borrowing can make such a long-term development process very risky. The temporal specificity of this activity is significant. For example, in the early 1970s, interest charges were low and private developers were active and held land banks.

"If I invested £25,000 in land, after a year it may be worth £27,000, if it was worked [developed] it would be worth considerably more" (D15).

In the mid 1980s, due to these conditions, development was mainly confined to land already developed. Even if a developer already owned some land it might only be possible to develop it in small stages. The case of D6 is a worth examining.

A large plot of agricultural land was purchased in the early 1970s, a small proportion of which received planning permission. The development of this small plot, it was hoped, would more than cover the initial purchase price of the whole plot. In the 1980s, the company was considering development, but servicing and building for industrial uses was not considered viable. The planned strategy was to secure planning per-mission for retailing; develop and sell-off this part of the site and then, by using the infrastructure investment as a lever, open up a further industrial site. Of course, this immediately presents planners with a dilemma, as it implicates the use of industrial land for retailing which was contrary to planning policy. But, at the same time, it may create more industrial development.

Generally, even if they can afford to service the land, developers will often choose serviced land simply because it can be developed immedi-ately. They do not have to wait for planning permission which incurs risk (in terms of time taken to develop the site, and extra borrowing costs incurred). The advantages to the small developer are stated by D15;

"it makes it possible to develop a plot at a time."

Grants and tax relief

A final element in the elaboration of costs is subsidy, either in the form of grants or tax relief. It is important to note that developers have differential access to these subsidies and they are differentially affected by the same subsidies. Indirect taxation relief can work in a variety of ways. Investors or developers falling into a high tax bracket can use the Industrial Building Allowances (IBA) to claim against taxation; a form of relief. Initially, this can make yields seem very attractive, improving them by 5 or 10%. However, it is a 'once and for all' payment. A subsequent decision to trade property or to invest in it can affect the developer's liability to taxation. D16 claimed that changes in Capital Gains Taxation had had a direct effect on the amount of development he carried out, making it possible to increase the scale of development activities.

Surprisingly, not all developers were willing to accept grants, confessing concern about 'interference' from the government. Perhaps this is because taxation is considered by many as taking away what is perceived as rightful income, whereas grants are perceived as a subsidy, indicative of some sort of inefficiency. The attitude is perhaps summed up in the aphorism quoted by developer D10

> "tax evasion is a crime, tax efficiency is an art".

A version which was, perhaps, closer to the real reason was communicated by both developers D3 and D10 who indicated that they would not take grants because this led to interference in both their own and their clients affairs. D10 and D15 had a rather more paternalistic approach, indicating that they would claim a grant if "a client was struggling".

In other cases where the margins are smaller it is perhaps indicative that D2, took grants and "... couldn't afford to pass them on to the client". Another dimension is added by D3 who complained that it had taken more than two years to actually get the appropriate forms and full details of a grant. In the end it may actually be more costly to hold-up a development and wait for a grant proposal to be processed.

Generally, developers considered that grants were more trouble than they were worth: in terms of applying for them, the uncertainty involved, and the extent to which the process exposed their dealings to wider inspection. This is perhaps why indirect grants, with their certainty, were more popular with developers undertaking developments.

The Structuring of the Location and Form of Development

As noted above, local authorities are often the only agencies willing or able to develop large plots of land, mainly as a result of being able to negotiate lower cost loans. In many cases, even the advantageous borrowing arrangements are insufficient to overcome total cost of development for local authorities. Many could not afford to service land without the 50% European Regional Development Fund grant. In one case, a 100% Derelict Land Grant has also been used to service industrial land. Larger plots are preferred in such cases to achieve economy of scale, but large plots can be difficult to assemble.

The fragmented nature of land ownership and mineral rights in Cornwall can cause considerable legal problems. More conventional problems of negotiating land sales can also add to the time and cost of land assembly. Again, this points to the reasons why, with such low land prices, larger developers are not attracted to develop and service land in Cornwall. Interestingly, it also suggests why most private industrial development is piecemeal, and not in the form of full industrial estates.

If a local authority is laying-out a site, then economies of scale would dictate land use approximating an industrial estate. With the expenditure limits, imposed by central government upon local authority spending over £60,000 under 'ratecapping' legislation, laying out an industrial estate of 6 hectares or more in size can be problematic due to the costs involved. A tactic adopted by some local government developers was to purchase land on the last and first days of consecutive tax years. This tactic is also attractive to land owners as it enables them to minimize the total capital gains made in any one year within the Capital Gains Tax threshold.

Another local authority tactic that has been used in the past, is historical purchase where land is sold-off at lower prices (a form of subsidy). A large land purchase is required to facilitate this. Although hardly used in Cornwall, this was a central concept in the Community Land Act's implementation. This procedure is not possible within the current struc-ture planning process as it would require an assembly of land in excess of that allowed for the current structure plan period.

Generally, these actions by both levels of government create a bias towards the creation of industrial estates, even though no local authority in Cornwall has an explicit policy to create them. The lack of explicit concern with industrial estates has had an adverse side effect in that there has been a lack of adequate guidelines on the development of estates. Most local authorities are so short of money that they can not adequately service the sites with lighting and refuse collection, let alone landscape them. Central government agencies seldom get involved in servicing land, preferring to buy it from local government. This state of affairs effectively limits the range of potential sites for industrial development activity at any one point in time. The practical choices available to developers are limited to a few possible new sites, or extensions of existing ones.

Most developers responded that any site would do, as long as it was not too remote, near a town and had reasonable access to main roads;

"[t]here's always a local firm if you're developing small sites" (D21).

As has already been noted, the area of search of most developers was limited by other factors, such as being within a specific area (often their home town) or a specific size of site. In many cases this would mean that the number of possible sites would be very small indeed. Even where the scale of operations was significantly larger, as with D13, the desire to develop within a specific locality can mean that site acquisition is ex-tremely problematic. Delays can run into years. This leads into the second issue of concern: the availability of the site.

Few land banks are held due to rises in interest rates which were not echoed in rises in land prices. The exception to the rule are local government developers, for whom the only way to develop land is by maintaining a land bank. Thus, for most developers the immediate availability of sites is of key importance. As Goodchild and Munton (1985) note, the seller is in a crucial position regarding the availability of possible sites for development. Slowe (1981, p. 70) has emphasized elsewhere the consequences of this: the location of industry is dependant upon the operation of the land market. This point is echoed by developer D22,

"site location is determined by sellers of land".

A common view expressed by developers was that agricultural land was offered at too high a price to justify industrial development. Even if agricultural land was for sale, the risk entailed in terms of cost and time of waiting for planning permission and the possibility of a public enquiry, was enough to dissuade all but the most determined developers. The most determined were local authorities. As has previously been noted, public sector developers also had problems financing development. But, they have a powerful tactic, the threat of compulsory purchase. Whilst seldom actually used, its existence can be used to force a landowners' hand (D24). Generally, in Cornwall, developers will take the easiest route, to avoid conflict with the community or the planners in order to avoid excessive delay and, hence, increased risk to development.

The third issue worth consideration is the form of the development. There seems to be general agreement that location on an industrial estate minimizes risks. Most obviously, economies of scale have to be considered. In most cases developments are small accretions rather than totally new sites;

"our development is always on the back of others" (D15).

Proximity to other successful developments was explicitly cited as liable to increase the chances of a successful letting, even if it was just with 'poached' tenants from the main development. From the point of view of an appraisal of risk, a location on an industrial estate is attractive as there are comparable buildings whose value can easily be estimated (for valuation purposes) by comparison with other similar developments. Thus, the likely return on investment can thus be calculated with more certainty by the developer.

With regard to the internal layout of the estate, little was said by developers; apart from the mention of economies of scale, layout was considered to be determined by the configuration of the actual site. Some of the larger developers had concerns regarding the density of development, but this depended upon the buildings developed. Larger developments required more space for expansion or storage. Smaller units were provided with an 'apron' (a concrete yard, usually combined with parking spaces) shared with others.

The final issue concerns the design of the premises themselves. Generally, the way for developers to reduce their liability to risk is to maintain the greatest flexibility of use of the premises, subject to other restraints.

This means favouring the lowest common denominator. In terms of larger premises, as noted in Chapter 4, the institutional standard may be crucial if a building is likely to be sold-on in the future.

"If the design is not of institutional standard, then they won't touch it. In Cornwall, if anything is wrong [outside the institutional parameters], they won't touch it"(D4).

Basically, this means that the design will be warehousing with limited office space. In terms of smaller buildings, the bulk of those developed in Cornwall, the standard is a unit for the starter business or small employer. Flexibility, from the developer's point of view, is still important,

"it can't be too specialized . . . with small units they're so expensive to build . . . flexibility is the key . . . we use movable walls" (D6).

Design requirements are considered to be basic. The unit is, to all intents and purposes, ". . . like a box" (D1). In fact developers make a virtue of this, claiming that it reduces rentals and the risk to them. Developers' perceptions are that smaller firms don't deserve 'appropriate' premises, "when a firm starts up 'beggars can't be choosers', they get what they're given" (D11). Clearly, such an attitude will reduce risks and costs for the developer.

The availability of sites, physically and legally, is clearly a key factor in terms of location. This can act as an absolute limit on the location of an estate in a locality at any time. If the developer seeks to challenge planning permission, or bargain with a landowner, risks are increased. Furthermore, the site itself will limit the choice of the form of the development. Extensive earthworks or levelling, will introduce extra costs and impose a time penalty on the development. Both increase risk, one in terms of outlay, and the other in terms of the period of the exposure to debt.

Contiguous development of land (an industrial estate) will benefit the developer in terms of economies of scale in infrastructure costs. Furthermore, certainty of value, and the likelihood of letting or sale may be increased due to proximity to other development. Additional risks can be reduced if the buildings on the plot are 'flexible' in use, and if the total outlay is low. Hence, the standard 'box' unit. Developers may reduce their risks by giving the unit potential appeal to a larger market. However, the selection of the specific tenant may be considered to be a liability and other means have to be used to modify risks; this entails what may be termed 'shifting the risk' to the occupants. Instead of the physical restraints discussed above, legal restraints are used.

Shifting the Risk: The Implications of the Occupancy of Industrial Estates for the Developer

This section is concerned with a further means by which developers' risks are minimized, via the legal control of the occupants. It is argued that this

can effectively 'shift the risk' from the developer to the user of the
buildings. There are two ways by which legal means can be used to
influence the occupancy of estates: by statutory procedure, and by contract.

The statutory procedures that affect the occupancy of industrial buildings relate to the Industrial Building Allowance (IBA) and the Use Classes
Order (UCO). If finance was released as part of a tax relief under the IBA,
then if the scheme is to qualify, the occupant must be a 'Section 7
qualifier'.[3] Despite the more recent liberal interpretation of these regulations to include some service sector activities, they are a significant
constraint on occupancy. Nevertheless, it must be noted that some
developers, after initial application for an IBA have considered the risk of
empty property too great and have, after a time, accepted noncomplying
occupants, and thus lost their eligibility.

The UCO is a far more wide-ranging restriction on occupancy, being
part of the planning development control. Permission is granted for
specific uses on a site. The UCO is used selectively by planners in
Cornwall to control 'nuisance' users (car repairers or other 'messy'
activities) on industrial estates, and to regulate the density of land use.[4]
Developments that can accommodate manufacturing activities are
favoured; warehousing is excluded on grounds of excessive land use, and
nonindustrial uses on the grounds of provision already being made
elsewhere (in town centres). Given the expressed desire to be flexible in the
use of premises, the exclusion of warehousing and retailing activities—
both activities are common amongst small firms—can be considered to
increase a developer's risk of letting.

The other means of restricting activity on estates is by the use of a
contract (the lease). The lease goes beyond simply imposing the statutory
regulations on the tenants and offers a clear insight into the practical
means by which developers can 'shift their risk'. There are three ways in
which contracts can restrict occupants; selective granting of leases, the
lease itself, and additional restrictive covenants.

Developers will not generally let their units to simply anybody; in
addition to statutory obligations they will want to ensure as far as possible
that they will secure reliable tenants. As noted in Chapter 4, financial

---

[3]Section 7 of the 1968 Capital Allowances Act (see Chapter 4): basically, manufacturing
activities. This designation limits the potential occupants and thereby increases the risk for
the developer.
[4]The common application of this regulation to industrial developments is permission for
Classes III and IV (light industry not injurious to residential amenity, and general
industry) and exclusion for Classes V to IX (Special industry where the processes are
noxious), and Class X (Wholesale warehouses) and all other non-industrial uses (including
offices and retailing). As noted in Chapter 4, the UCO has been revised since the survey
work reported in this chapter was carried out. The result is a relative liberalisation of this
control, particularly for smaller premises (smaller than 235 m^2).

institutions–when they act as landlords–operate an informal selection procedure, restricting access to public limited companies. This is not practical on small-scale developments, nevertheless, developers often run credit checks on potential occupants, in effect favouring more established firms. In some cases (D16) developers will only accept those users who will accept personal liability for the rental payments. For developers this insures them, or acts as a first line of defence, against the risk of potential losses if the property is void.

The details of the lease itself are fairly standard, what is of concern here are premiums, rentals and reviews. Premiums are a down payment requested by a developer to 'secure access' to the property. Although often used in other commercial property settings in Cornwall they were not requested by developers; this is indicative of the weak market for industrial premises obtaining at that time. The rental levels themselves are variable by property type and location. Although they are nominally related to yields, they are variable. Developers seemed willing to drop their rentals if premises were vacant for a period. However, 'rent-free' periods were frowned upon. It was felt that 'rent-free' periods established a bad precedent for small firms, encouraging 'weak firms' which were more liable to fail. As a compensation for taking the lower initial rental income for the developer usually makes clear provision in the lease for upward rental reviews at the end of three years. In the case of the lengths of leases, the commonest was between 15–25 years, occasionally with 'break clauses' after 5 years, with a caveat that 6 months advance notice (or compensatory rental payments) was required.

As noted above, leases can be used to restrict certain activities relating to statutory regulations, they are also used to impose further restrictions to safeguard developers (i.e. shift the risk). One common restriction is the imposition of the Fully Repairing and Insuring (FRI) Covenant. As it suggests, this leaves the tenant fully liable for repair and insurance of the building. Covenants may also specify certain activities that are restricted, common ones being car repairs or car spraying. Two reasons were given for the exclusion of such activities (where they were not restricted by UCO or IBA): insurance and image of the estate.

Insurance premiums on the rest of the site are likely to be increased due to the risk of explosion of paint propellants. This is a liability for the other users and imposes a surcharge on rentals, making them less attractive. Image is important to some developers who are charging higher rents for a 'higher quality' development. This image is maintained by controlling development, and 'messy' activities, including external storage, that may either dissuade potential tenants or bring down the rental level.

Finally, if a developer was also carrying out production activities on the site that was being let, a clause would usually be written into the covenant excluding an occupant of the premises from carrying out activities that would be in direct competition with the developer. This can also be construed as risk minimization of the developer's wider activities.

Conclusion: The Re-production of the Property Development Process

The aim of this chapter has been to 'get inside' the property development process; to dispel the myth that is reproduced in much research on property development that focuses on either 'agents' or 'structures'. The value of careful conceptualization of relationships and using these as a guide to empirical analysis has been emphasized. As has been shown, developers take a variety of forms: in many cases they are either not identifiable as developers in an 'idealist' sense, or separable from construction or manufacturing activities in an empirical sense. This highlights the value of the critical realist analysis presented here. It can perhaps be characterized as an analysis that goes beyond the empirical categories, taxonomies, or empirically generated concepts that are characteristic of so much research. This chapter has emphasized how, if one is bound to such conceptualizations, much of what makes for an adequate explanation of property development is lost: the significance of organizational form for the practice and outcome of the development process; the 'cross-subsidization' of activities and the shifting of the risk between agents.

Just as developers are not reducible to any one 'ideal type', so their activities are not reducible to rationalistic costing exercises. It is important to stress that a 'behaviourial factor' is not being resurrected here. Rather it stresses what might be referred to as the uneven re-production of the development process. The term risk has been used to stress the empirical ways in which particular relations become enabling and constraining depending upon the particular resources of developers. This underscores the fundamental unevenness of the social relations of property development. Nevertheless, uneven development is not reducible to, or exclusively concerned with, property development; this process — important though it is — is part of an explanation of the re-production of space: in this case the re-production of a particular form of the industrial built environment, the industrial estate. This is not a 'universal' state of affairs, it is necessary to be sensitive to the social, spatial and temporal context of development activity. This is why so much time was spent in Chapters 4 and 5 outlining this context. This leads back into the central argument of this book, that property development and industrial location are both embedded in context and internally related to one another; they can not simply be abstracted (in the conventional use of the term).

The final sections of this chapter have shown how the social relations of building production can impact directly upon the users of that property. The impact is not that of restriction of size or location (Fothergill *et al.*,

1987), these factors are of negligible importance for small firms, rather it is the legal and financial relationships that they are implicated in which may constrain their provision activities. It is in this way that the social relations of building production can be seen to involve the users; in effect the risk is being passed onto the occupants. The following chapter moves on to focus more closely upon the relationship between industrial property and economic development, exploring the implications of the development of industrial estates in Cornwall.

7

The Role and Evaluation of the Industrial Built Environment in Cornwall

The Evaluation Problem

The aim of this chapter is to evaluate the role of the industrial built environment, specifically industrial estates, in the re-production of Cornish economy and society. This task is not as straightforward as it may at first seem, primarily because of the methodological problems associated with evaluation. These can be considered as falling into two categories. The first relates to the conceptualization of what evaluation is itself; monitoring and assessment of the efficiency, or effectiveness, of policies and programmes. The crucial point here is the definition of 'efficient' and/ or 'effective', which implies a subsidiary question regarding for whom, and on what terms, it is 'efficient' or 'effective'? The second relates to the conceptualization of the objects to be evaluated; in terms of empirical regularities and narrow economic criteria divorced, for the most part, from the wider social and political arena. In short, conventional evaluation is constructed on a foundation of positivism. The question that is addressed in the first part of this chapter is why positivist evaluation methodology is inadequate and what a critical realist evaluation might look like. The remaining part of the chapter outlines such an evaluation.

Positivist Evaluation Methodology: a Critique

Despite the variety of evaluation techniques available in the realm of 'spatial and economic policy evaluation' (see for example Diamond and Spence, 1983; Turok, 1990) they are predominantly based upon a variant of the scientific method. They can be characterized as a form of experimentation, usually on the basis of predicting what would have happened if the policy under investigation had not been applied and comparing this with what actually happened.[1] Some classic examples of this approach as applied to UK regional policy can be found in the work of Moore *et al.* (1986). It is useful to take this as an example. Moore and his colleagues attempt to model one indicator of regional policy, such as employment, over time covering both the periods when the policy was applied (the 'policy-on' period) and when it was not (the 'policy-off' period). The difference between the two measures is deemed to be the 'policy effect'.

There are two technical problems — internal to positivist methodology — with this sort of approach. The first is concerned with the actual identification of the policy objective, and consequently a means of expressing it in measurable (quantifiable) terms. There are two subsidiary points. First, that policies are notoriously vague in their specification of policy goals, second, that even when goals are clearly specified they may not be immediately measurable and substitute, indirect, or surrogate measures have to be used. In this latter case an additional problem is introduced; that of the relationship between the surrogate measure and the actual measure.

In many micro-economic evaluation techniques the technical problem of measurement is 'solved' by resolving all factors to common terms: usually monetary value (see Willis, 1983, 1985). The technique is to model the likely benefits of a policy initiative and to discount the future costs to present values.[2] It is then argued that such findings provide a basis upon which alternative policies can be compared against a cost 'yard-stick'; a commonly used measure is the 'cost-per-job' created by the policy.

From a critical realist point of view these conventional, positivist, approaches are problematic; one reason is related to the problem of system closure. For a positivist experiment to be valid, the experimenter must be sure that the change in the object under investigation is due exclusively to the introduction of the experimental condition (the policy) and not due to other, extraneous, factors. The way that this is achieved in physical science is by insulating or controlling the environment within which the experiment takes place: the laboratory. Clearly, such control — known as system closure — is more difficult, if not impossible, in the social realm.

In the examples of spatial and economic policy evaluation noted above the system is defined as including only a narrow economic realm, even when multiplier effects are taken into account. Recent critiques of micro-

---

[1]This is referred to as *ex-post* evaluation as it takes place after the event. Strictly, this is not an experiment but a quasi-experiment; it is only one part of the process (see (iv) below). Proper experiments should include events both before and after the application of experimental condition, this: (i) the specification of the population and the system, (ii) the division of the population into an experimental group and a control group, (iii) the application of the experimental condition to the experimental group, (iv) comparison of the experimental and control groups; and difference being inferred as being caused by the experimental condition.
[2]An evaluation carried out prior to the launch of a policy, on the basis of forecast expenditure or income, is referred to as *ex-ante* evaluation.

economic evaluation techniques have highlighted this issue—namely those advocating social audits (Harte, 1986; Geddes, 1988)—arguing for the system to be more widely defined. For example, when evaluating the effect of a single manufacturing plant closure it is argued that the exchequer costs of social security payments and unemployment benefits, a wider spatial extent of the impact, and longer timescale of evaluation be taken into account.[3] Whilst these modifications do offer a broader technical interpretation, albeit at the cost of introducing greater practical difficulties into the evaluation process, they still flounder on the logical limitations of the evaluation of 'closed systems'. Critical realist analyses are not prone to such problems as they are premised upon an open system.

A second problem underlying the positivist experimental form, and consequently all positivist evaluation, is that of induction. An implicit assumption in extrapolations and predictions is that the future will be like the past. For example, in macro-economic evaluation of regional policy it is assumed that the economy would have continued to perform in a way consistent with the prior policy-off period when the policy-on is operating. In this way the experimental condition and the control are generated. As noted in Chapter 1, critical realism avoids the problem of induction.

The third point of critique is one that characterizes critical realist approaches; the relationship between politics, theory and method. Diamond and Spence (1983, p. 4) recognizing this problem within a conventional positivist framework suggest that the identification of practical goals by the researcher is related to the theoretical conception of the problem addressed. For example, in the case of regional policy they suggest that it is not exactly clear what constitutes balanced national development: different theories would suggest different explanations. They concede that it is at this point that 'political pressure' may be bought to bear on evaluation. In an attempt at theoretical and hence political pluralism they review a variety of typologies of regional development theory and thus develop a range of criteria by which they suggest that the outcome of regional development policy can be evaluated. Once past this uncertainty of the political sphere, they turn back to measuring the 'effects' of policies in terms of these criteria (see above). As such they attempt to rescue the objectivity and hence the validity of positivist approaches by insulating themselves from political processes by evoking pluralism. Critical realists disagree with such a separation of the political realm and argue that it is, in fact, part and parcel of the explanation.

It is significant that Diamond and Spence's range of alternative theories of regional development are all neoclassical in origin. Whilst the individual

---

[3]Some processes may conceivably take many years to operate, an arbitrary 'cut-off' point may thus fail to identify the empirical outcomes of a long term policy process. More specifically, in micro-evaluation where future values are discounted to the present, project viability can rest as much upon the rate of return or the time period used in the evaluation.

adequacy of these theories may be questioned, they are all consistent with a nominalist ontology. A conspicuous omission from their typology is any discussion of theories in which explanation is related to the restructuring of production which are based upon a realist ontology. Appropriately, Massey and other authors sympathetic to critical realism, have argued that traditional evaluation methodology based upon location decisions and the locational environment can not provide an insight into the processes identified by theories concerned with the restructuring of production. The importance of Massey's (1979, p. 239) contribution in this context is that she suggests that not all theories can be evaluated by the same methodologies.

This problem can perhaps best be considered by looking at Keeble's (1980) evaluation of the 'restructuring thesis'[4] using positivist methodology and Sayer's (1982b) reply to it. Sayer objects to Keeble's premise that the 'restructuring thesis' would give rise to outcomes of universal empirical regularity or that such outcomes would necessarily co-vary with aggregate economic indicators. The nub of this disagreement is that critical realists hold that the 'restructuring thesis' is formulated on a realist ontology. Explanation is dependent upon the identification of causal mechanisms (which may or may not be empirically observable). An appropriate means of evaluation must be sensitive to ontological depth. However, as has been noted, positivism is founded upon a nominalist ontology where causality must be inferred from constant conjunctions of empirical events, not from causal mechanisms. A crude analogy of Keeble's approach might be the use of an ordinary camera (as opposed to an X-ray camera) to assess the condition of a broken limb. The implication of critical realists' criticisms of conventional—positivist—approaches to evaluation is that the evaluation methodologies used must be appropriate for the theoretical frameworks that generate the explanations upon which policies are based.

A consequence of the critical realist conception of society is that questions concerning the production of knowledge itself are also problematized. In an attempt to examine this relationship, albeit not explicitly in a critical realist framework but one consistent with it, Lewis and Melville (1978) draw upon the literature of critical theory to develop a critique of regional science. The crucial step in the development of a critical theory is not just to be critical of other theories, but also to be critical of the objective of the theory itself: knowledge production. Lewis and Melville argue that the concepts of explanation used by regional scientists (which can be closely equated with positivists generally) in the evaluation of policies cause knowledge to be structured in a particular manner that reasserts, rather than challenges, the status quo. They highlight that regional science

---

[4]Broadly the 'restructuring thesis' is the approach advocated by Massey (1984).

has a particular view of what constitutes explanation, one that excludes the social ends or consequences. It is in this way, they argue, that epistemologies are inherently political and are not objective. Their conclusion is that if regional science is to be reconstructed as a critical theory then the social ends must be incorporated into explanation. To these ends Carney and his colleagues have developed alternative explanations of the 'regional under-development' of the North East of England in which they highlight the relationship between the coal industry, the state and civil society.[5]

An indication of the internal relationship between regional policy and social and economic change is provided by Dunford *et al.* (1981). In the latter part of their paper they argue that regional policies are themselves divisive (setting one group of workers, or/and one locality, against another) and distort (by the imposition of bourgeois forms on class struggles) struggles against uneven development. They argue that regional policy is directed towards the maintenance of capitalist production for profit and the maintenance of its social relations. In effect Dunford *et al.* are relocating the source of the problem from a simple distributional cause to a social structural one. In a similar context Harte (1986) has argued that the development of alternative evaluation methods is central to the development of alternative economic strategies.

Whilst those writing on restructuring have generally taken a more satisfactory line of argument on the development process by involving discussion of political processes, there has been a tendency towards reduction of these processes to relations of production or the labour process. Several writers have highlighted the importance of the consideration of the social relations that lie 'outside of' production as well as those that lie within it (see Bagguley *et al.*, 1990, p. 134). Hence, the emphasis in this book is on the importance of the state and civil society (reproduction) as well as production in explaining development. Although prone to reductionism in parts, Massey's (1984) work highlights nonproductive relations through the sensitive discussion of space. A key point of focus in the analysis presented here is the mediation of the 'top-down' imposition of the relations of production by the local social and economic structure; specifically through struggles around the re-production of the industrial built environment.

The conclusion of this section is the importance of reframing the initial question of how to evaluate policies.[6] First, one needs to consider what problems policies are meant to ameliorate and whom the problem affects.

---

[5]See (Carney *et al.*, 1976; Carney and Lewis, 1977; Carney *et al.*, 1977; Carney, 1980). Massey (1984) also draws upon this work, and elaborates with further examples from South Wales and Cornwall in her elaboration of the 'restructuring thesis'.
[6]In this sense a policy need not be a codified statement, but may be widened to any set of linked activities and actions by a group.

Positivist evaluation methodology casts questions as technocratic problems to be solved by the application of quantitative methods. The critical realist responses highlight the broader social relationships involved in evaluation and that evaluation is not exhausted by simple or limited empirical monitoring; rather, it should be directed at the elaboration of causal mechanisms. Thus, it may be argued that the object of analysis needs to be shifted from the immediate employment or floorspace developed on an industrial estate to the process of the production of those estates set within the wider context of an examination of the regulation of social and economic transformation of society. The following section outlines such an analysis in relation to industrial estates in Cornwall.

A Critical Evaluation of Industrial Estate Development in Cornwall

This section sets both the development and role of industrial estates back into the wider context of struggles over the reproduction of the locality of Cornwall introduced in Chapter 5. In this sense the aim is to plot a course between cultural and economic determinism. The argument so far is that industrial estates have acted as a site for the restructuring of economic activity, in other words they have facilitated, or enabled, rather than caused the restructuring. By suggesting that industrial estates have acted as a site for the relocation of industry and as a means of promoting or attracting certain types of economic activity we must not loose sight of the point made in Chapter 6; namely that the re-production of industrial estates is itself a site of struggle in the realm of property development and investment. The aim of this part of this chapter is to explore some of the issues relating to the struggles over the nature of industrial estate development within and between the state and civil society. This will illuminate the wider setting of the struggles underlying the social and economic reproduction of the Cornish locality.

A classic text on the nature of uneven development within the 'Celtic' periphery is Hechter's (1975) where regional exploitation is expressed in terms of cultural oppression. However, as Nairn (1981, p. 165) notes, its core–periphery analysis overlooks issues of class. In order to explore the lines of cleavage in Cornwall, it is useful to explain the particular social, economic and political history that forms the context.

The degree of external landownership in Cornwall is a significant factor in its history. The major landowner in Cornwall is 'The Duchy'[7] which

---

[7]The Duchy was created in 1337 to provide an income for the next-in-line to the throne of England. Although associated with Cornwall, the Duchy's landowning is not confined there. Estates are held in various counties, principally Devon. The Duke of Bedford also owns substantial estates in the county. Spring (1971, p. 28) notes that the Duchy owned one sixth of the tin and one eighth of the copper mined in the county in 1830.

holds some 10,000 hectares of land, and 22,700 hectares of mineral rights in Cornwall (Dalton, 1987, p. 27). One consequence of external ownership has been the substantial leakages of capital out of the economy. At the other end of the land ownership spectrum there were a large number of small holdings, which although not profitable in themselves, were often farmed by miners to supplement mining income (Rose, 1987, p. 113). This system gave rise to a very particular social formation, the resonances of which are still to be felt in the present day.

Mining and development rights were obtained by action and formed the basis of the notorious 'tribute' system. Under this system 'free miners' organized themselves into gangs or 'pares' and had to bid against one another for pitches to mine. Thus, much of the extraction was carried out by small organizations, or individuals with a small capital base, while much of the profit went directly out of the county in the form of rents. Moreover, it was common practice to operate a 'cash-book' system, whereby reserves were not invested in future development of the mine.

Whilst apparently quite autonomous, the miners had little real control over their circumstances. As voting and access to a seat in parliament was dictated by landownership and the ancient boroughs the people who actually lived in the locality had little real democratic representation.[8] Halliday (1975, p. 258) summarizes the consequence of the mining activity on the locale, albeit in a slightly nostalgic light, as

> ". . . upsetting a simple economy based primarily on agriculture and fishing, when there was neither a philosophy nor a political machinery to prevent the grotesque maldistribution of wealth and the exploitation of labour that helped to produce it".

A consequence of the low level of capital retention in the locality, and the petty-capitalist basis of mining led to the classic problem of processing and added value activities being relocated away from the locality.

Mining activity declined rapidly in the mid- and late-nineteenth century with little to replace it in terms of employment apart from falling back upon agriculture and fishing; and by the 1840s agriculture itself was suffering from a succession of bad harvests; the response, for many, was migration. Migration was particularly devastating for the west of the county; some districts lost over one quarter of their population in a ten year period. It is estimated that nearly one third of the mining population left between 1861–71 (Cornwall County Council, 1952, p. 27). Some of course did get jobs elsewhere in Cornwall; it is estimated that nearly one third of the miners from the west of the county were able to find jobs in the new mining industry of the china clay industry around St Austell (Rallings and Lee 1978, p. 7). The Cornish population declined continuously until 1960.

---

[8] As late as 1832 Cornwall returned 44 members of parliament, compared with 45 in the whole of Scotland (Rowse, 1986, p. 6).

Rallings and Lee (1978) argue that the instability in the tin and copper mining industry led to social unrest. However, the organization of the industry—which was antithetical to unionization—did not lead to this being expressed in the form of industrial unrest, but by individualistic means.[9] Rose (1987, p. 150) suggests that the tradition of dual occupation (farming and mining), and the associated land tenure further mediated industrial struggles. But more significantly, both the scattered settlement pattern and the out-migration, undermined the building of collective action in the locality. This long history of social instability, external economic and political control contributed to the late integration of the county into both the polity and cultural aegis of England (Rallings and Lee, 1978, p. 3). It is perhaps for this reason that issues relating to the locus of control and locality are key issues in the political fabric of the county.

The issue of regional definition in the mid-1960s provides a useful insight into the local political character. Most of Cornwall was contained in the West Cornwall subdivision of the Western subregion of the Standard Economic Planning Region. This division represents an imposition of a particular political will and homogeneity on the inhabitants of the region and subregions. A significant point made by various official bodies concerned with reviewing the administration of the region—the Redcliffe-Maud Committee, the Kilbrandon Committee and the South West Economic Planning Council—have all noted the problems of this regional classification, recognizing the economic and cultural diversity within the region (see Rallings and Lee, 1978, p. 13). This brings to the surface a very interesting point, an active struggle over the definition and articulation of the means of reproducing the locality, both economically and socially.

A common strand of this definition of regional identity is the discourse of control from 'up country'. This position may be dismissed as the view of a minority, numerically speaking, of the local nationalist movement, but the influence of such views run through the spectrum of political opinions, and are articulated in a variety a ways. For example, Rallings and Lee (1978), note that many candidates in local elections—even supporters of national parties—stood at local elections as independents, distancing themselves form national politics, and also that most of the members of parliament were also members of Mebyon Kernow (MK), the main Celtic nationalist party.

As has already been noted traditional English political divisions are not relevant to Cornwall. With the low degree of unionization and the lack of traditional working class formation, support for the Labour Party may be expected to be negligible in the county. More traditional capitalist interests are represented by the Conservatives, with a high degree of

---

[9]This is an important point, one that contradicts Massey's (1984, p. 225) claim that the same kind of unionization developed in the Cornish mining industry to that of South Wales.

opposition to central control, even from favourable governments. It is not surprising that the Liberals with their traditional emphasis upon localism have good support. Perhaps the best way to consider the dominant political divisions in the locality are around issues based on the reproduction of that locality which cut across traditional party-political lines.

A central issue of Cornish politics is that of self-determination. It is an issue that cuts through all struggle in civil society. The two view points that will be considered are those of MK and the Cornwall Industrial Development Association (CIDA). CIDA is a loose grouping of industrialists and representatives of local Chambers of Commerce. It is not being suggested that these views (of both CIDA and MK) are polar opposites, in fact both views share common points and they are both apparently supported at one and the same time by political representatives; rather what is being demonstrated is an important tension in the political fabric represented by these views.

One view of the mode of reproduction is expressed by MK, who want to create a Celtic culture and autonomous rule by the reintroduction of the Cornish language and by treating Cornwall as a separate economic unit (Williams, 1985). On these grounds they oppose both the County Council and the central government regional policy initiatives (such as industrial estates) as they argue that they create dependency and remove control as economic and administrative decisions are taken far away, in the interests of the wider economy and at the expense of Cornwall. In particular, there is concern about the emergence of "...a new social situation of nonCornish management and skilled men [sic] and nonskilled Cornish workers" (Plummer, 1978). In other words both a spatial and a social division of labour. Economically, it may be argued that there is dependence and instability as firms "...come in pick up the grants, and then move away" (Plummer, 1978).

The MK response to the 'branch-plant problem' would be to allow such companies to operate only through registered subsidiaries, and elsewhere to promote cooperatives run by their workforces (Mebyon Kernow, 1984). This policy is not as radical as it might suggest. For example, Deacon *et al.* (1988, p. 178) argue that co-operatives are important in as much as they can not easily be taken over by outside bodies, especially those from outside of the county.

CIDA (1976) also oppose branch plants and industrial estates, but for other reasons; their opposition is based upon a different sort of power struggle to that advanced by MK. CIDA are protectionist as it is feared that the penetration of large-scale, external, capital might threaten the local social and economic order, possibly leading to the loss of control of the locality to outside capitals. The dominance of local capitals is also dependent upon the maintenance of existing forms of social reproduction.

This can perhaps be most clearly seen in the case of the reproduction of divisions of labour along lines of gender.

Massey (1984, p. 231) notes how CIDA policies promote the ideology of the family where women are encouraged to preform a caring role inside the home, and thus to reproduce their family's labour. In this context a limited amount of locally obtained, part-time work, might not be considered as a threat to the dominant interests of local capitals as it does not substantially challenge the reproduction of the traditional family roles. For example, children can still be picked up from school and housework still carried out. This is contingent upon the part-time work being available locally so that women are not absent from the home for long. Thus, the support for localized industrial opportunities and the lack of support for the improvement of local passenger transport are consistent.

Part-time or seasonal work, associated with low wages, informal contracts and lack of fringe benefit payments is not considered to be a serious problem because, from CIDA's perspective, it may contribute to the reduction of labour costs for local firms and thus counter-balance their adverse transport costs to central markets. Small firms are also supported as they may force down costs by competition as a result of the greater self-exploitation of labour. On both of these points CIDA's views are in line with Conservative Party thinking as expressed in the 1983 white paper on regional policy (HMSO, 1983, p. 3).

A further complication has to be added to these basic positions by the population changes and economic restructuring that have occurred since the 1960s, particularly in respect of the recomposition of class fractions that has followed from this migration. Research by Shaw *et al.* (1983, p. 256) indicates that in-migrants generally have a higher educational attainment and have often moved to Cornwall in search of an 'alternative lifestyle'. Moreover, that the 'incomers' tend to have a less direct interest in economic reproduction. This would seem to indicate an active and accelerated process of class restructuring, and the potential for a cleavage of interests in the economy and the reproduction of the locality. Interestingly, MK's transformation from a pressure group to a political party in 1967 was precipitated by a debate over the proposed accommodation of population 'overspill' from Greater London (Deacon, 1985, p. 243). One example of this restructuring is the action of other local interest groups, such as conservation lobbies. The ranks of these groups have been swollen by the inmigration of retirees and 'alternative lifestylers' in search of a rural idyll. These groups may be expected to oppose new development, particularly if it is close to residential areas. Again, there is potential for conflict with the indigenous population, CIDA uses the tactic of arguing that jobs of 'locals' are taken by incomers. Environmental concerns also have to be assuaged. Wight (1981) notes that CIDA's formation in 1974 was prompted as a response to a growth of antibusiness feeling amongst environmentalists. By the late 1970s they had sought to incorporate environmentalism within their own agenda arguing that small-scale development would satisfy environmentalists and CIDA supporters (quoted in Wight, 1981).

Some commentators argue that structure plan policies which accommodate population growth (in-migration) are effectively supporting the interests of migrants against the indigenous population (CIDA, 1976, p. 94; Dean *et al.*, 1988). It may be argued that the interests of large-scale capital are met by structure plan policies that allow limited expansion of industrial development in rural areas, but seek to concentrate it in urban areas, thereby providing access to a new labour market.[10] Other structure plan policies make provision for distribution activities on national and county transport routes. On one hand, these developments suit groups such as CIDA as they subsidize local business, making it more 'competitive' in the national market. However, on the other hand, centralized developments may threaten the reproduction of 'traditional' family roles, by drawing in females to the workforce (see Massey, 1984, p. 231). Hence, the struggle over the exact form of promotion of local business, and where it is located. The industrial estate can be seen to be centrally situated in such a struggle. It could be suggested that smaller, more remote, industrial estates often of a very 'basic' quality and with low cost accommodation may more closely support the interests of local capital.

Whilst there is no directive in the Structure Plan to develop industrial estates, policies do refer to the need to maintain a choice of sites for industry (in both location and size), as well as an adequate supply of land in total. In terms of the allocation of the use of this land, planners resist the allocation of industrial and serviced land to 'low density users' — defined as warehousing and distribution activities — in order to conserve farmland. Conveniently, this avoids threatening the interests of another powerful lobby of local capital in the County: farmers and landowners.

At different periods, the central and local state have supported various competing interests in the social and economic reproduction in order to maintain accumulation. Local government, organized on a different electoral basis to central government, may pursue conflicting policies to central government in order to satisfy its perceived electoral base. The interests of the nation may not be in the local interest; a good case in point may be regional policy. In Cornwall the resolution of this situation has necessitated heavy local investment in infrastructure, in recent years this has been supplemented by EC funds.

It can be concluded that local and national interests cut across, or

---

[10]Cornwall County Council (1979) *Structure Plan*, written statement; Chapter 7: Industrial Policies

infuse, lines of class conflict. Collective labour has been effectively margi-
nalized in Cornwall, the major line of cleavage which defines local politics
is that between local and national capital. Industrial estates are implicated
in the way in which these struggles for the control and location of
reproduction are carried out. Developing estates at all is seen by some as a
concession to national capitals, a policy that undermines local control. A
key component of the local social order is the specific nature of the
composition of the labour force along gender lines; again the opposition is
to female full-time working as it is considered to 'upset' the social order and
create competition for labour. The following section considers the nature
of industrial floorspace and employment changes more closely and to what
extent this can be attributed to the development of industrial estates.

Industrial Estate Development in the Context of Floorspace Changes in Cornwall

In Chapter 5 a detailed analysis of the emergence of the physical form of
industrial estates in Cornwall was presented. The aim of this section is to
complement the social and political context already covered earlier in this
chapter with a discussion of the immediate context of the development of
industrial floorspace and its associated employment. This will achieve the
objective of placing the development and use of industrial estates back into
their context. It was noted earlier that a comprehensive critical realist
analysis of the development of industrial estates requires—in addition to
an intensive survey of developers—an extensive survey of the industrial
estates themselves. An extensive survey of the condition of industrial
buildings was reported in Chapter 5. However, a further detailed survey of
employment and floorspace was necessary due to the lack of appropriate
data directly linking industrial floorspace, employment and economic
activity at either the establishment or industrial estate level (see Pratt,
1994). The survey carried out in June 1984 consisted of a questionnaire
implemented via a 'post and collect' method.[11] A 100% coverage of details
of all buildings situated on industrial estates was achieved for items such as
floorspace, site area, ownership, and the economic activity carried on at
each site. A 74% response rate was achieved for other information

---

[11] A key problem in the operationalization of this survey was the lack of an up to date
directory of the occupants and owners of buildings and sites on industrial estates. Both maps
of estates and the names of some occupants collated over a period of time from planning
records were made available by Cornwall County Council Planning Department. Unfortunately, this source was at least one year out of date, and partial in its coverage. The strategy
adopted for the survey was to send questionnaire forms to all of the occupants on the list.
Questionnaires were sent by post to occupants of industrial units on industrial estates, a date
was then specified when the form would be collected by hand. When the responses were
collected errors of occupation were rectified and new questionnaires distributed as appropriate.

TABLE 7.1. *Floorspace Changes 1974–1984 by District and Type*

	% Floorspace change 1974–1984		
	Manufacturing	Warehousing	All industry
Caradon	58.5	13.4	28.5
Carrick	8.4	13.4	10.8
Kerrier	5.4	21.7	11.3
North Cornwall	−0.5	35.5	17.4
Penwith	1.8	7.6	4.9
Restormel	41.2	30.2	35.0
Cornwall	14.2	21.9	18.0
England	−0.4	40.5	11.3

Source: DoE (various).

collected via the questionnaire, most significantly employment. This response rate was judged to be very good in the circumstances (see Healey, 1991).[12] The survey of industrial estates both updated and expanded upon an earlier sample survey of industrial estates carried out by Shaw and Williams in 1981 (see Shaw and Williams, 1981, 1982, 1985).

Information on industrial floorspace[13] collected by the Inland Revenue Office for rating and valuation purposes indicates that the growth of floorspace in Cornwall outstripped that of England for the period 1974–84 (see Table 7.1). However, these figures should not be taken at face value; considerable caution is required in the interpretation of the Inland Revenue statistics; especially with respect to the differences between the reporting of manufacturing and warehousing data.[14] As Table 7.1. indicates, the changes in the growth of warehousing floorspace obscure that of manufacturing change. The Inland Revenue classification results in a rather broader range of actual buildings being included in the warehousing category; from traditional warehouses to a large number of smaller stores and workshops (many associated with retail establishments) that

[12]As the main unit of analysis was the industrial estate, follow-up questionnaires were sent to estates where the total response rate fell below 50% of occupied premises in order to maintain an representative spread of responses.
[13]The term 'industrial floorspace' is used here as a generic term that includes those buildings classified by the Inland Revenue (IR) as covered warehouses, stores and workshops, and industrial. When referred to separately the usage followed here is to term manufacturing what the IR call industrial; warehousing covers what the IR call covered warehousing, stores and workshops.
[14]These statistics provide information on the floorspace and numbers of hereditaments at the county and district level for industrial and warehousing, stores and workshops (covered), warehouse (open storage), offices and retail establishments. These data are available for the years 1967, 1969 and annually from 1974–85. The statistical series was discontinued in 1985. The main drawbacks of their use are that the lowest spatial level of disaggregation is the local authority district, and that floorspace statistics are not linked, nor can they easily be, to specific employment data on individual firms, travel to work areas, or by specific land uses or agglomerations such as industrial estates (see Pratt, 1994).

TABLE 7.2. *Comparison of Average Sizes of Industrial Units 1974 and 1984*

Use	Average size of industrial units (m^2) 1974	1984
Manufacturing		
England	2317	2109
Cornwall	1129	936
Warehousing		
England	480	557
Cornwall	180	213
Industry		
England	1091	1032
Cornwall	310	340

Source: DoE (various).

would not normally be associated with industrial buildings. This makes the warehousing statistics a less reliable or representative indicator of change in industrial floorspace.

The components of total floorspace change in Cornwall and England have a markedly different character. England has experienced, as outlined in Chapter 4, a huge growth in warehousing floorspace and a decline in manufacturing floorspace. Whereas in Cornwall there was a smaller growth in warehousing[15] but a counter national trend — a substantial growth — in manufacturing floorspace. Much of the new manufacturing space in Cornwall, it will be argued, can be accounted for by the emergence of industrial estates. The average size of individual industrial buildings also accounts for differences between the amounts of floorspace devoted to warehousing and manufacturing (see Table 7.2). Generally, unit sizes devoted to warehousing have been getting larger, and those devoted to manufacturing have been getting smaller. Moreover, on average units are at least 50% smaller in Cornwall than in England as a whole.

At a smaller scale than county level considerable variation can be seen between different local authority districts with Caradon, Restormel and North Cornwall registering significant increases in floorspace (see Table 7.1). Once again the aggregated 'industrial' statistic obscures the volatile manufacturing changes. The most dramatic growth of manufacturing floorspace has been experienced in Caradon and Restormel. Notably North Cornwall has actually lost manufacturing floorspace, all of its industrial growth being accounted for by a greater than average warehousing growth. Table 7.3 illustrates the relative importance of floorspace by district; the distribution is surprisingly even, the only district performing

---

[15]A smaller growth in warehousing in Cornwall can be related to the peripheral location; if much of the national warehousing growth was in regional distribution centres, it is not surprising that Cornwall has failed to benefit as much as other more centrally located and better connected to the motorway network.

TABLE 7.3. *Percentage Distribution of Floorspace by District 1974, 1984*

District	1974			1984		
	Mfg.	W'hsg	All Ind.	Mfg.	W'hsg	All Ind.
Caradon	3.7	7.4	11.1	5.0	7.1	12.2
Carrick	10.1	9.6	19.6	9.3	9.2	18.5
Kerrier	13.3	7.6	21.0	12.0	7.9	19.8
N. Cornwall	9.3	9.2	18.5	7.9	10.5	18.4
Penwith	5.5	6.3	11.9	4.8	5.8	10.6
Restormel	7.9	10.0	17.9	9.4	11.1	20.5
Cornwall	49.9	50.1	100.0	48.3	51.7	100.0

Source: DoE (various).

TABLE 7.4. *Relationship of Industrial Floorspace Growth in Cornwall with the Stock of Industrial Estate Floorspace, 1984*

District	Ratio of industrial estate totals to that of all floorspace growth (1974–84)	Floorspace on ind. ests as % of all floorspace	Number of ind. ests	Number of units on ind. ests
Caradon	1.7	38	8	107
Carrick	1.9	18	7	123
Kerrier	5.4	55	8	212
N. Cornwall	2.8	41	13	245
Penwith	4.1	19	5	67
Restormel	0.7	18	5	67
Cornwall	2.1	32	46	821

Source: Survey, DoE (various).

out of character over the decade 1974–84 was Restormel which grew at a dramatic rate from an already significant base level. Interestingly, Caradon's growth is from a small initial base. Once again, North Cornwall can be seen as a relative, and well as a net, loser of manufacturing floorspace.

There is no comparable statistical source of industrial floorspace data that covers industrial estates. However, survey work carried in 1981 does suggest that industrial estates accounted for some 29% of all industrial floorspace; this had grown to 32% by 1984. At the district level Kerrier, North Cornwall and Caradon were notable in having a dominant representation of floorspace on industrial estates (see Table 7.4). Given the fact that the warehousing statistics are likely to be an over-representation, industrial estates may well account for a greater proportion of industrial floorspace in practice. Moreover, as noted in Chapter 5 much of the development of industrial estates has occurred in the years 1979–84. If we compare the floorspace found on industrial estates and that developed in

TABLE 7.5. *Average Sizes of Industrial Buildings on Industrial Estates in Cornwall, by Use, in 1984*

Use	Floorspace (m²)	%	Average size of unit (m²)	Industrial estates as % of all Cornish floorspace
Manufacturing	403,109	77	759	47
Warehousing	59,938	12	487	15
Vacant	56,883	11	390	62
All industrial units	519,930	100	650	32

Source: Extensive survey, DoE (1985), CCC (1986).

the decade 1974–84 it can be noted that the ratio of floorspace on industrial estates (most of which will have been developed post-1974) to that of all floorspace growth is greater than two to one (see Table 7.4). Thus, even allowing for demolition, industrial estates must account for a major proportion of the total growth experienced 1974–84. Significantly, the exception to the rule is Restormel. It is not surprising that this distortion should occur given, at that time, the relatively buoyant nature of the china clay industry dominating employment in that district.[16]

Table 7.5 shows that the major activities carried out on industrial estates in terms of the actual uses that the buildings are put to: manufacturing or warehousing.[17] The average manufacturing unit on an industrial estate was smaller, and that of the warehouse larger, than that for the Cornish average (compare with Table 7.2), this would suggest that buildings developed on estates are more likely to be representative of national trends than those not located on industrial estates. Nevertheless, industrial estates still account for a greater proportion of larger buildings than more generally in Cornwall; the average industrial unit located on an estate is more than twice the average size for Cornwall. The dominance of manufacturing floorspace on industrial estates is consistent with the larger than average manufacturing unit size. In this context it is not surprising that whilst industrial estates account for 32% of all floorspace in Cornwall, 47% of the manufacturing floorspace is located on industrial estates.

It is clear that industrial estates have become an increasingly important location for new industrial buildings particularly in Kerrier, North Cornwall and Caradon. This confirms the fact that industrial estates have

---

[16]The 1981 floorspace statistics originate from unpublished data collected by Shaw and Williams.

[17]This classification was derived from the responses by occupants to the survey. Basically activities classified under the Standard Industrial Classification (1980) as class 61,67,77, and 84 and activity 723 were allocated as warehousing, all others (mainly divisions 2,3 and 4) were allocated to manufacturing. No comparable data is available for earlier years.

TABLE 7.6. *Employment Change in Cornwall 1973–84*

Year	Male	Female	Total
1973	67,122	34,578	101,700
1977	72,093	53,220	125,313
1981	67,499	50,536	118,035
1984	67,108	53,714	122,822

Source: Census of employment.

played a significant role in the restructuring of the available locations of industrial activity in Cornwall over the period 1974–84. A further implication, one that is pertinent to the consideration of wider reproductive issues that are the focus here, is for the people seeking work from those firms which have become increasingly tied to industrial estates as locations. The following sub-section considers whether this pattern of increasing dominance in industrial estate floorspace is replicated with respect to employment.

Industrial Estate Development in the Context of Employment Changes in Cornwall

This section begins by considering the general context of employment change in Cornwall before moving on to both the differences between male and female employment, and the distribution of employment. Census of population data for the period 1971–81 indicates that the increase in the numbers of economically active persons in Cornwall (14%) was greater than the overall population increase in the same period (12%). The difference can be accounted for by the rapid growth in economic activity rates; predominantly amongst women. Statistics collected from the Census of Employment for the period 1981–84 show a further increase of 4% in overall employment numbers. The dynamics of change are also highlighted; significant increases are noted both in female and part-time employment, along with decreases in all male and full-time female employment. Whilst these trends are replicated at the national level, the rates of change are far greater for Cornwall.

Detailed figures[18] show that employment grew by 20.7% in the period 1973–84 (see Table 7.6). The overall contribution to total employment in Cornwall by those firms located on industrial estates grew from 4% in 1973

---

[18]The employment figures given by the Census of Employment (CE) are different to those of the Census of Population. CE figures do not include self-employed persons (estimated at 20% of the Cornish workforce), and the method of sampling used in the CE only samples firms employing more than 5 persons; this was increased to 20 in 1984 (in Cornwall 50% of firms employ 5 persons or less). On both counts this may lead to considerable inaccuracy. Data was not available for the CE for 1974, so 1973 was used. Publication of CE data is restricted by the 1947 Statistics of Trade Act. The data is used here with permission.

TABLE 7.7. *Employment Change in the Industrial Estates Subgroup in Cornwall 1973–84*

Year	Male	Female	Total	Sub-group as % of all employment
1973	n.a.	n.a.	35,426	35
1977	15,823	7,402	23,226	18
1981	20,965	6,117	27,082	23
1984	24,084*	7,350*	31,439*	19

n.a.—data not available.
*These figures do not correspond to those in Fig. 7.11 as they use the Census of Employment rather than the Census of Population as a base.
Source: Census of Employment (various); Census of Population, 1981.

to over 7% in 1984. However, it would be inappropriate to use these total employment figures as a point of comparison for the growth of employment on industrial estates as it would not be comparing like with like. Accordingly, an industrial estates subgroup has been derived. This subgroup contains all of the employment in those activities that might be considered likely to locate on an industrial estate.[19] This subgroup accounted for some 19% of total employment in the county 1984. As might be expected in a county with a historically weak manufacturing base the subgroup is smaller in Cornwall than it is in Great Britain as a whole where it accounts for 38% of all employment. Table 7.7 shows that the subgroup experienced variable performance in Cornwall; numerically, dramatic decline was observed in the period 1973–7, followed by recovery—almost to 1973 levels—through to 1984.[20]

Data derived from previous survey work undertaken on industrial estates in Cornwall suggests that an increasingly significant contribution to the accommodation of the employment in the subgroup has been made throughout the period 1973–84 (see Table 7.8). Given that the whole local economy was growing and that the subgroup still lagging behind the 1973 figures, in this period the consistent growth of industrial estates employment should be considered as significant.

<hr/>

[19]Those economic activities that are considered likely to occupy industrial estates are Divisions are 2–4 excluding Classes 21, 23 and 24 (mineral extraction and processing); plus Classes 61, 67, 77, 84 and Activity 723 (wholesale distribution and haulage) of the SIC (1980).
[20]The subgroup data for 1981 and 1984 (see Table 7.11) are different from Tables 7.7, 7.8 and 7.9 as they were modified to account for the under-representation of the Census of Employment data (the Census of Employment does not collect information on the self-employed, and it is a sample survey). The correction, +40%, was derived from a comparison with the 1981 Census of Population and the 1981 Census of Employment. Whilst the Census of Employment figure is satisfactory for longitudinal analyses, the corrected figure is more accurate for point in time comparisons of the employment totals both on industrial estates and in the subgroup.

TABLE 7.8. *Total Employment on Industrial Estates Compared to the Sub-group 1973–84*

Year	Subgroup	Industrial estates	Industrial estates as% of the subgroup
1973	39,323	5,673	14.4
1977	25,781	8,020	31.1
1981	30,610*	10,870	35.5
1984	35,542*	11,636	32.7

* these figures do not correspond to those in Figure 7.11 as they use the Census of Employment rather than the Census of Population as a base.
Sources: Shaw and Williams (1985), Survey, Census of Employment (various), Census of Population (1981).

TABLE 7.9. *Percentage of Women Employed in all Activities, Industrial Estates Subgroup, and on Estates 1977–1984 in Cornwall*

Year	All activities	Subgroup	Industrial estates
1977	42	32	n.a.
1981	43	23	27
1984	44	23	31

n.a.—no data available.
Sources: Census of employment, derived from Shaw and Williams (1985), extensive survey.

We can take this analysis a stage further and explore the breakdown of employment in terms of gender. Tables 7.6 and 7.7 (above) have already shown that female employment has increased significantly in Cornwall since 1973. However, this growth has been less significant in the subgroup. This is perhaps not surprising given the predominance of female employment in the service sector; plus, the greater propensity for part-time and casual employment in that sector. Nevertheless, Table 7.9 shows that the firms located on industrial estates have employed a progressively greater proportion of females than those in the subgroup more generally.

Data from both the 1981 and 1984 industrial estate surveys indicates that whilst firms locating on industrial estates have increased the numbers of persons working part-time, this sector of the workforce has not grown as much as in the subgroup as a whole. Male full-time employment has been greater on industrial estates than in the subgroup, and female employment has increased at a greater rate than in the subgroup (see Table 7.10). Overall, we can note a shift towards female employment on industrial estates. Significantly, given the concerns expressed by supporters of CIDA referred to above, those estates with greater than 40% female employment

TABLE 7.10. *Proportion of Male to Female Employment in Full-time and Part-time Work on and off Industrial Estates 1981, 1984*

Employment group	On estates		Estates subgroup	
	1981	1984	1981	1984
Full-time				
Male	71.5	65.2	71.3*	88.8
Female	24.7	27.7	28.7*	22.0
Part-time				
Male	1.0	2.3	n.a.	3.2
Female	2.8	4.8	n.a.	6.0

n.a.—data not available.
*full-time employment refers to both full and part-time employment.
Source: Calculated from Pratt *et al.* (1986; p. 38), Survey, Census of Employment 1981, 1984.

tended to be located away from larger towns and in more isolated settlements.

The spatial distribution of employment in 1984 is shown in Table 7.11. Generally, this pattern echos the distribution of floorspace on industrial estates detailed in Chapter 5 (see Fig. 5.14). Considered at the district level, North Cornwall and Kerrier have the largest representation in the subgroup, and Caradon the smallest (see Table 7.12). In terms of the gender of employees; notably higher representations of women can be found in North Cornwall and Kerrier. The impact of industrial estates on employment at the district level in 1984 is shown in Table 7.13. The broad distribution of employment is remarkably evenly balanced between districts, however, employment on industrial estates shows a rather greater variation by district than in the subgroup. Notably North Cornwall, Caradon and Kerrier have significant proportions of all of the subgroup employment located on industrial estates. Industrial estates play a relatively insignificant role in the distribution of employment in Carrick and Penwith.

In summary, it can be seen that industrial estates have progressively accounted for a greater proportion of employment in Cornwall. Moreover, they are structuring the location and distribution of employment opportunities both at an inter- and intra-district level. Employment change on industrial estates has shown a less significant trend towards casualization and part-time employment that might be expected (compared with the subgroup). The firms providing employment on industrial estates would appear to be faster growing and more buoyant generally than the subgroup; there is the possibility that growing firms are choosing an industrial estate location above a nonestate location, rather than there being better growth *in situ*. Nevertheless, it does indicate that industrial estates are the forum for a modernising trend in the structure of employment in the local economy.

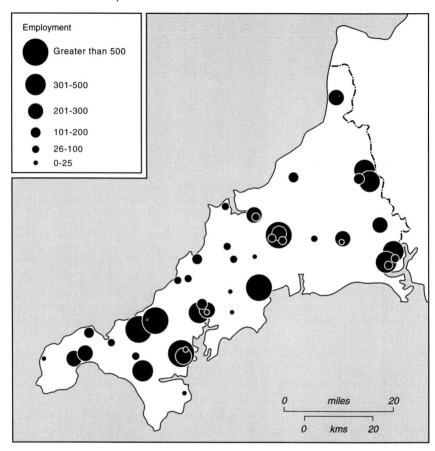

Fig. 7.1. Distribution of employment on industrial estates in Cornwall

Conclusion

The aim of this chapter has been to indicate the role that the industrial built environment may play in the re-production of one locality. As noted in earlier chapters, the industrial estate is an historically specific form of the industrial built environment. So, its impact—or role—will likewise be socially and historically situated. One of the problems in examining the role that the built environment has played in a locality is selecting the means of evaluation. This chapter has highlighted the fact that traditional evaluation methodology is infused with positivist assumptions which are antithetical to the sort of comprehensive evaluation sought here. More-over, the critical realist critique of the positivist position situates the

TABLE 7.11. *Relative Employment in Subgroup and all Employment, by District, by Gender in Cornwall 1984*

District	All employees			Industrial estates subgroup			Subgroup as % of all employment		
	Male	Female	Total	Male	Female	Total	Male	Female	All
Caradon	13187	12046	25251	2622	1520	4141	20	13	16
Carrick	17950	20644	38594	4594	2216	6809	26	11	18
N. Cornwall	14882	14487	29370	3863	2378	6241	26	16	21
Kerrier	19001	15891	34892	4988	2830	7818	26	18	22
Penwith	11502	11222	22724	2633	1554	4188	23	14	18
Restormel	20301	17982	38282	3932	2413	6345	19	13	17
Cornwall	96824	92290	189114	22632	12911	35542	23	14	19

Source: Census of Population (author's projection).

TABLE 7.12. *Relative Employment in Subgroup and on Industrial Estates by District, by Gender, in Cornwall 1984*

District	Industrial estates			Industrial estates subgroup			Industrial estates as % of Cornish total
	Male	Female	Total	Male (%)	Female (%)	All (%)	
Caradon	1155	681	1836	44	45	44	7
Carrick	687	205	892	15	9	13	2
N. Cornwall	2110	989	3099	55	42	50	11
Kerrier	2161	926	3087	43	33	39	9
Penwith	422	306	728	16	20	17	3
Restormel	1038	956	1994	26	40	31	5
Cornwall	7573	4036	11636	33	31	33	6

Source: extensive survey: Census of Population (author's projection).

production of knowledge about uneven development *within*, or as a part of, the process of development itself; not outside, or external to it. The implication of this insight that has been specifically explored in this chapter is to widen the realm of evaluation from the economic to include the political and the social.

What has emerged from this analysis is that the production of industrial estates should be considered to be situated within the local social formation. This chapter fleshes out the implication of the ways in which 'space matters' in such a context. As noted in Chapter 3, space can not be considered to exist in the abstract, only in concrete situations. Concrete situations are produced through the struggle over the process of the reproduction of industrial buildings (see Chapter 6) and the local political, social and economic context. In turn these buildings and their locations may enable or restrict the possible activities of industrialist, which in turn opens up possibilities for the employee.

In conclusion we can say that the development of industrial estates in Cornwall has facilitated the development of indigenous industry and in-migration of industry. In many cases it has opened up new employment opportunities, notably for women. This is, of course, not a neutral act but a highly political one. It may in time change the local balance of political power and social struggle in the locality. Whilst the Cornish economy has been restructured in the decade 1974–84 industrial estates have not been the 'cause'; nevertheless they have played a role in enabling and shaping the ways in which this restructuring has occurred. Perhaps the most obvious way has been in enabling the relocation of industry on to industrial estates.[21] As noted earlier, this has led to firms being subjected to potentially restrictive covenants on their activities. However, these new productive spaces may well have facilitated productive activities that might not otherwise have been possible. At present this question remains open, but it is one that will benefit from further research (see Ball and Pratt, 1994).

---

[21] Of those firms located on industrial estates in 1984 31% were new firms, 15% were branch plants and 54% were relocating firms (this latter figure contrasts with 45% in an earlier survey – see Pratt, Shaw and Williams, 1985, p. 36). Significantly, amongst those firms relocating to industrial estates the median distance moved was just 3 km.

8
Conclusion

Introduction

The objective of this chapter is to draw together the emergent themes of the book and to set them into a wider context. These themes do not only concern the form and location of industrial estates in Cornwall, but also more general issues such as the methodological and theoretical analysis of the uneven re-production of localities. The focus of discussion here has been limited to just one aspect of this wider argument—one that has previously been neglected in this context—that concerning the industrial built environment.

The production of space has been dealt with—particularly in relation to the urban environment—quite extensively by geographers, albeit at the abstract level. However, concrete forms of space—for example, the industrial built environment—have been ignored on the whole. Accordingly, the process of the provision and equipment of actual spaces and how they mediate, and are mediated by, the social, economic and political processes of reproduction have been inadequately addressed. Where the industrial built environment has received consideration it has been as an appendage to other aspects of development; as a commodity of the property development sector, or as part of the means of production of manufacturing activities. The relatively autonomous nature of the production and form of the industrial built environment—how and why it has changed and what relation this may bear to uneven development—has not been explored. Consequently, a key theme of this book has been to demonstrate how such considerations are important in any adequate explanation of the re-production of localities in their unique social, economic, political and spatial forms. The way that I have gone about exploring these issues rests heavily on the use of critical realism.

On Putting Critical Realism to Work

A significant amount of effort has been expended in the writing of this book in the exploration of what a critical realist methodology might constitute and how it may be operationalized. I have argued that one can only have critical realism when it is operationalized. In a nonoperational form it might simply be termed realism—signifying the lack of one half of what may best be called the dialectical process. The practicalities of putting critical realism to work—to derive adequate explanations—presents a stumbling block for prospective researchers.

I have found it useful to conceptualize the research process implied by critical realism as a consecutive engagement of theory and methodology, spiralling between the abstract and the concrete. This is represented in diagrammatic form in Fig. 8.1. This suggests a constant confrontation of method and theory—re-evaluating the adequacy of explanation of concrete events and the causal mechanisms that produce them—through all levels of abstraction. The process is permanently reiterative. This mode of proceeding might be compared with the more markedly linear and rigid form suggested by the, positivist, scientific method.

One of the practical problems that the critical realist research process throws up is how it should be reported. An important point of critique of positivism advanced by critical realists is the diurnal model of science which suggests that a gap—sometimes a canyon—exists between the rhetoric of scientific discovery (as recommended by the scientific method) and the actual practice. Both modes are based upon different ontological and causal logic. Hence, the imperative of bringing together research practice and its presentation.

The mode of research as presented in Fig. 8.1 is both cyclical and recursive. However, the structure of reading and writing is linear. If we force the research process into a linear mode for the purposes of presentation its logic will be misrepresented. At the same time the written presentation must be comprehensible. Whilst the presentation of jottings or a diary may be true to the practice, they may conceal the logic and philosophical basis of the argument. There is no immediate resolution to this problem other than cautioning the reader and raising the awareness of the restrictions of written forms and the way that communication is thus structured.

The implication is that the written form of this book does not immediately, or easily, disclose the research process that it is based upon. For example, the theoretical chapter, Chapter 3, could not have been written before the analytical chapters that follow. Whilst some earlier theoretical analysis was developed preceding the main analytical section, several reformulations took place as the analysis proceeded. Likewise the critical review of the literature on the industrial built environment, Chapter 2, although it is presented here before the theoretical section, Chapter 3, actually partially evolved out of that reformulation. These notes should

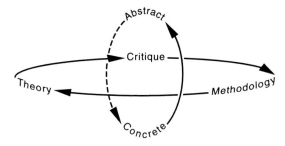

Fig. 8.1. The critical realist mode of research.

not be considered either as trivial or vain comments, but are offered in the spirit of a critical reflection on the social production of knowledge.

More specifically, methodology conceived in this way does allow the resolution of the type of difficulty Moos and Dear (1986) encountered with respect to idealist conceptions of actors. Just because one identifies a necessary relationship it does not mean that that role will always have the same form. For example, a rational abstraction identifies the development process as a set of necessary relations of capital, the means of production (land and materials), and labour. Exactly how these elements will be combined at any one time or place are clearly contingent upon the form of that society and the nature of class combination at any one time. Thus, in the concrete situation the developer may be one individual or a trans-national corporation. In other words, there are a variety of forms that the 'developer' may take. The exact specification of the developer will depend upon a whole range of contingent conditions, and so cannot be identified a priori. In the analysis detailed earlier, a developer's role was identified at the abstract level, but, in practice the activity of property development was found to be performed in a variety of different ways through both time and space. Hence, it was considered misleading (a contentless abstraction) to view the 'property developer' as a unitary category but one with a variety of expressions. Alertness to this variability was a key in the explanation of the variety of different outcomes of property development activity in the form of industrial estates.

The close integration of theory and methodology is implicit in the critical realist approach adopted in this book. It may be useful to make some comments on the implications of this integration in practice. A key stage in critical realist research is that of retroduction: the use of causal mechanisms to explain concrete events. As discussed above this is an iterative process, and one that it has been found useful to conceptualize in terms of 'levels' of theory. At the most abstract level, processes are decontextualized: the specificity of space and time are lost. At the most concrete level it is context that is everything. In order to conceptualize change a midpoint must be reached, whereby processes are set in their context. The notion of space-time distanciation is of particular use here: the sense of some continuity of institutions and practices across spatial and temporal boundaries.

A note of caution must be sounded here. Structures, although enduring, are constantly in the process of transformation. It is difficult to capture the idea of structure and the process of change at one and the same time. This translates into a practical research problem, in practice, institutions constituted by structures may be identified, but, they are themselves undergoing change. An example may illustrate this point. The practice of property development is necessary for the creation of new spaces and forms. But, property development is articulated differently at various places and times depending upon local contingencies. Different actors have carried out property development, while confusingly some are actually called property developers. The exact articulation of the practice of property development is contingent upon which actors are involved and how they are organized, as well as the particular historical and spatial context. It is this specificity that gives rise to the various industrial built environment 'events', one subgroup of which are industrial estates.

A further point relating to the role of theory in critical realist research concerns the understanding of inter-relationships. Whilst this emphasis on inter-relationships is very illuminating it can initially throw up too many of them and thus obscure rather than clarify analysis. Hence, for practical research reasons it is often useful to bracket out whole areas of process. It is important that this bracketing out is not an arbitrary 'cut' but one based upon rational abstraction: one involving causally related mechanisms. In this book the wider social and economic repercussions of the development of industrial estates: labour market restructuring, the labour process, class restructuring, state–civil society relationships, and capital–civil society relationships were touched upon in Chapter 8, but they would clearly ideally benefit from more sustained analysis in their own right.

Finally, there is the issue of the relationship between critical realism and social theory more generally. There have been numerous calls for the integration of mainstream social theory and human geography. However, many advise caution. For example, Gregson's (1987a) critique of previous attempts, specifically with respect to the integration of structuration and realism, were discussed in Chapter 3. Whilst rejecting Gregson's specific point about realism, a note of caution is still maintained here in the sense that 'free floating' theories are not compatible with critical realism if they are not rooted in a methodology consistent with it. Critical realism offers a guide to the practice of research and theory generation, both of which are inter-related. Thus, the adequacy of theories generated by other (metho-dological) practices may be questioned. Theorization is a mode of expla-nation; not an end in itself. Turning from the subject of theorization to its object, the following section moves on to discuss the explanation of the reproduction of the industrial built environment.

From Production to Re-production: Finding a Place for Space

Whilst much has been written about industrial location and economic development it has been viewed predominantly from the perspective of industry. One aspect of this fixation has been challenged by other writers, namely the uncritical acceptance of an identification with the political and economic interests of 'industry' (see Massey, 1977). The second aspect, which has as yet gone unchallenged, could perhaps be best expressed as the 'subject position'. The idea of a subject position conveys the idea of the locus of interest and concern of the reader/analyst; in this case from the point of view of the firm. Consequently analyses from this particular subject position are exclusively concerned with working out the processes and effects of a particular instance of the organization of production. All other things might be considered to be more or less related to this concern. Historically, geographers have been very concerned with one particular 'effect': that of space. Unfortunately, it is not the case that a simple shift of subject position—from industry to space—will resolve this problem. Rather, it is the conception of space and industry as separate analytical objects that constitutes the problem. This issue can be resolved by considering a reconceptualization of space.

Traditionally, space has been conceived of as a 'thing' within which objects are situated. One has only to scan a library shelf for titles of economic geography to get the point, for example, Lloyd and Dicken's (1977) *Location* in *Space* (my emphasis). Such a conception of space places it in a dualistic relationship with production: they are two separate realms. In this book I have attempted to present an alternative conception, one that considers space as part of, and internal to, social and economic processes: not as an optional extra.

Within such a reconceptualization, space is not longer just 'context' or 'contingency'; it is—in its reconceptualized social-spatial mode—something that is constructed by, and in turn constructs, social conditions. Space is no longer just 'there'. To paraphrase Bhaskar (1989, p. 38); we cannot create space[1] but we are constantly engaged in its transformation and its reproduction. A consequence is that in conventional analyses what is 'outside of production'—often termed reproduction—must now be considered to be inside or part of a whole. In fact the dualistic division of production and reproduction breaks down and is better resolved as a duality. Moreover, production, as a discrete and once and for all process, is

---

[1]Bhaskar is actually referring to society not space; but the argument still stands.

thus opened up into a dynamic, ongoing, process. Space is not static but dynamic, each moment new sites and buildings are created or destroyed, thereby opening up new realms of social struggle.

The Industrial Built Environment

So far all of this discussion of space may seem to have been very abstract. This will not do; I have argued earlier that to talk of space in abstraction is meaningless—a contentless abstraction. The task of reconceptualization is only half complete unless we consider actual, concrete, practices and outcomes. I have tried to show how, analytically, such an analysis foregrounds the role of the built environment and its re-production in explanations of industrial location and development. It is important to note that it is not being suggested that all other aspects of industrial location and development should be discarded; clearly there is still place for work on labour markets, industrial organization etc. though they may need to be reformulated to incorporate this reconceptualization of space. I would suggest that the key point of change in the nature of analyses of industrial location should be to consider the actual form of the industrial built environment, the relationship of its occupants to it, and the uses that it is put to. This must *inter alia* involve an analysis of how the industrial built environment *is itself* produced. In following through such an analysis it is necessary to consider the changing socio-spatial relations of industrial building provision.[2]

There is little previous research on private (or public) industrial landlordism, industrial building finance and structures of provision. This situation contrasts markedly with the existing body of research on residential building and, to a lesser extent, with that on commercial offices. In mitigation it might be added that the industrial rented sector has only really emerged in the UK in the last 25 years.[3] Research on industrial buildings, finance and structures of provision must necessarily begin from scratch; one of the major obstacles to carrying out such an analysis is the lack of data (see Pratt, 1994). The analysis that has been presented here, in Chapters 4 and 6, suggests that the structures of provision of industrial premises have changed over time and that new forms of development outcome have emerged; namely, industrial estates and science parks. These outcomes can be associated with particular changing relationships both *within and between* structures of provision and particular modes of

---

[2] I take this phrase from Ball's (1981; 1984) work on housing; however, crucially, I replace his *social* relations of provision with *socio-spatial* relations of provision to stress the incoorporation of the spatial dimension.
[3] Moreover, the UK is generally ahead of most other developed economies in developing such a trend in rented industial accomodation

industrial organization.[4] The main focus of this book has, obviously, been on aspects of building provision. Clearly, more work needs to be done on the detailed inter-relationships between the changing organization of industry and the structures of provision of industrial buildings.

Some significant events which characterize the changing structures of provision of the industrial built environment are the emergence of a relatively autonomous property sector, the growing autonomy of the production and ownership of industrial buildings; of those agents concerned more with dealing in the circulation of capital, rather than the production of commodities. Clearly, the variety of actors involved in property development and the roles that they have played have also changed over time. However, the specificity of these relationships is indicative of a distribution of economic power to control the re-production of the built environment. Examples include the domination of large financial institutions in some places and forms of industrial property, or the domination of property and production by transnational corporations, or the domination of the production of particular industrial units by the state. It is the specificity of these relationships and the associated structures of provision that give rise to the variety of development outcomes. The differential outcomes of the property development process may also be accounted for by the degree of risk undertaken by individual actors, which may in turn be dependent upon their organizational structure and institutional context. For example, there will be choices to be made about investments, but these will be more or less constrained by the locality operated within and the individual firm's use of productive technology (be they a 'developer' or an 'industrialist').

The concept of risk was found to be a useful one in the analysis of industrial property development presented in Chapter 6 as it emphasized the internal relationships between both the organization of the production of property and its eventual form and location. The temporal aspect of development activity was also highlighted, with particular respect to how actors might be able to act differently as risks change, or how they may reorganize themselves to bear different degrees of risk.

Industrial Estates in Context

The conclusion of the early chapters of this book was that there was a need for a more adequate explanation of the development of particular forms of the industrial built environment; specifically the most popular and numerous form, the industrial estate. It was argued that as industrial estates are a chaotic conception and, as such, it was not appropriate to develop an

---

[4]The popular conception of the restructuring of (manufacturing) production ought to be extended to include the restructuring of (industrial property) production. Analysis of the changing structures of provision wil be key to explaining such processes.

autonomous theory of industrial estates. Rather, it was considered more appropriate to identify the processes and mechanisms that give rise to the 'event' of an industrial estate, and to explain their development in specific places and times with recourse to the structures of provision and the contingent conditions pertaining there.

The argument presented in Chapter 3 emphasized the importance of conceptualizing industrial estates as temporally and spatially specific outcomes of the restructuring of the property development sector; this is an integral part of the restructuring of society more generally. The historical specificity of the changing mode of production of industrial space in particular localities—specifically industrial estates in Cornwall—was considered in the second half of this book. The industrial estate, the outcome of much of this activity is not a fixed event. Its form and specificity is changeable depending on the nature of the development and its relationship to industrial production and the role of the state. The eventual forms are at one and the same time past evidence of struggle within civil society and the setting for future struggles.

The industrial estate was set firmly in a wider context of other reproductive struggles in civil society. Social and economic restructuring were not considered to be the result of the development of industrial estates but rather as facilitated by them. The very nature of the struggle to support or oppose their development was considered to be an aspect of wider struggles over the exact nature of the social and economic reproduction of a particular locality. Moreover, the analysis points to the fact that there is a necessary spatial dimension to these social relations of production—the specific structures of provision—and that the location, form and terms of provision of such buildings have implications: for the potential users of those buildings, those who gain direct employment from firms using them, and the localities dominated by such employment.

It is impossible to specify, in the abstract, what actual form development will take in any one locality without detailed, theoretically informed, empirical analysis. Accordingly, Chapters 5, 6 and 7 sought to show how the emergence of this form played out in one locality, and how it affected the reproduction of that locality. They demonstrated the complex way in which property development operates. Above all they showed that the industrial built environment becomes situated—necessarily—within other struggles, forming the theatre for them. The built environment may also be used as a tool to regulate and control social reproduction. Hence, the importance of analyses of the struggles over the control of the provision of the built environment. I would not pretend to have more that scratched the surface of such an analysis here. However, I hope that the analysis presented here has been sufficient to demonstrate the value of using a critical realist approach to develop a more adequate explanation and understanding of the nature of uneven re-production.

Appendix

Industrial Estates: A Catalogue of Ideal Forms

Introduction

Researchers, managers and planners charged with establishing or managing industrial estates have sought to establish—in vain—a set of universal criteria of the factors contributing to their success. For the most part these criteria have consisted of various empirical measures of the physical dimensions and layout of the infrastructure. On one hand there is the assumption that infrastructure will be developed—seemingly, automatically—because there is a real or anticipated demand for it. Precious little concern is directed at the nature or the means of provision of the infrastructure. On the other hand, the nature or selection of the firms that occupy these developments or the significance of the inter-relationships established between firms and how these might be further encouraged or facilitated is neglected. This appendix represents an uneasy catalogue of the idealized nature of industrial estates; it is a testament to their under-analysis.

Management and Zoning

In most of the literature, the subdivision of land uses is taken as a self-evident fact of the existence of industrial estates. It is worth exploring the idea in a little more detail as it links two important concepts; control and zoning. In order to justify zoning Holford (1938, p. 233) argues that, despite being disrupted by the early industrial revolution, historical precedence shows that the zoning of industry is 'natural'. Holford is arguing for a market intervention by making it seem natural. However, free-marketeers who might otherwise be expected to argue that zoning constitutes a barrier to free competition, were not opposed to the idea. As Goodman explains

"... zoning might put controls on entrepreneurial abilities to develop their land in whatever way they wished, but even more importantly it could stabilize and increase property values" (Goodman, 1972, p. 189).

Roterus (1956, p.1) shares such a view comparing the industrial estate with the residential subdivision where, he argues, it benefits the occupant, developer and the community. Wagner (1957, p. 132) supports this idea with particular reference to the industrial estate — ". . . owners of larger and more stable factories . . . maintain the property values of their investments". Hartshorn (1973, p. 3) also suggests that ideally, industrial estates should be,

> ". . . suitably zoned to protect the area surrounding it from being devoted to lower uses. The management is charged with the continuing responsibility of preserving compatibility between park [industrial estate] and community as well as protecting the investment of the developers and tenants".

There is clearly an association of subdivision of land (zoning) and control of space (through management and planning) by particular groups. In this case the unequal power relationship is seen as legitimate and even desirable.

Bredo (1960) also pays considerable attention to the need for industrial estates to be managed or planned, particular areas include the layout, location, selection of occupants, and financing. This practice has been elevated to a generalized policy in reports by the United Nations (1962a,b), where the need for restrictive covenants on occupants, and admission policies are stressed. On a larger scale research in the United States indicates the nature of competition between 'good' and 'bad' industrial estate developments.

By ignoring the differential power relationships, the theoretical benefits of monopolies to both the estate developer in financial terms, and the individual firm in terms of infrastructure and linkages, are presented as mutually beneficial. However, there is disagreement over the exact size that estates should be in practice to best achieve these benefits.

Size

One way of tackling the issue of ideal size has been to adopt a naturalistic approach and simply take an average of existing estates and express this as the ideal. Others are more concerned with explanation rather than description, and have related size specifically to agglomeration economies. Holford (1939, p. 158) suggested a figure of between 20 and 40 ha for the ideal size of an estate.[1] It was argued that too small an area can lead to the scattering of industry on numerous estates as well as being an uneconomic size for the provision of communal services and transport. Industrial

---

[1]To give some idea, a football pitch is about 4 ha in area.

estates larger than 60 ha only succeed, Holford argued, in areas of special advantage such as near large towns or ports. Many commentators have simply repeated, or quoted Holford's figures (see United Nations 1962a, b, 1968). In other contexts different size ranges have been recommended, for example in rural areas Quigly (1968, p. 201) suggests a size range of 12–40 ha as ideal, and Brown (1966, p. 17) 80 ha as a maximum in British New Towns.

Clearly firm size will be an important factor in determining the 'ideal size'. This is implicitly articulated by Bredo (1960, p. 31) who notes that both tangible (evaluated in monetary terms) and intangible benefits, similar to those gained by the internal economies of scale of large firms, can be achieved by grouping small firms together on an estate. By acknowledging this inter-relationship Bredo (1960, p. 33) also suggests that the optimum size of estates will depend upon the facilities provided there. The United Nations (1968, p. 29) note that "...generally the bigger the estate the more economic the provision of services". Elsewhere it is suggested that larger estates benefit by making more economic use of infrastructure, and attracting capital investment (United Nations, 1962b, p. 432).

On the other hand, it may be argued that estates should not be too large as they will be prone to traffic congestion and complicate the administration of the estate. However, Quigly (1968, p. 202) notes that on small-scale estate the dis-economies of scale may be offset by social (intangible) benefits. The United Nations (1962b, p. 25) consider that 12–20 ha should be the minimum size unless there is a social policy, and that there are few cases where the construction of estates over 40 ha is appropriate.

The optimum size will clearly be dependent upon the objectives of the estate, and the type of industry on it as well as wider social and cultural factors. For example, in India it was noted that 12 ha could be regarded as large (United Nations, 1962a, p. 432), whereas in Britain it would have been small (Quigly, 1968). One set of United Nations (1966, p. 24) guidelines simply suggest that the estate should be large enough to achieve economies of scale in provision of the services and special buildings .

Design

Drawing upon the new standards of urban design being developed with respect to housing at the time, Holford also had firm views as to the appropriate width of roads to carry traffic and the amount of space left for expansion of premises. Holford suggested the practice, later adopted by English Estates, of allowing 100% expansion space on developed plots (except in the case of smaller 'workshop units'). Much later similar concern for design and circulation was expressed by the United Nations (1962a, p. 28) who recommended that equal proportions of space be given up to factory units, transport/circulation, and open space on an industrial estate as a whole. They were less generous than Holford in their recommendation that no more than two thirds of any individual plot be occupied by factory units.

As with size, these recommendations are subject to variation in the size of the estate overall. For example, on smaller estates it was argued that there should be more open space. As estates get larger, it is argued, a smaller proportion should be given over to administration and ancillary uses and a greater proportion to factories (Lang Wong, 1962, p. 215). Provision of expansion space can be problematic, giving estates an unfinished appearance which may be considered as a disincentive to potential occupants. McConnell (1967, p. 961) suggests the need for landscaping to avoid this problem. More recently the degree of landscaping has been related to image. Generally the greater the anticipated 'office' content the greater the amount of green open space, this is conveyed by the substitution of 'estate' with 'park', i.e. 'Business Park' and 'Science Park'.

There has been debate amongst planners as to the appropriate 'density' of accommodation of industrial land use generally (see Tempest, 1982). In this case density refers to the number of persons employed per area of building or plot of land. Much of the information collected fails to adequately distinguish between estate and non estates situations, although Gentleman and Clark (1977, p. 8) and Lever (1974) offer some interesting observations, noting that densities are two and a half times higher on estates than off. The reason given is that nonproductive land is externalized, in other words: economies of scale. Historical material has been collected by Lever (1974, p. 37), who suggests that densities have fallen over time. This is also supported by Fothergill and Gudgin's (1982, p. 104) findings of increasing capital intensity of manufacturing activity in the post-1960 period. However, it must be noted that Fothergill and Gudgin's findings are not supported by Tempest's (1982) analysis. This review, of both on and off estate employment densities, was disaggregated at the local level whereas Fothergill and Gudgin's work uses gross employment statistics for the country as a whole.[2]

Communal Facilities

A point that is much emphasized in the planning literature concerns the benefits of a wide range of infrastructure services for firms.

---

[2]Collections of density figures for British estates can be found in Logie (1952), Adeolu (1961), and Bale (1972), and internationally in Muncy (1954), Bredo (1960), and United Nations (1962a, 1965). However, caution is needed in their interpretation due to the multiplicity of definitions of density used. A recent concern over the densities of manufacturing and nonmanufacturing users on industrial estates has been reported by Shaw and Williams (1985). However, their research indicates that there is little difference in densities between manufacturing and service users (Shaw and Williams, 1985, Table 5).

"Dispersion nullifies the advantages of communal services, the planned expansion space, of cheaper power, of feeder factories, and of the practice so common amongst the lighter type of industries and industrial services, of the taking in of one another's washing" (Holford, 1938, p. 234).

It is suggested by some that the provision of communal facilities is crucial to the success of industrial estates (Bredo, 1960). It is this point that the early descriptive reviews considered important (PEP, 1936; Wolton, 1938).

Whilst regarded as fundamental to the industrial estate, few estates have in practice provided communal facilities. Kirkby Estate, established by a local authority, is an interesting case in point. Originally, it had many communal facilities provided (bank, post office, and canteen). However, due to lack of support they quickly fell into disuse. Gentleman (1970) links this fact to the balance of firm sizes on the estate . He argues that larger firms internalize such facilities, whilst the rapid turnover of smaller firms made continuity of support for the facilities problematic. Smaller estates were not considered large enough to make the provision of communal facilities economical (Wrigley, 1959, p. 479). Ironically, it is the smaller firms that should have most to gain from locating on estates, both through inter-trading and access to communal facilities to enable them to compete with larger firms with their internal economies.

Advance Factory Units

The availability of factory units for rent in advance of demand is central to the concept of the industrial estate (Niesing, 1970, p. 7 and Henderson, 1980). The first rented units at Slough came about by chance circumstances (Slough, 1970), but were successfully copied elsewhere. In particular they were being cited by the committee that called for the establishment of the first British industrial estates (HMSO, 1936, p. 13). Many researchers have confirmed the point that vacant factory space is important to attract firms.[3] Allen (1951) explained that in the case of small firms the availability of buildings 'plugged the credit gap' that many small firms experience in their early days. This has been supported by recent material looking at small firms more generally (Falk, 1982).

In many of the papers cited above, the provision of buildings is considered important, or second in importance to the availability of labour in an area. The design of advance factory units (as used on estates) has been influenced by the perceived need of firms to get into them with the minimum delay (Slowe, 1981). Thus, a rather standard, but flexible design

---

[3]See Trottman-Dickinson (1961, p. 50), Castree (1966, p. 151), Cameron and Clark (1966, p. 163), Keeble (1965, p. 21), and Cloke and Edwards (1983, p. 16).

has been favoured.[4] The idea of rented property is that firms can quickly expand and move a short distance with the minimum of disruption. Considerable emphasis has been placed within publicly funded estates, on the benefits of allowing for expansion space. This objective implies that a range of different size factory units will be available on the estate at any given time. There are two objectives to such policies; to support small firms and to maintain tenants in a landlord's properties. The exact size of building that should be provided has also been a point of contention. As with the size of estates in practice, smaller buildings have become most popular in the UK in the 1980s and 1990s. Most researchers fall back—in teleological desperation—on an argument supporting the necessity of the considering local circumstances as well as the objectives of setting up the estate in the first place.

---

[4]See Holford (1938) and McConnell (1967, p. 959). See also Brett (1984) on the architectural styles employed.

References

AIC (1965) *The Economy and Industrial Development of the South West*, Wheaton, Exeter.

ADAMS, D. (1990) Meeting the needs of industry? The performance of industrial land and property markets in inner Manchester and Salford. In Healey, P. and Nabarro, R. (eds) *Land and Property Development in a Changing Context*, Gower, Aldershot.

ADEOLU, O. (1961) Kirkby industrial estate: an instrument for industrial planning. Unpublished MA dissertation, Department of Civic Design, University of Liverpool.

AGLIETTA, M. (1979) *A Theory of Capitalist Regulation: The US Experience*, New Left Books, London.

ALLEN, G. (1929) *The Industrial Development of Birmingham and the Black Country, 1860–1927*, George Allen and Unwin, London.

ALLEN, G. (1951) The growth of industry on trading estates 1920–39, with special reference to Slough trading Estate. *Oxford Economic Papers New Series* 3, 272–300.

ALLEN, J. (1983a) In search of a method: Hegal, Marx and realism. *Radical Philosophy* 35, 26–33.

ALLEN, J. (1983b) Property relations and landlordism—a realist approach. *Environment and Planning* D1, 191–203.

ALLEN, J. and McDOWELL, L. (1989) *Landlords and Property: Social Relations in the Private Rented Sector*, Cambridge University Press, Cambridge.

ALONSO, W. (1964) *Location and Land Use: Toward A General Theory of Land Rent*, HUP, Cambridge, Mass.

ALTHUSSER, L. (1969) *For Marx*, Penguin, Harmondsworth.

AMBROSE, P. (1986) *Whatever Happened to Planning?*, Methuen, London.

AMBROSE, P. and COLENUTT, B. (1975) *The Property Machine*, Penguin, Harmondsworth.

AMIN, A. and ROBINS, K. (1990) The re-emergence of regional economies? The mythical geography of flexible accumulation. *Environment and Planning* D8, 7–74.

APPLEYARD, K. (1938) The future of trading estates. In Wolton, D. (ed.) *Trading Estates*, 30–36, Ed Burrow, London.

ARMSTRONG, H. and FILDES, S. (1989) Industrial development initiatives in England and Wales: the role of district councils. *Progress in Planning* 30(2), 91–156.

BAGGULEY, P., MARK-LAWSON, J. SHAPIRO, D., URRY, J., WALBY, S. and WARDE, A. (1990) *Restructuring: Place, Class and Gender*, Sage, London.

BALCHIN, W. (1983) *The Cornish Landscape* (revised edn), Hodder and Stoughton, London.

BALE, J. (1972) The development of industrial estates with special reference to South Wales 1936–69. Unpublished M.Phil thesis, University of London.

BALE, J. (1974a) Towards a definition of the industrial estate: a note on a neglected aspect of urban geography, *Geography* 59, 31–34.

BALE, J. (1974b) Toward a geography of the industrial estate, *The Professional Geographer* 26(3), 291–297.

BALE, J. (1976) *Industrial Estates: A Bibliography and Geographical Information*, Council of Planning Librarians Exchange Bibliography No. 1022, Monticello, Illinois, U.S.A.

216   *Uneven Re-production*

BALE, J. (1977) Industrial estate development and location in post-war Britain, *Geography* 62, 87–92.

BALE, J. (1978) Externality gradients, *Area* 10, 334–336.

BALL, M. (1981) The development of capitalism in housing provision, *International Journal of Urban and Regional Research* 5, 145–177.

BALL, M. (1983) *Housing Policy and Economic Power: The political economy of owner occupation*, Methuen, London.

BALL, M. (1984) Forms of housing production—the birth of a new concept or the creation of a cul-de-sac, *Environment and Planning* A16, 261–268.

BALL, M. (1986) The built environment and the urban question, *Environment and Planning* D4, 447–464.

BALL, R. and PRATT, A. C. (1994) (eds) *Industrial Property: Policy and Economic Development*, Routledge, London.

BARR, B. (1983) Industrial parks as locational environments: a research challenge. In *Spatial Analysis, Industry and the Industrial Environment*, Volume 3, Regional economics and industrial systems, 423–440, Wiley, London.

BARR, B. and MATTHEWS, A. (1982) Agglomeration economies in public and private industrial parks: possible differences in firm's utilization of metropolitan location environments. In Collins, L. (ed.) *Industrial Decline and Regeneration*, pp. 187–201.

BARRAS, R. and FERGUSON, D. (1985) A spectral analysis of building cycles in Britain, *Environment and Planning* A17, 1369–1391.

BARRAS, R. and FERGUSON, D. (1987) Dynamic modelling of the building cycle: 1. Theoretical framework, *Environment and Planning* A19, 353–367.

BARRETT, S., STEWART, M. and UNDERWOOD, J. (1978) The land market and the development process, *Occasional Paper No. 2*, School for Advanced Urban Studies, University of Bristol.

BARRETT, S. and WHITING, G. (1983) Local authorities and land supply, *Occasional Paper No. 10*, School for Advanced Urban Studies, University of Bristol.

BARRINGTON, G. (1970) *West Cornwall Study*, Cornwall County Council, Truro.

BATEMAN, M. (1985) *Office Development: A Geographical Analysis*, Croom Helm, London.

BEAUREGARD, R. (1988) In the absence of practice: The locality research debate, *Antipode* 20(1), 52–59.

BELLANDI, M. (1989) The industrial district in Marshall: Goodman *et al.* (op cit), 136–152.

BERGER, J. and LUCKMANN, T. (1972) *The Social Construction of Reality*, Penguin, Harmondsworth.

BHASKAR, R. (1978) *A Realist Theory of Science*, (2nd edn), Harvester, Brighton.

BHASKAR, R. (1979) On the possibility of social scientific knowledge and the limits to naturalism. In Mephan, J. and Ruben, D. (eds) *Issues in Marxist Philosophy*, 55–106.

BHASKAR, R. (1986) *Scientific Realism and Human Emancipation*, Verso, London.

BHASKAR, R. (1989) *The Possibility of Naturalism: A Philosophical Critique of the Contemporary Human Sciences* (2nd edn), Harvester Wheatsheaf, Brighton.

BLUNDEN, J. (1970) The renaissance of the Cornish tin industry, *Geography* 55, 331–335.

BLUNDEN, J. (1972) The decision-making process. In *Economic Geography: Industrial Location Theory D281, Block 11, Unit 7*, 61–81, Open University Press, Milton Keynes.

BODDY, M. (1979) Investment by financial institutions in commercial property, pp. 17–19. In Boddy, M. (ed.) *Land, Property, Finance, Working Paper No. 2*, School for Advanced Urban Studies, University of Bristol.

BODDY, M. (1981) The property sector in late capitalism: the case of Britain. In Dear, M. and Scott, A. (eds) *Urbanisation and Urban Planning in Capitalist Society*, 267–287, Methuen, London.

BODDY, M. (1982) Local government and industrial development. *Occasional Paper No. 7*, School for Advanced Urban Studies, University of Bristol.

BODDY, M. (1983) Changing public-private sector relationships in the industrial development process. In Young, K. and Mason, C. (eds) *Urban Economic Development*, 34–52, Macmillan, London.

BODDY, M. and BARRETT, S. (1980) Local government and the industrial development process. *Working Paper No. 6*, School for Advanced Urban Studies, University of Bristol.

BOGDEN, R. and TAYLOR, S. (1975) *Introduction to Qualitative Research Methods: A Phenomenological Approach to the Social Sciences*, Wiley, London.

BOURDIEU, P. (1977) *Outline of a Theory of Practice*, Cambridge University Press, Cambridge.

BOURDIEU, P. (1984) *Distinction*, Routledge & Keegan Paul, London.

BOURN, M. (1978) The increasing importance of industrial parks and their role in intermediate size urban areas. *A.I.D.C. Journal* 8(1), 41–88.

BRADLEY, T. and LOWE, P. (1984) (eds) *Locality and Rurality: Economy and Society in Rural Areas*, GeoBooks, Norwich.

BREDO, W. (1960) *Industrial Estates — Tool for Industrialisation*, The Free Press, Glencoe, U.S.A.

BRETT, P. (1984) Evolution of the species, *Building* 247(50), Industrial Buildings Supplement, 10–13.

BROWN, C. (1966) Successful features of the planning of new town industrial estates, *Journal of the Town Planning Institute* 51(1), 15–18.

BURROWS, R. (1989) Some notes towards a realistic realism: the practical implications of realistic philosophies of science for social research methods, *The International Journal of Sociology and Social Policy* 9(4), 46–63.

BYRNE, T. (1985) *Local Government in Britain* (3rd edn), Penguin, Harmondsworth.

CADMAN, D. (1984) Property finance in the UK in the post-war period. *Land Development Studies* 1, 61–82.

CADMAN, D. and AUSTIN-CROWE, L. (1983) *Property Development*, (2nd edn) Spon, London.

CADMAN, D. and CATALANO, A. (1983) *Property Development in the UK: Evolution and Change*, Centre for Advanced Land Use Studies, Spon, London.

CAESAR, A. (1949) Devon and Cornwall. In Daysh G. (ed) *Studies in Regional Planning*, 197–223, Philip, London.

CAMERON, G. and CLARK, B. (1966) Industrial movement and the regional problem, *Occasional Paper No. 5*, University of Glasgow social and environmental studies, Oliver and Boyd, Glasgow.

CAMINA, M. (1974) Local authorities and the attraction of industry. *Progress in Planning* 3, 83–182.

CANNADINE, D. (1980) *Lords and Landlords, Aristocracy and the Towns*, Leicester University Press, Leicester.

CARDOSO, A. and SHORT, J. (1983) Forms of housing production: initial formulations, *Environment and Planning* A15, 917–928.

CARNEY, J. (1980) Regions in crisis: accumulation, regional problems and crisis formation. In Carney, J., Lewis, J. and Hudson, R. (eds) *Regions in Crisis*, Croom Helm, London.

CARNEY, J. and LEWIS, J. (1977) Accumulation, the regional problem and nationalism. In Batey, P. (ed.) *London Papers in Regional Science 8: Theory and Method in Urban and Regional Analysis*, Pion, London.

CARNEY, J., HUDSON, J., IVE, G. and LEWIS, J. (1976) Regional underdevelopment in late capitalism: a study of North East England. In Masser, I. (ed.) *London Papers in Regional Science 6: Theory and Practice in Regional Science*, Pion, London.

CARNEY, J., LEWIS, J. and HUDSON, R. (1977) Coal combines and inter-regional uneven development in the UK. In Massey, D. and Batey, P. (eds) *London Papers in Regional Science 7: Alternative Frameworks for Analysis*, Pion, London.

CASTELLS, M. (1977) *The Urban Question*, Edward Arnold, London.

CASTELLS, M. (1983) *The City and the Grassroots*, Blackwell, Oxford.

CASTELLS, M. (1989) *The Information City*, Blackwell, Oxford.

CASTREE, J. (1966) An investigation of industrial estates in Wales. Unpublished MA Thesis, University of Wales, University College Swansea.

Central Statistical Office (1987) *Economic Trends Annual Supplement*, HMSO, London.

Central Statistical Office (1992) *Economic Trends Annual Supplement*, HMSO, London.

CHALKEY, B. and PERRY, M. (1982) On using social geographical concepts and approaches in the study of industrial location. *Discussion Papers No. 14*, University of Southampton, Department of Geography.

CHALMERS, A. (1982) *What is this Thing Called Science?* (2nd edn), Open University Press, Milton Keynes.

218 Uneven Re-production

CHAMBERLAIN, W. (1938) Builders in the trading estates scheme. In Wolton, D. (ed.) *Trading Estates*, 73–74, Burrow, London.

CHERRY, G. (1982) *The Politics of Town Planning*, Longman, London.

CHRISTALLER, W. (1966) *Die zentralen orte in Suddeutschland*, Jena (1933), transl. C. Baskin as *Central Places in Southern Germany*, Prentice Hall, London.

CLARKE, L. (1980) Subcontracting in the building industry. In: The production of the built environment, 35–53, *Proceedings of the Bartlett International Summer School, No. 2*, University College, London.

CLARKE, L. (1991) *Building Capitalism*, Routledge, London.

CLARKE, G. and DEAR, M. (1981) The state in capitalism and the capitalist state. In Dear, M. and Scott, A. (eds) *Urbanisation and Urban Planning in Capitalist Society*, 45–51, Methuen, London.

CLOKE, P. and EDWARDS, G. (1983) The industrial estate business in Newtown, Mid-Wales. *Planning Outlook* 26(1), 14–17.

COCHRANE, A. (1987) What difference the place makes: the new structuralism of locality. *Antipode* 19(3), 354–363.

COCHRANE, A. (1989) Britain's political crisis. In Cochrane, A. and Anderson J. (eds) *Politics in Transition*, 34–66, Sage, London.

COCKBURN, C. (1977) *The Local State*, Pluto, London.

COOKE, P. (1983) *Theories of Planning and Spatial Development*, Hutchinson, London.

COOKE, P. (1986) The changing urban and regional system in the UK. *Regional Studies* 20(3), 243–251.

COOKE, P. (1987) Clinical inference and geographic theory. *Antipode* 19(1), 69–78.

COOKE, P. (1989) (ed.) *Localities*, Unwin Hyman, London.

Coopers and Lybrand/Drivers Jonas Associates (1980) *Provision of Small Industrial Premises*, Department of Industry, London.

CORNELIUS, A. and SMITH, G. (1986) RTZ to axe 1000 at Cornish tin mines. *The Guardian* 29.4.86.

Cornwall County Council (1952) *Development Plan, Report of Survey, Part I: The County*, Wheaton, Exeter.

Cornwall County Council (1981) *Structure Plan: Explanatory Memorandum*, Cornwall County Council, Truro.

Cornwall County Council (1985) *Economic Policies and Programmes 1985*, Cornwall County Council, Truro.

Cornwall County Council (1986) *Economic Policies and Programmes 1986*, Cornwall County Council, Truro.

Cornwall County Council (1988) *Economic Policies and Programmes 1988*, Cornwall County Council, Truro.

Cornwall Industrial Development Association (1976) *The Economy of Cornwall*, Cornwall Industrial Development Association, Truro.

COLEMAN, A. (1990) *Utopia on Trial* (2nd edn), Hilary Shipman, London.

CONZEN, M. (1983) Historical geography: changing spatial structure and social patterns of Western cities. *Progress in Human Geography* 7, 88–107.

COX, K. and MAIR, A. (1989) Levels of abstraction in locality studies. *Antipode* 21, 121–32.

CRAIB, I. (1992) *Anthony Giddens*, Routledge, London.

CSO (1991a) *Business Monitor MQ5: Insurance Companies' and Pension Funds' Investments*, Third Quarter, Tables 4 and 17, HMSO, London.

CSO (1991b) *Financial Statistics*, May, HMSO, London.

CULLEN, G. (1961) *Townscape*, Architectural Press, London.

CULLINGWORTH, J. (1983) *Town and Country Planning in Britain* (9th edn), Allen and Unwin, London.

CZARTORYSKI, R. (1975) Factories—for sale or rent. *Trade and Industry* 19, 757–753.

DALE, A. *et al.* (1988) *Doing Secondary Analysis*, Unwin Hyman, London.

DALTON, A. (1987) *Turn Left at Land's End*, Red book publications, London.

DARLOW, C. (1982) (ed.) *Valuation and Development Appraisal*, Estates Gazette, London.

DARWENT, D. (1969) Growth poles and growth centres in regional planning—a review. *Environment and Planning* A1, 5–32.

DAVIS, W. (1951) The nature and significance of trading estates with special reference to the Treforest and Slough estates. Unpublished MA Thesis, University of Wales, Aberystwyth.

DAWE, A. (1970) The two sociologies. *British Journal of Sociology* 21, 207–218.

DEACON, B. (1985) The electoral impact of Cornish nationalism. In Luain C. O. (ed.) *For a Celtic Future*, pp. 243–252, Celtic Leauge, Dublin.

DEACON, B., GEORGE, A. and PERRY, R. (1988) *Cornwall at the Crossroads?*, CoSERG, Redruth.

DEAN, K., BROWN, B. and PERRY, R. (1984) Counterurbanisation and the characteristics of persons migrating to West Cornwall. *Geoforum* 15(2), 177–190.

DEAR, M. (1988) The postmodern challenge: reconstructing human geography. *Transactions of the Institute of British Geographers* 13(3), 262–274.

DEAR, M. and CLARK, G. (1978) The state and geographical process: a critical review. *Environment and Planning* A10, 173–183.

DEAR, M. and MOOS, A. (1986) Structuration theory in urban analysis: 2 empirical application. *Environment and Planning* A18, 351–373.

DEAR, M. and SCOTT, A. (eds) (1981) *Urbanisation and Urban Planning in Capitalist Society*, Methuen, London.

DEAR, M. and WOLCH, J. (eds) (1989) *The Power of Geography*, Unwin Hyman, London.

Debenham, Tewson and Chinnocks (1982) *Money into Property 1970–1982*, Debenham, Tewson and Chinnocks, London.

Debenham, Tewson and Chinnocks (1988) *Money into Property*, Debenham, Tewson and Chinnocks, London.

Debenham, Tewson and Chinnocks (1989a) *Money into Property*, Debenham, Tewson and Chinnocks, London.

Debenham, Tewson and Chinnocks (1989b) *Banking on Property*, Debenham, Tewson and Chinnocks, London.

Department of Trade and Industry (1988) *Releasing Enterprise*, HMSO, London.

Department of the Environment (various) *Commercial and Industrial Floorspace Statistics*, HMSO, London.

Department of Trade and Industry (1973) Memorandum of the DTI minutes to the select committee of regional development initiatives, *House of Commons Papers*, HMSO, London.

Department of Industry (1982) *A Survey on the Effect of the 100% IBA on the Supply of Small Industrial Premises*, HMSO, London.

Department of the Environment (1987) *Town and Country Planning (Use Classes) Order 1987*, SI 1987/764.

Department of the Environment (1989) *Housing and Construction Statistics 1978–88*, DoE, London.

DIAMOND, D. and SPENCE, N. (1983) *Regional Policy Evaluation: A Methodological Review and the Scottish Example*, Gower, Aldershot.

DREWETT, R. (1973) The developer's decision process. In Hall, P., Gracey, H., Drewett, R. and Thomas, R. (eds) *The Containment of Urban Britain*, 163–193, Allen and Unwin, London.

DUNCAN, S. (1986) What is locality? *Working Paper No. 51*, University of Sussex, Urban and Regional Studies.

DUNCAN, S. and GOODWIN, M. (1982) The local state and re-structuring social relations: theory and practice. *International Journal of Urban and Regional Research* 8, 157–185.

DUNCAN, S. and GOODWIN, M. (1988) *The Local State and Uneven Development*, Polity, Cambridge.

DUNCAN, S. and SAVAGE, M. (1989) Space, scale and locality. *Antipode* 21, 179–206.

DUNFORD, M., GEDDES, M. and PERRONS, D. (1981) Regional policy and the crisis in the UK: a long run perspective. *International Journal of Urban and Regional Research* 5(3), 377–340.

EDGE, C. (1972) External costs. In *Economic Geography—Industrial Location Theory*, 49–75, Open University Press, Milton Keynes.

ESTALL, R. and BUCHANAN, R. (1966) *Industrial Activity and Economic Geography* (revised edn), Hutchinson, London.

Estates Times (1978) Plumbing the depths in search of industry, p. 21, 21.4.78.

EVANS, P. and PLUMB, C. (1984) The property requirements of knowledgebased industries. *Land Development Studies* 1(3), 131–144.

FALK, N. (1982) Premises and the development of small firms. In Watkins, D., Stannworth, J. and Westrip, A. (eds) *Stimulating Small Firms*, pp. 127–163, Gower, Aldershot.

FARNIE, D. (1980) *The Manchester Ship Canal and the Rise of the Port of Manchester 1894–1975*, Manchester University Press, Manchester.

FEAGIN, J. (1982) Urban real estate speculation in the United States: implications for social scientists and urban planners. *International Journal of Urban and Regional Research* 6, 35–60.

FIELDING, N. and FIELDING, J. (1986) *Linking Data*, Sage, London.

FIELDING, N. (ed.) (1988) *Action and Structure*, Sage, London.

Financial Times (1970) Industrial estates survey, 8.9.70.

Financial Times (1979) The South West, 23.2.79.

FISHER, J., HANINK, D. and WHEELER, J. (1979) *Industrial Location Analysis: A Bibliography 1966–79*, Department of Geography, University of Georgia, Athens, U.S.A.

FLANAGAN, I. and SHILLER, R. (1980) Contour map shows rental variations. *Chartered Surveyor* November, 256–257.

FOGARTY, M. (1945) *Prospects of the Industrial Areas of Great Britain*, Methuen, London.

FOGARTY, M. (1947) *Plan Your own Industries: a Study of Local and Regional Development Organisations*, Blackwell, Oxford.

FORESTER, T. (1979) The great jobs hunt. *New Society* 48, May, 252–255.

FORM, W. (1954) The place of social structure in the determination of land use: some implications for a theory of urban ecology. *Social Forces* 32(4), 317–323.

FOTHERGILL, S. and GUDGIN, G. (1982) *Unequal Growth: Urban and Regional Employment Change in the UK*, Heinemann, London.

FOTHERGILL, S., KITSON, M. and MONK, S. (1982) The role of capital investment in the urban-rural shift in manufacturing industry. *Working Paper No. 1*, Department of Land Economy, University of Cambridge.

FOTHERGILL, S., KITSON, M. and MONK, S. (1985a) The supply of land for industrial development. In Barrett, S. and Healey, P. (eds) *Land Policy, Problems and Approaches*, 27–40, Gower, Aldershot.

FOTHERGILL, S., KITSON, M. and MONK, S. (1985b) *Urban Industrial Change*, Department of the Environment/Department of Industry, London.

FOTHERFILL, S., MONK, S. and PERRY, M. (1987) *Property and Industrial Development*, Hutchinson, London.

FRANKLIN, P. (1976) Insurance into property. *The Banker* 126, 1127–1129.

FRASER, W. (1984) *Principles of Property Investment and Pricing*, Macmillan, London.

FROBEL, F., HEINRICHS, J. and DREYE, O. (1980) *The New International Division of Labour: Structural Unemployment in Industrialised Countries and Industrialisation in Developing Countries*, CUP, Cambridge.

FULCHER, M. (1973) British industrial estates: an anotated bibliography, *Research Paper, TRP5*, Department of Town and Regional Planning, University of Sheffield.

GEDDES, M. (1988) Social audits and social accounting in the UK: A review. *Regional Studies* 22(1), 60–5.

GEERTZ, C. (1973) *The Interpretation of Cultures*, Basic Books, New York.

GEERTZ, C. (1983) *Local Knowledge: Further Essays in Interpretive Anthropology*, Basic Books, New York.

General Records Office (1934) *Industrial Tables of the 1931 Census of Population*, HMSO, London.

General Records Office (1957) *Industrial Tables of the 1951 Census of Population*, HMSO, London.

GENTLEMAN, H. (1970) Kirkby industrial estate: Theory v's practice. In Lawton, R. and Cunningham, C. (eds) *Merseyside: Social and Economic Studies*, 411–449, Longman, London.

GENTLEMAN, H. and CLARK, H. (1977) *The Use of Industrial Land: A Report of a Case Study in North Lanarkshire in 1973–4*, Central research unit, Scottish development department, Edinburgh.

GIDDENS, A. (1976) *New Rules of Sociological Method*, Hutchinson, London.

GIDDENS, A. (1979) *Central Problems in Sociological Theory*, Macmillan, London.
GIDDENS, A. (1981) *A Contemporary Critique of Historical Materialism, Vol. 1: Power, Property and the State*, Macmillan, London.
GIDDENS, A. (1984) *The Constitution of Society*, Polity, Cambridge.
GILBERT, A. (1988) The new regional geography in English and French speaking countries. *Progress in Human Geography* 12(2), 208–228.
GLASER, B. and STRAUSS, A. (1967) *The Discovery of Grounded Theory: Strategies for Qualitative Research*, Aldine Publishing, Chicago.
GOODCHILD, R. and MUNTON, R. (1985) *Development and the Landowner: An Analysis of British Experience*, Allen and Unwin, London.
GOODMAN, R. (1972) *After the Planners*, Penguin, Harmondsworth.
GOODMAN, E., BAMFORD, J. and SAYNOR P. (eds) (1989) *Small Firms and Industrial Districts in Italy*, Routledge, London.
GOODWIN, M. (1989) The politics of locality. In Cochrane, A. and Anderson, J. (eds) *Politics in Transition*, 141–172, Sage, London.
GORE, T. and NICHOLSON, D. (1991) Models of the land development process: a critical review. *Environment and Planning* A23, 705–730.
GOSS, A. (1962) *British Industry and Town Planning*, Fountain Press, London.
GOTTDEINER, M. (1985) *The Social Production of Urban Space*, University of Texas Press, Austin, U.S.A.
GRANT, A. (1937) *A Study of the Capital Market in Post-war Britain*, Macmillan, London.
GRANT, A. (1970) Locations are bedevilled by motorway myth. *Financial Times*, 8.9.70.
Grant and Partners (1982) *A Report on the Industrial Property Market*, Grant and Partners, London.
Greater London Council (1986) *Financial Strategy*, GLC, London.
GREEN, C. (1986) Rural development areas—progress and problems. *The Planner* 72, 18–19.
GREEN, H. and FOLEY, P. (1982) Small industrial units: is conversion a viable alternative? *Estates Gazette*, August, pp. 574–575.
GREEN, H. and FOLEY, P. (1986) *Redundant Space–A Productive Asset*, Harper and Row, London.
GREEN, H., FOLEY, P. and BURFORD, I. (1985) *Putting Spare Space to Work*, Small business research trust, London.
GREGORY, D. (1978) *Ideology, Science and Human Geography*, Hutchinson, London.
GREGSON, N. (1986) On duality and dualism: the case of structuration and time geography. *Progress in Human Geography* Vol. 10, pp. 184–205.
GREGSON, N. (1987a) Structuration theory: some thoughts on the possibilities for empirical research. *Environment and Planning* D5, pp. 73–91.
GREGSON, N. (1987b) Locality research: a case of conceptual duplication. *Discussion Paper No. 86*, Centre for urban and regional studies, University of Newcastle.
HACKING, I. (1983) *Representing and Intervening*, Cambridge University Press, Cambridge.
HALL, P. (1975) *Urban and Regional Planning*, Penguin, Harmondsworth.
HALL, S. (1984) The rise of the representative/interventionist state 1880s–1920s. In McLennan, G., Held, D. and Hall, S. (eds) *State and Society in Contemporary Britain*, 7–49, Polity, Cambridge.
HAMMERSLEY, M. and ATKINSON, P. (1983) *Ethnography: Principles in Practice*, Tavistock, London.
HARRE, R. (1970) *Principles of Scientific Thinking*, Macmillan, London.
HARRE, R. (1979) *Social Being: A Theory for Social Psychology*, Blackwell Science, Oxford.
HARRE, R. (1984) *The Philosophies of Science* (2nd edn), Oxford.
HARRE, R. and MADDEN, E. (1975) *Causal Powers*, Blackwell, Oxford.
Harris, L. (1984) State and economy in the second world war. In McLennan, G., Held, D. and Hall, S. (eds) *State and Society in Contemporary Britain*, 50–76, Polity, Cambridge.
HARTE, G. (1986) Social accounting in the local economy. *Local Economy* 1(1), 45–56.
HARTSHORN, T. (1973) Industrial/office parks: a new look for the city. *Journal of Geography* 72, 33–45.
HARVEY, D. (1969) *Explanation in Geography*, Edward Arnold, London.
HARVEY, D. (1973) *Social Justice and the City*, Edward Arnold, London.

HARVEY, D. (1978) The urban process under capitalism. *International Journal of Urban and Regional Research* 2, 101–131.

HARVEY, D. (1982) *The Limits to Capital*, Blackwell, Oxford.

HARVEY, D. (1985) *The Urbanisation of Capital*, Blackwell, Oxford.

HARVEY, D. (1987) Flexible accumulation through urbanisation: reflections on 'Post Modernism' in the American City. *Antipode* 19(3), 260–86.

HAYTON, K. (1990) The future of local economic development. *Regional Studies* 22, 549–557.

HEALEY and BAKER (1986) *The Workplace Revolution*, Healey and Baker, London.

HEALEY and BAKER (1990) *Industrial Land Value Survey*, Healey and Baker, 29 St. George Street, Hanover Square, London W1A 3BG.

HEALEY, M. (1983) (ed.) *Urban and Regional Industrial Research*, Geobooks, Norwich.

HEALEY, M. (1991) (ed.) *Economic Activity and Land Use: The Changing Information Base for Local and Regional Studies*, Longman, Harlow.

HEALEY, P. (1990) Models of the development process *Mimeo*: Draft 1, Department of Town and country planning, University of Newcastle Upon Tyne, see Land Dev Studies.

HEALEY, P. (1991) Urban regeneration and the development industry. *Regional Studies* 25(2), 97–110.

HEALEY, P. and BARRETT, S. (1990) Structure and agency in the land and property development process: some ideas for research. *Urban Studies* 27(1), 89–104.

HECHTER, M. (1975) *Internal Colonialism: The Celtic Fringe in British National Development*, Routledge and Keegan Paul, London.

HECK, H. (1964) New industries for Cornwall. *Town and Country Planning* 32(1), 453–457.

HELD, D. (1980) *An Introduction to Critical Theory*, Hutchinson, London.

HENDERSON, R. (1980) The location of immigrant industry within a UK Assisted Area: The Scottish experience. *Progress in Planning* 14(2), 126–187.

HENNEBERRY, J. (1985) The use classes order and high technology developments. *The Planner* 71, 23–25.

HENNEBERRY, J. (1988) Conflict in the industrial property market. *Town Planning Review* 59(3), 241–262.

HENNEBERRY J. (1994) High technology firms and the property market. In: Ball, R. and Pratt, A. C. (eds) *Industrial Property: Policy and Economic Development*, Routledge, London.

HMSO (1980) *Standard Industrial Classification*, HMSO, London.

HMSO (1983) *Regional Industrial Development*, Cmnd 9111, HMSO, London.

HMSO (1991) *Regional Trends* 26, HMSO, London.

HOARE, Q. and NOWELL-SMITH, G. (1971) (eds) *Selections from the Prison Notebooks of Antonio Gramsci*, Lawrence and Wishart, London.

HOBSBAWM, E. (1969) *Industry and Empire*, Penguin, Harmondsworth.

HOLFORD, W. (1938) Notes on the segregation of industry with special reference to trading estates. *Journal of the Town Planning Institute* 24(7), 230–237.

HOLFORD, W. (1938) The location and design of trading estates. *Journal of the Town Planning Institute* 25(5), 151–167.

HOOVER, E. (1948) *The Location of Economic Activity*, McGraw-Hill, New York.

HOWARD, E. (1965) *Garden Cities of Tomorrow*, Faber & Faber, London.

HOYT, H. (1939) (ed.) *The Structure and Growth of Residential Neighborhoods in American Cities*, Federal Housing Administration, Washington DC.

HUDSON, R. and WILLIAMS, A. (1986) *The United Kingdom*, Harper & Row, London.

Investment Property Databank (1989) *The IPD Annual Review 1988*, IPD, London.

ISARD, W. (1956) *Location and Space Economy: A General Theory Relating to Industrial Location, Market Areas, Land Use, Trade and Urban Structure*, Chapman and Hall, London.

IVE, G. (1980) Capital accumulation, the built stock and the construction sector: an economic overview. In *The Production of the Built Environment*, pp. 1–14, *Proceedings of the Bartlett International Summer School*, No. 2, University College, London.

JAMES, C. (1984) Occupational pensions: the failure of private welfare. *Fabian Tract*, No. 497, Fabian Society, London.

JESSOP, B. (1977) Recent theories of the capitalist state. *Cambridge Journal of Economics* 1, 353–373.

JESSOP, B. (1982) *The Capitalist State*, Martin Robertson, Oxford.

JESSOP, B. (1987) *The State and Political Strategy*, mimeo.

JOHNSON, T., DANDEKER, C. and ASHWORTH, C. (1984) *The Structure of Social Theory*, Macmillan, London.
JOHNSTONE, R. (1982) *Geography and the State*, Macmillan, London.
JONAS, A. (1988) A new regional geography of localities. *Area* 20(2), 101–110.
KARL, K. (1968) *Industrial Parks and Districts: An Annotated Bibliography*, Council of planning librarians exchange.
KAUNITZ, R. (1950) The British trading estate: A study in commercial, local and central government enterprise. Unpublished PhD Thesis, Radcliffe College, Harvard, Cambridge, Mass. U.S.A.
KAY, N. (1980) The growth and development of industrial estates within Leeds County Borough 1960–78. Unpublished M.Phil. Thesis, School of Geography, University of Leeds, Leeds.
KEAT, R. and URRY, J. (1975) *Social Theory as Science*, Routledge & Keegan Paul, London.
KEEBLE, D. (1965) Industrial migration from North West London 1940–64. *Urban Studies* 2, 15–32.
KEEBLE, D. (1980) Industrial decline, regional policy and the urban–rural manufacturing shift in the UK. *Environment and Planning* A12, 945–962.
KING, N. (1986) *Novel and Unorthodox*, English Estates, Team Valley.
King and Co. (various) *Industrial Floorspace Survey*, King and Co., 7 Stratford Place, London.
KNORR-CERTINA, K. and CICOUREL, A. (eds) (1981) *Advances in Social Theory and Methodology: Towards an Integration of Micro- and Macro-Sociologies*, Routledge & Keegan Paul, London.
KUHN, T. (1970) *The Structure of Scientific Revolutions*, (2nd edn) University of Chicago Press, Chicago.
LABAW, P. (1980) *Advanced Questionnaire Design*, ABT Books, Cambridge, Mass., U.S.A.
LAMARCHE, F. (1976) Property development and the economic foundations of the urban question. In Pickvance, C. (ed.) *Urban Sociology: Critical Essays*, 85–118, Tavistock, London.
LAYDER, D. (1990) *The Realist Image in Social Science*, Macmillan, London.
LEFEBVRE, H. (1991) *The Production of Space*, Blackwell, London.
LEVER, W. (1974) Planning and manufacturing industry. In Forbes, J. (ed.) *Studies in Social Science and Planning*, 183–220, Scottish Academic Press, Glasgow.
LEWIS, J. and MELVILLE, B. (1978) The politics of epistemology in regional science. In Batey, P. (ed.) *Theory and Method in Urban and Regional Analysis*, 35–54, Pion, London.
LICHFIELD, N. (1970) Evaluation methodology of urban and regional plans: a review. *Regional Studies* 4, 151–165.
LIPIETZ, A. (1987) *Mirages and Miracles: The Crises of Global Fordism*, New Left Books, London.
LIPSEY, R. (1963) *An Introduction to Positive Economics*, Weidenfield and Nicholson, London.
LLOYD, P. and DICKEN, P. (1977) *Location in Space: a Theoretical Approach to Economic Geography*, (2nd edn), Harper and Row, London.
Local Economic Development Information Service (1982) *Science Parks, Bibliography C1*, Planning Exchange, Glasgow.
Local Economic Development Information Service (1983) *Science Parks, Bibliography C1b*, Planning Exchange, Glasgow.
Local Economic Development Information Service (1984) *Science Parks, Overview B5*, Planning Exchange, Glasgow.
LOGIE, G. (1952) *Industry in Towns*, Allen and Unwin, London.
LÖSCH, A. (1954) *Die Raumliche Ordnung der Wirtschaft* (1940), Jena transl. by W. Woglom as *Economics of Location*, Oxford University Press, Oxford.
LOVERING, J. (1989) Postmodernism: Marxism and locality research; the contribution of critical realism to the debate. *Antipode* 21, 1–12.
MacLAREN, A. and BEAMISH, C. (1985) Industrial property development in Dublin 1960–82. *Irish Geography* 18, 37–50.
MacLAREN, A. (1986) Property and the institutional investor in Ireland. *Irish Geography* 19, 69–73.
MALONE, P. (1981) Office development in Dublin 1960–80. *Occasional Paper, No. 1*, Department of geography, Trinity College, Dublin.
MARRIOTT, O. (1967) *The Property Boom*, Pan, London.

MARSHALL, A. (1919) *Industry and Trade*, Macmillan, London.

MARSHALL, A. (1974) *Principles of Economics* (1890), Macmilan, London.

MARSHALL, M. (1987) *Long Waves of Regional Development*, Macmillan, London.

MARX, K. (1954) *The Eighteenth Brumaire of Louis Bonaparte*, Progress, Moscow.

MARX, K. (1973) *Grundrisse*, Penguin, Harmondsworth.

MASSEY, D. (1977) Towards a critique of industrial location theory. In Peet, R. (ed.) *Radical Geography*, 181–197, Methuen, London.

MASSEY, D. and CATALANO, A. (1978) *Capital and Land: Landownership by Capital in Great Britain*, Edward Arnold, London.

MASSEY, D. (1979) In what sense a regional problem? *Regional Studies* 13, 233–000.

MASSEY, D. and MEEGAN, R. (1979) The geography of industrial reorganisation. *Progress in Planning* 10(3), 155–237.

MASSEY, D. and MEEGAN, R. (1982) *The Anatomy of Job Loss*, Methuen, London.

MASSEY, D. (1984) *The Spatial Division of Labour*, Macmillan, London.

MASSEY, D. and MEEGAN, R. (1985) (eds) *Politics and Method*, Unwin Hyman, London.

MASSEY, D. (1985) A British region in a world context. *Introduction and Themes, D205, Block 1*, 2–38, Open University Press, Milton Keynes.

MASSEY, D. and QUNITAS, P. (1992) Science parks: a concept in science, society and 'space' (a realist tale). *Environment and Planning*, D.

MASSEY, D., QUINTAS, P. and WIELD, D. (1992) *High-tech Fantasies: Science Parks in Society, Science and Space*, Routledge, London.

McCONNELL, A. (1967) Industry in towns. *Official Architecture and Planning* 30, 954–961.

McCRONE, G. (1969) *Regional Policy in Britain*, Allen and Unwin, London.

McINTOSH, A. (1986) Investment in office and industrial property. In *The Workplace Revolution*, 111–130, Healey & Baker, London.

McINTOSH, A. and KEEDIE, V. (1979) *Industry and Employment in the Inner City*, Department of the Environment Inner City Directorate, Inner Cities Research Programme Volume 1, DoE, London.

McKENNA, T. (1986) Managing business premises in the next decade. In *The Workplace Revolution*, 173–180, Healey & Baker, London.

McKINNON, A. and PRATT, A. (1986) Jobs in store: an examination of the employment potential of warehousing. *Occasional Paper No. 11*, Department of Geography, University of Leicester, Leicester.

McLOUGHLIN, J. B. (1969) *Urban and Regional Planning: A Systems Approach*, Faber and Faber, London.

McNAMARA, P. (1990) The changing role of research in investment decision making. In Healey, P. and Nabarro, R. (eds) *Land and Property Development in a Changing Context*, Gower, Aldershot.

McNAMARA, P. (1984) The role of local estate agents in the residential development process. *Land Development Studies* 1, 101–112.

McRAE, H. and CAIRNCROSS, F. (1984) *Capital City* (2nd edn), Methuen, London.

Mebyon Kernow (1984) *Making our Own Decisions*, Gwerthro Mebyon Kernow, Helston.

MILES, M. and HUBERMANN, A. (1984) *Qualitative Data Analysis: A Sourcebook of New Methods*, Sage, London.

MILLER, E. and MILLER, R. (1984) *Industrial Location and Planning: A Bibliography*, Vance bibliographies, Monticello, Illinois, U.S.A.

MILLS, L. and YOUNG, K. (1986) Local authorities and economic development: a preliminary analysis. In Hausner, V. (ed.) *Critical Issues in Urban Economic Development* 1, pp. 89–144, Clarendon Press, Oxford.

MINAY, C. (1986) The Development Commission and English rural development. Paper presented at a Conference of the Rural Economy and Society Study Group, Oxford University, December, Mimeo.

MOHUN, S. (1989) Continuity and change in state economic intervention. In Cochrane, A. and Anderson, J. (eds) *Politics in Transition*, 67–94, Sage, London.

MOORE, B., RHODES, J. and TYLER, P. (1986) *The Effects of Government Regional Economic Policy*, Department of Trade and Industry, London.

MOORE, B. and SPIERS, R. (1983) The experience of the Cambridge sciencepark. Paper presented at OECD workshop on research, technology.

Moos, A. and Dear, M. (1986) Structuration theory in urban analysis: 1 Theoretical exegesis. *Environment and Planning* A18, 231–252.

Morgan, K. and Sayer, A. (1988) *Micro-circuits of Capital: Sunrise Industry and Uneven Development*, Polity, Cambridge.

Moser, C. and Kalton, G. (1971) *Survey Methods in Social Investigation*, Heinemann, London.

Moser, C. and Kalton, G. (1979) *Survey Methods in Social Investigation*, (2nd edn), Heinemann Educational Books, London.

Muncy, D. (1954) Land for industry—a neglected problem. *Harvard Business Review* 32, 51–63.

Nairn, T. (1981) The crisis of the British state. *New Left Review* No. 130, 37–44.

Newman, R., Bacon, V., Hudson, J. and Jenks, M. (1982) *Small Factories in Rural Areas: Final Report*, Buildings research team, Department of architecture, Oxford Polytechnic, Oxford.

Niesing, N. (1970) Industrial estates as a means of regional industrialisation policy. *Discussion Paper No. 3*, Seminar fur wirschsftspolitik und struckturferschung der Universitat Kiel, West Germany.

Norcliffe, G. (1975) A theory of manufacturing places. In Collins, L. and Walker, D. (eds) *Locational Dynamics of Manufacturing Activity*, pp. 19–57, Wiley, London.

Ogden, C. (1979) *Buildings for Industry*, Centre for advanced land use studies, University of Reading, Reading.

Oppenheim, A. (1966) *Questionnaire Measurement and Design*, Heinemann, London.

Outhwaite, W. (1987) *New Philosophies of Social Science: Realism, Hermeneutics and Critical Theory*, Macmillan, London.

Pahl, R. (1975) *Whose city?* (2nd edn), Penguin, Harmondsworth.

Pahl, R. and Craven, E. (1975) Residential expansion: the role of the private developer in the South East. In Pahl, R. (ed.) *Whose City?*, 105–123, Penguin, Harmondsworth.

Park, R., Burgess, E. and McKenzie, R. (eds) (1925) *The City*, University of Chicago Press, Chicago.

Parsons, T. (1968) *The Sociological Imagination*, Penguin, Harmondsworth.

Parsons, D. (1986) *The Political Economy of British Regional Policy*, Croom Helm, London.

Percival, G. (1978) *The Government's Industrial Estates in Wales 1936–75*, Information department of the Welsh Development Agency, Treforest, Wales.

Perroux, F. (1950) Economic space, theory and applications. *Quarterly Journal of Economics* 64, 89–104.

Perry, M. (1986) *Small Factories and Economic Development*, Gower, Aldershot.

Perry, M. and Chalkey, B. (1982) The geography of recent small factory provision in Cornwall. In Shaw, G. and Williams, A. (eds) *Economic Development and Policy in Cornwall*, 67–82. Proceedings of a Regional Studies Association and Institute of Cornish Studies joint conference, South West papers in Geography, No. 2, University of Exeter, Exeter.

Perry, R., Dean, K. and Brown, B. (eds) *Counterurbanisation*, Geobooks, Norwich.

Philipp, A. (ed.) (1985) *Pension Funds and their Advisers*, A & P Information Services Ltd., London.

Pickvance, C. (1976) Introduction: Historical materialist approaches to urban sociology. In Pickvance, C. (ed.) *Urban Sociology: Critical Essays*, 1–32, Tavistock, London.

Piore, M. and Sabel, C. (1984) *The Second Industrial Divide*, Basic Books, New York.

Plender, J. (1982) *That's the Way the Money Goes*, Andre Deutch, London.

Plender, J. (1983) The £30bn property conundrum. *Financial Times* 5.12.83.

Plummer, J. (1978) Current problems for the Cornish economy caused by the promotion of the "branch factory" economy. *Cornish Nation*, Winter.

Political and Economic Planning (1939) *Report on the location of Industry in Great Britain*, Political and Economic Planning, London.

Pratt, A. C. (1983) Finance for industry. *Town and Country Planning* 52(1), 111–113.

Pratt, A. C. (1989) Toward an explanation of the location, form and development of industrial estates in Cornwall: a critical realist approach. Unpublished PhD Thesis, Department of Geography, University of Exeter.

Pratt, A. C. (1991) Discourses of locality. *Environment and Planning* 23, 257–266.

Pratt, A. C. (1993) Putting science parks in their place: accounting for the development of science parks and high tech property in Britain. In Simmie, J and Hard, D. (eds) *Technopoles and Regional Development*, Papers in Planning, UCL, London.

PRATT, A. C. (1994) Information sources for non-commercial research on industrial property and industrial activity. In Ball, R. and Pratt, A. C. (eds) *Industrial Property: Policy and Economic Development*, Routledge, London.

PRATT, A., SHAW, G. and WILLIAMS, A. (1986) The changing role of industrial estates in the Cornish economy. *Journal of Cornish Studies* 12, 31–46.

PRATT D. (1994) New land uses; the recommodification of land uses on the city fringe. In: Ball, R. and Pratt, A. C. (eds) *Industrial Property: Policy and Economic Development*, Routledge, London.

Property Advisory Group (1975) *Commercial Property Development: First Report*, Department of the Environment, London.

Property Advisory Group (1980) *Structure and Activity of the Development Industry*, Department of the Environment, London.

PUDUP, M. (1988) Arguments within regional geography. *Progress in Human Geography* 12(3), 269–290.

PUNTER, J. (1985) Aesthetic control within the development process: a case study. Mimeo, School of Planning, University of Reading.

RALLINGS, C. and LEE, A. (1978) Cornwall: The Celtic fringe in English politics. Paper presented at the British Sociological Association Sociology of Wales conference, Gregynog, Wales, Mimeo.

RAVETZ, A. (1986) *The Government of Space*, Faber, London.

RORTY, R. (1980) *Philosophy and the Mirror of Nature*, Blackwell, Oxford.

ROSE, J. (1985) *The Dynamics of Urban Property Development*, Spon, London.

ROSE, D. (1987) Home ownership, subsistence and historical change: the mining district of West Cornwall in the late nineteenth century. In Thrift, N. and Williams, P. (eds) *Class and Space: the Making of Urban Society*, 108–153, Routledge & Keegan Paul, London.

ROTERUS, V. (1956) Planned industrial districts. *Proceedings of the American Society of Civil Engineers* 82, 1–4.

ROWSE, A. (1986) *The Little Land of Cornwall*, Alan Sutton, Gloucester.

SABEL, C. (1989) Flexible specialization and the re-emergence of regional economies. In Hirst, P. and Zeitlin, J. (eds) *Reversing Industrial Decline? Industrial Structure and Policy in Britain and Her Competitors*, pp. 17–69.

SACK, R. (1973) The concept of physical space in geography. *Geographical Analysis* 5, 16–34.

SACK, R. (1980) *Conceptions of Space in Social Thought*, Macmillan, London.

SARRE, P. (1987) Realism in practice. *Area* 19, 3–10.

SAUNDERS, P. (1981) *Social Theory and the Urban Question*, Hutchinson, London.

SAUNDERS, P. (1983) The 'regional state': a review of the literature and agenda for research. *Urban and Regional Studies, Working Paper No. 35*, University of Sussex, Brighton.

SAYER, A. (1979) Theory and empirical research in urban and regional political economy: a sympathetic critique. *Urban and Regional Studies Working Paper*, No. 14, University of Sussex, Brighton.

SAYER, A. (1981) Abstraction: a realist interpretation. *Radical Philosophy* 28, 6–15.

SAYER, A. (1982a) Explanation in economic geography: abstraction versus generalisation. *Progress in Human Geography* 6(1), 68–89.

SAYER, A. (1982b) Explaining manufacturing shift: a reply to Keeble. *Environment and Planning* A14, 119–125.

SAYER, A. (1983) Review: a contemporary critique of historical materialism. *Environment and Planning* D1, 109–114.

SAYER, A. (1984) *Method in Social Science: A Realist Approach*, Hutchinson, London.

SAYER, A. and MORGAN, K. (1985) A modern industry in a declining region: links between method, theory and policy. In Massey, D. and Meegan, R. (eds) *Politics and Method*, pp. 144–168, Methuen, London.

SAYER, A. (1985a) Realism and geography. In Johnston, R. (ed.) *The Future of Geography*, 159–173, Methuen, London.

SAYER, A. (1985b) The difference that space makes. In Gregory, D. and Urry, J. (eds) *Social Relations and Spatial Structures*, 49–66, Macmillan, London.

SAYER, A. (1988) The 'new' regional geography and problems of narrative. *Research Papers in Geography* 17, University of Sussex, Brighton.

SAYER, D. (1979) *Marx's Method*, Harvester, Brighton.
SAYER, D. (1987) *The Violence of Abstraction*, Blackwell, Oxford.
SCARRETT, D. (1983) *Property Management*, Spon, London.
SCOTT, A. (1988) Flexible production systems and regional developments: the rise of new industrial spaces in N. America and W. Europe. *International Journal of Urban and Regional Research* 12(2), 171–186.
SCOTT, A. and STORPER, R. (1986) (eds) *Production, Work and Territory*, Unwin Hyman, London.
SHAW, D., BROWN, B. and PERRY, R. (1983) A tide that's turning in the rural south west. *Town and Country Planning* 5(9), 255–256.
SHAW, G. and WILLIAMS, A. (1981) Creating a data bank for Cornish industrial estates. In Shaw, G. and Williams, A. (eds) *Industrial Change in Cornwall: Proceedings of a Seminar on the Collection and the Analysis of Data, South West Papers in Geography, No. 1*, 41–54, University of Exeter, Exeter.
SHAW, G. and WILLIAMS, A. (1982) Industrial estates and the recession: The Cornish experience 1973–1982. In Shaw, G. and Williams, A. (eds) *Economic Development and Policy in Cornwall*, Proceedings of a Regional Studies Association and Institute of Cornish Studies joint conference, *South West Papers in Geography, No. 2*, 51–66, University of Exeter, Exeter.
SHAW, G. and WILLIAMS, A. (1985) The role of industrial estates in peripheral areas: The Cornish experience 1973–81. In Healey, M. and Ilberry, B. (eds) *Industrialisation of the Countryside*, 221–241, Geobooks, Norwich.
SHORTER, A., RAVENHILL, W. and GREGORY, K. (1969) *South West England*, Thomas Nelson & Sons, London.
SHREWING, T. (1970) A study of industrial estates in the regional development of industrial South Wales. Unpublished MSc Thesis, University of Wales.
SILVERMAN, D. (1985) *Qualitative Methodology and Sociology*, Gower, London.
SIM, P. (1983) Choosing areas of property investment. In Philipp, A. (ed.) *Pension Funds and their Advisers*, 105–111, A & P Financial registers, London.
SIMMIE, J. and JAMES, N. (1986) Will science parks generate the fifth wave? *Planning Outlook* 29(2), 54–57.
Slough Estates (1970) *1920–1970*, Greenaway, London.
Slough Estates (1978) *Slough Estates*, Slough Estates, Slough.
SLOWE, P. (1981) *The Advance Factory in Regional Development*, Gower, Aldershot.
SMITH, D. (1981) *Industrial Location*, (2nd edn), Wiley, London.
SMITH, N. (1984) *Uneven Development*, Blackwell, Oxford.
SMITH, N. (1987) Dangers of the empirical turn: some comments on the CURS initiative. *Antipode* 19(1), 59–68.
SMYTH, H. (1985) *Property Companies and the Construction Industry in Britain*, Cambridge University Press, Cambridge.
SOJA, E. (1980) The socio-spatial dialectic. *Annals of the American Association of Geographers* 70(2), 207–225.
SOJA, E. (1985) The spatiality of life: towards a transformative retheorisation. 90–000.
South West Economic Planning Counil (1967) *A Region with a Future a Draft Strategy for the South West*, Department of Economic Affairs, London.
SPOONER, D. (1971) Industrial development in Devon and Cornwall 1939–67. Unpublished PhD Thesis, St Catherine's College, University of Cambridge, Cambridge.
SPOONER, D. (1972) Industrial movement and the rural periphery: the case of Devon and Cornwall. *Regional Studies* 6, 197–215.
SPRING, D. (1971) English landowners and nineteenth century industrialism. In Ward, J. and Wilson, R. (eds) *Land and Industry*, 16–23, David & Charles, Newton Abbot.
STARBUCK, J. (1976) *Recent Articles on Office and Industrial Parks*, Council of planning librarians exchange bibliography, Monticello, Illinois, U.S.A.
STEVENS, T. (1947) *Some Notes on the Development of Trafford Park, 1897–1947*, Manchester University Press, Manchester.
STORPER, M. (1985) The spatial and temporal constitution of social action: a critical reading of Giddens. *Environment and Planning* D3, 407–424.

STORPER, M. and SCOTT, A. (1989) The geographic foundations and social regulation of flexible production complexes. In Wolch, J. and Dear, M. (eds) *The Power of Geography*, pp. 21–40, Unwin Hyman, London.

STORPER, M. and WALKER, R. (1983) The theory of labour and the theory of location. *International Journal of Urban and Regional Research* 7, 1–43.

TAYLOR, M. and THRIFT, N. (1983) The role of finance in the evolution and functioning of industrial systems. In Hamilton, F. and Linge, G. (eds) *Spatial Analysis and the Industrial Environment, Vol. 3: Regional Economies and Industrial Systems*, 359–385, Wiley, London.

TEMPEST, I. (1982) Warehousing as an employment source—a study of employment density figures and local authority estimates. *Planning Outlook* 25(3), 105–110.

THOMAS, I. and DRUDY, P. (1987) The impact of factory development on 'growth town' employment in Mid-Wales. *Urban Studies* 24, 361–378.

THOMPSON, G. (1984a) Economic intervention in the post-war economy. In McLennan, G., Held, D. and Hall, S. (eds) *State and Society in Comtemporary Britain*, 77–118, Polity, Cambridge.

THOMPSON, G. (1984b) "Rolling back" the state? Economic intervention 1975–82. In McLennan, G., Held, D. and Hall, S. (eds) *State and Society in Contemporary Britain*, 274–298, Polity, Cambridge.

THRIFT, N. (1983) On the determination of social action in space and time. *Environment and Planning* D1, 23–57.

THRIFT, N. (1984) Review: a contemporary critique of historical materialism. *Progress in Human Geography* 8, 139–42.

THRIFT, N. (1985) Bear and mouse or bear and tree? Anthony Giddens' reconstruction of social theory. *Sociology* 19, 609–623.

THRIFT, N. (1986) The internationalisation of producer services and the integration of the Pacific Basin property market. In Taylor, P. and Thrift N. (eds) *Multinationals and the Restructuring of the World Economy*, 142–182, Croom Helm, London.

THRIFT, N. (1987a) The fixers: The urban geography of international commercial capital. In Henderson, J. and Castells, M. (eds) *Global Restructuring and Local Areas*, 203–233, Sage, London.

THRIFT, N. and WILLIAMS, P. (1987) The geography of class formation. In Thrift, N. and Williams, P. (eds) *Class and Space: the Making of Urban Society*, 1–24, Routledge & Keegan Paul, London.

TOTTERDILL, P. (1989) Local economic strategies as industrial policy: 1980s Britain. *Economy and Society* 18(4), 478–526.

TOWNROE, P. (1971) Industrial location decisions. *Occasional Paper No. 15*, Centre for urban and regional studies, University of Birmingham, Birmingham.

TOWSE, R. (1985) Accreditation and certification of industrial parks: experiences in the state of Michigan. *Economic Development Review* Winter, 58–69.

TRICKER, M. and MARTIN, S. (1984) The developing role of the Commission. *Regional Studies* 18(6), 507–514.

TROTTMAN-DICKINSON, D. (1961) The Scottish industrial estates. *Scottish Journal of Political Economy* 8, 45–56.

TURNER, J. (1978) Out of work in Cornwall. *New Society* 477–478.

TURNER-SAMUELS (1970) Package deals and tighter cost control. *Financial Times*, 8.9.70.

TUROK, I. (1990) Evaluation and accountability in spatial economic policy: a review of alternative approaches. *Scottish Geographical Magazine* 106, 4–11.

United Nations (1962a) *Seminar on Industrial Estates in the Region of the Economic Commission for Asia and the Far East*, Department of economic and social affairs, United Nations, New York.

United Nations (1962b) *The Physical Planning of Industrial Estates*, Department of economic and social affairs, United Nations, New York.

United Nations (1965) *Industrial Estates in Africa*, United Nations, Department of economic and social affairs, New York.

United Nations (1966) *Industrial Estates: Policies, Plans and Progress: A Comparative Analysis of International Experience*, United Nations, Department of economic and social affairs, New York.

United Nations (1968) *Industrial Estates in Europe and the Middle East*, United Nations, Department of economic and social affairs, New York.

University College of the South West (1947) *Devon and Cornwall: A Preliminary Survey*, Wheaton, Exeter.

URRY, J. (1981) *The Anatomy of Capitalist Societies: The Economy Civil Society and the State*, Macmillan, London.

URRY, J. (1983) Some notes on realism and the analysis of space. *International Journal of Urban and Regional Research* 7(1), 122–7.

URRY, J. (1985) Social relations, space and time. In Gregory, D. and Urry, J. (eds) *Social Relations and Spatial Structures*, 20–48, Macmillan, London.

URRY, J. (1986) Locality research: the case of Lancaster. *Regional Studies* 20, 233–242.

VALENTE, J. and LEIGH, R. (1982) Local authority advance factory units: a framework for evaluation. *Planning Outlook* 24(2), 67–69.

VAN BUYNDER, E. (1971) Industrialisatiebeleid in de province Antwerpen. *Tijdschrift Voor Econ. en Soc. Geografie* 25(1), 21–28.

VANCE, M. (1961) *Planned Industrial Districts*, Council for planning librarians exchange bibliographies, Monticello, Illinois, U.S.A.

VON THÜNEN (1966) *The Isolated State*, translated by C. Wartenbery and edited by P. Hall, Pergamon, Oxford (original version *Der Isolierte Staat* 1826).

WAGNER, C. (1957) Planned industrial districts. *Journal of Geography* 56, 129–132.

WAINMAN, D. and BROWN, H. (1978) *Leasing: The Accounting and Taxation Implications*, Guild Press, St Helier, Jersey.

WALKER, R. and STORPER, M. (1981) Captial and industrial location. *Progress in Human Geography* 5(4), 473–509.

WARD, S. (1988) *The Geography of Inter-war Britain*, Routledge, London.

WARD, S. (1970) Local industrial promotion and development policies 1899–1940. *Local Economy* 5(2), 100–118.

WARDE, A. (1988) Industrial restructuring, local politics and the re-production of labour power: some theoretical considerations. *Environment and Planning* D6, 75–95.

WATTS, H. (1987) *Industrial Geography*, Longmans, London.

WEBER, A. (1929) *Theory of the Location of Industries*, Chicago.

WEBER, M. (1964) The south west—a well defined field of industry. *Board of Trade Journal* 187, 615–621.

WHITEHAND, J. (1987) *The Changing Face of Cities: A Study of Development Cycles and Urban Form*, Blackwell, Oxford.

WIGHT, I. (1981) Territory versus function in regional development; the case of Cornwall, paper presented at the 6th International Marginal Regions Seminar, Norway.

WILLIAMS, S. (1981) Realism, Marxism, and human geography. *Antipode* 13(2), 31–38.

WILLIAMS, P. (1982) Restructuring urban managerialism: towards a political economy of urban allocation. *Environment and Planning* A12, 95–105.

WILLIAMS, G. (1984) Rural advance factories: a programme in search of a policy, *The Planner* 70(3), 11–13.

WILLIS, K. (1983) New jobs in urban areas—an evaluation of advance factory building. *Local Government Studies* 9(2), 73–85.

WILLIS, K. (1985) Estimating the benefits of job creation from local investment subsidies. *Urban Studies* 22, 163–77.

WILSON, S. (1984) *Science Parks: A Select Bibliography*, Department of Trade and Industry, London.

WIRTH, L. (1938) Urbanism as a way of life. *American Journal of Sociology* 44, 1–24.

WOLTON, D. (ed.) (1938) *Trading Estates*, Ed Burrow, London.

WOOD, P. (1969) Industrial location and linkage. *Area* 1(2), 32–38.

WOOLGAR, S. (1988) *Science: The Very Idea*, Tavistock, London.

WRIGLEY, R. (1959) Organised industrial districts. In Meyer, H. and Kohn, H. (eds) *Readings in Urban Geography*, 478–495, Chicago, U.S.A.

Author Index

Subject Index